THE EXAMINED LIFE

—CHINESE PERSPECTIVES

THE EXAMINED LIFE

—CHINESE PERSPECTIVES

Essays on Chinese Ethical Traditions

Edited, with Introduction, by Xinyan Jiang
Foreword by Robert C. Neville

Global Publications, Binghamton University
Binghamton, New York
2002

A Volume in *the ACPA Series of Chinese and Comparative Philosophy.*
Sponsored by the Association of Chinese Philosophers in America.
http://www.acpa-online.org

Cover design by Peimin Ni.

Library of Congress Cataloging-in-Publication Data:

The examined life : Chinese perspectives : essays on Chinese ethical
traditions / edited, with introduction, by Xinyan Jiang ; foreword by
Robert C. Neville.
    p. cm. -- (ACPA series of Chinese and comparative philosophy ;
1)
Includes bibliographical references and index.
  ISBN 1-58684-223-4 (pbk. : alk. paper)
   1. Ethics, Chinese. 2. Confucian ethics. 3. Philosophy, Chinese.
I. Jiang, Xinyan, 1958- II. Series.
BJ117 .E93 2002
170'.951--dc21

                                                         2002006619

Published by:
Global Academic Publishing
Binghamton University, LNG 99
Binghamton, NY 13902-6000 USA
Phone: (607) 777-4495; Fax: (607) 777-6132
E-mail: globlpub@binghamton.edu

ACPA Series of Chinese and Comparative Philosophy

Contents

Foreword

The very title of this volume advertises that its contributors belong to a new and exciting generation of philosophers. "The examined life" is a phrase from Socrates that is close to the inauguration of the Western philosophic tradition. "Chinese perspectives" indicates that the positions discussed are those arising from China, and also that the contributors are of Chinese background. "Essays on Chinese Ethical Traditions," a Western genre of philosophy if there ever was one, indicates that this group of Chinese philosophers is at home in Western as well as Chinese modes of thought, and are thinking for our own time, not merely about the past. These philosophers are normative thinkers for the contemporary global philosophic conversation.

The evolution of Chinese philosophy in the West continues to have a fascinating history in the 21st century. Chinese thinkers at the end of the 19th century and the beginning of the 20th carefully studied Western thought, and many sought to re-establish Chinese traditions of philosophy in modern language learned from the West. The Westernizing revolutions in China up to the formation of the People's Republic in 1949 drove many of their students from the mainland to Hong Kong, Taiwan, and the West where they conducted serious studies of Western philosophy from the perspective of the Chinese. The recent death of Mou Zong-san marked the passing of that generation of expatriates.

The next generation of creative Chinese philosophers was trained by these expatriates and also educated in the West, often at American universities; thinkers such as Cheng Chung-ying, Antonio Cua, Liu Shu-hsien, and Tu Weiming are leading representatives of this group that has established a serious dialogue in which both Western and East Asian thinkers grapple with contemporary issues using the resources of both traditions. The approach or style of these thinkers has been extremely catholic, embracing many kinds of philosophy both East and West and not drawing sharp distinctions between philosophy and neighboring disciplines and texts. In many respects, the leaders of this generation have functioned less as professional philosophers—though they hold academic appointments—than as public intellectuals creating an interpretation of the contemporary philosophical situation, from practical politics and the critique of the Enlightenment to the interpretation of newly discovered texts.

The authors coming to light in this volume, however, represent yet another generation, trained in Chinese universities and also Western ones. They do not identify so much with the expatriate Chinese philosophical tradition as it has been expelled from the mainland as with the contemporary recovery of Chinese philosophy in the mainland itself. And they teach or have taught in North American institutions as part of the Anglo-American mainstream of philosophy though all but Professor Goulding are of Chinese ethnic extraction. These are philosophers in the technical professional sense, at home in the disciplines of analytic philosophy and the schools of Chinese thought. They seem to think of themselves simply as philosophers whose resources include the traditions of Chinese philosophy as well as those of Greek, Western medieval, French, German, and English philosophy. There is little effort here to be "representative" of anything.

This said, it must be remarked that all of these essays are comparative philosophy, with the special issues of translation this involves. Some of the essays are directly comparative in the sense of bringing particular Chinese and Western thinkers into dialogue. Professor Yu compares Confucius and Aristotle while Professor Chen compares two philosophical movements, Chinese Confucianism and contractualism with Western roots. Professor Chan relates Confucian *Shu* to feminism with Western roots and Chinese branches; Professor Goulding not only compares Buddhism, Confucianism, and Daoism in the "Three Teachings," but discusses all of these as translatable into a Western vocabulary. Professor Mou compares pragmatism and Daoism.

All of the essays, even where comparison is not direct, address Chinese thinkers, texts, movements, or the language itself, from the standpoint of questions and methods raised within contemporary Western philosophy. The context for Professor Yu's comparison of Confucius and Aristotle is nothing ancient but rather the current interest in virtue ethics. Professor Ni's discussion of freedom in Confucius and Confucianism aims to enrich the contemporary Western understanding of freedom. Professor Jiang's analysis of Mencius' view of moral responsibility arises out of contemporary concerns for assigning responsibility relative to exculpating conditions. Professor Ding's analysis of human rights in Chinese philosophy from a fascinating matrix of angles is a contribution to the current political discussion. Contemporary issues of health care focus Professor Fan's discussion of Confucianism. Professor Huang appeals to Zhu Xi to mediate between contemporary liberals and communitarians. Professor Li's paper on filial piety is really about contemporary moral philosophy. Professor Mou's approach to Daoism is motivated by issues in contemporary pragmatism (or neo-pragmatism). The essay by Professor Chan is an extraordinary contemporary elaboration and defense of the usefulness of the so-called negative golden rule of Confucius with a careful analysis of its limitations. Professor Golding's paper is a bravura critical review of Chinese literary and philosophical traditions, showing the mediating role of Buddhist ethics, relevant to our time especially because of the frequent (but false) claim that Buddhism is less interested in ethics than in getting out of the world. In short, all of these essays are contemporary philosophy, some of which have the form of Chinese intellectual history.

The historical significance of these essays is that they represent a genuinely global philosophical conversation, not the effort to create such a conversation. I myself identify with the somewhat older generation for whom the global conversation remains problematic, something needing encouragement and frequent small speeches about its importance. It remains humorous to me that we Confucians in Boston self-consciously call ourselves "Boston Confucians." The authors in this volume so nicely assembled by Professor Jiang do not talk about the integration of Chinese and Western philosophy, they just do it. Those of us who have campaigned for this applaud with delight. The only ones who will be surprised are the American analytic philosophers who do not yet realize what is in their midst.

Xinyan Jiang is to be congratulated and thanked for assembling this generation of contemporary philosophers who are both Chinese and Western.

Robert Cummings Neville
Boston University
November, 1998
Revised in September 2001

Introduction

This anthology is a collection of essays on Chinese ethical traditions, including Confucian, Daoist, and Buddhist ethics. Most of its contributors are philosophers who are trained in both Chinese and Western philosophy. The anthology intends to provide readers with some new perspectives, especially comparative perspectives, and to make intelligible and dynamic dialogues between Western philosophy and Chinese philosophy. It includes eleven essays, more than half of which are on Confucian ethics. All essays in this volume are concentrated on discussions of philosophical issues in the classics of Chinese philosophy and their contemporary relevance rather than specialized textual research. Furthermore, all contributors are primarily occupied by issues of deep concern to both Chinese and Western moral philosophers: topics such as virtue, freedom, responsibility, rights, etc.

I

Philosophy has played an extremely important role in Chinese culture. As Feng Youlan (Fung Yu-lan) points out: "The place which philosophy has occupied in Chinese civilization has been comparable to that of religion in other civilizations. In China, philosophy has been every educated person's concern" (Fung 1948, 1). The main reason why philosophy has been so important to the Chinese is that Chinese philosophy is closely related to people's lives and its central theme is about how to live a good life and how to build a good society. Ethics or philosophy of life has always been the most important part of Chinese philosophy. For Chinese philosophers, philosophy should offer people guidance for life and provide principles for government. Unlike other kinds of study, the purpose of studying philosophy is not to enable a person to become a specialist in a particular area, but to become a fully developed and perfected human being.[1] In all major schools of Chinese philosophy, ideal personhood and ideal government are always the main topics. Although different schools offer different answers, they are all deeply concerned with these questions. For example, Confucianism is well-known for emphasizing self-cultivation and advocating benevolent government, while Daoism is famous for its praise of the natural state in both private and public life. Furthermore, as far as ideal personhood is concerned, Chinese philosophers offer people more than advice on how to be a moral person. They also teach people how to be wise. For example, in the *Daode Jing*, the best known Daoist text, there are many passages that talk about the unity of opposites. According to that idea, everything consists of opposite sides, and everything implies its negation and may turn into its opposite. Such a philosophy is so useful that anyone who truly believes it will never despair when he/she is in a very difficult situation and will never lose caution when he/she has achieved great success.[2]

In the old days, as Feng puts it, if a person were educated at all, the first education he received was in philosophy. When children went to school, the *Four Books*, consisting of Confucius's *Analects*, the *Book of Mencius*, the *Great Learning*, and the *Doctrine of the Mean*, were the first ones they were taught to read. In order for young children to learn philosophy there was a sort of textbook like the *Three Characters Classic*. Each sentence in the *Three Characters Classic* consists of three characters arranged so that when recited, they produced rhythmic effects and thus helped children to memorize them more easily. The first statement in it is that "the nature of man is originally good" which expressed one of the fundamental ideas of Mencius' philosophy.[3] The second sentence is an idea of Confucius: "By nature human beings are alike, but by practice they have become far apart" (*Three Characters Classics*, Zhong and Su comp., 1994, 2).

---

[1] This idea is derived from Fung's similar view. See Fung, 11.

[2] For a discussion on the effect this philosophy has had upon the Chinese people, see Fung 19-20. For a more detailed discussion on the unity of opposites, see my paper, "The Law of Non-Contradiction and Chinese Philosophy" (Jiang 1992).

[3] See Fung, 1.

Today, in China, the *Four Books* are no longer read as much as in the past, and young children can no longer recite the *Three Characters Classic*. Nonetheless, philosophy is still a significant part of Chinese life. For example, Confucian values still dominate Chinese moral life to a great degree. Anyone who notices how the Chinese deal with family relationships and how much Chinese intellectuals feel they have a duty to their country and their people will admit that this is the case. As for Daoism, the Chinese people's dialectical attitude toward the world and life shows that it also still has a great influence on Chinese daily life. No matter how different Confucianism and Daoism are, they work together in shaping Chinese character.

Although Chinese philosophy has been so significant to the Chinese, it has not received much recognition from philosophers in the West. In the United States and other Western countries, very few philosophy departments in major universities offer courses on Chinese philosophy. Very often when Chinese philosophy is taught in a major university, it is taught by those who are in an Asian studies program, religion department, or history department. This contrasts sharply with how Western philosophy has been received in China. There is hardly any philosophy department in China that does not teach Western philosophy and does not have faculty members specializing in Western philosophy. Among others, one of the reasons for less recognition of Chinese philosophy in the West is that many mainstream Western philosophers have denied that Chinese philosophy is true philosophy, classifying it instead as religion and excluding it from philosophy curricula. Part of their justification for claiming that Chinese philosophy is not philosophy seems to be that in writings of ancient Chinese philosophers they cannot find the kind of strictly rational argument to which Western philosophers are accustomed.

It is true that in writings of ancient Chinese philosophers there are very few arguments similar to those made by major Western philosophers. But philosophical persuasion is more than one or two types of argument and there are various ways of philosophizing. If we include various types of persuasion as legitimate ways of making philosophical argumentation, we will find that ancient Chinese philosophers are very philosophical. They are concerned with questions that are philosophically significant and have their own ways to argue for their views.

Ancient Chinese philosophers often argued for their views by appealing to people's shared emotions and intuitions. In other words, when ancient Chinese philosophers made their points and tried to persuade others, what they paid much attention to was not logical coherence but emotional or intuitive consensus. They were accustomed to express themselves in the form of aphorisms, apothegms, allusions, and illustrations.[4] They used analogical arguments more often than any other ways of persuasion.[5] By doing so, they effectively appealed to people's basic intuitions and common sentiments. Everyone familiar with the writings of Zhuangzi, one of the most important Daoist philosophers, may agree that the way Zhuangzi makes his points is very powerful, although analogy, metaphor, and story are his main tools. For example, when he argues that it is wrong to force different individuals to live in the same way and that we should let different beings live according to their natures, he uses a story of the prince of Lu and a bird. Although the prince loved the bird, he treated the bird in the way he treated a human being; i.e., he served the best food for human beings to the bird and played music that human beings loved rather than music loved by birds. So the bird died.[6] The point Zhuangzi makes by this story can definitely be made by another kind of argument, e.g., a deductive argument, but the latter may not convince readers as much as Zhuangzi's way can. What Zhuangzi does here is not to appeal to logical consistency but to shared intuitions. The advantage of making philosophical points by appealing to emotions or intuitions is that very often it can work in places where other arguments cannot. Take, for example, deductive argument, which we all know that it has its limitations. It will work only if its premises are accepted. But most premises from which we start deductive reasoning cannot be derived from deduction. They are usually from experience or intuition. In order to con-

---

[4] For a detailed discussion on this, see Fung 11-13.

[5] Zhang Dongsun (1886-1973) probably was the first one who discussed this aspect of Chinese philosophy. See Zhang 1946, 190.

[6] See *Zhuangzi*, "Supreme Happiness."

vince others to accept certain premises, one needs to appeal to people's emotions and intuitions. That seems to be what Chinese philosophers have done best.[7] Furthermore, making philosophical persuasion by appealing to emotion and intuition can affect people more deeply than deductive persuasion in the sense that it not only can convince people on the conceptual or theoretical level but also can touch people's hearts and strongly motivate them to act.[8] Because of this, to persuade people by appealing to emotion and intuition is also to invite people to practice, to cultivate, and to reach a better state of being.[9]

Clearly, if we understand philosophy as the critical examination of our basic beliefs and an attempt to formulate and answer fundamental questions, as Socrates did, and if we respect different forms of expression in philosophical writings, we will see that the lack of particular types of arguments should not be a plausible reason for denying that Chinese philosophy is true philosophy. To deeply understand Chinese philosophy, we need to appreciate the way Chinese philosophers do philosophy. Each essay in the present volume is partly an attempt to show that Chinese philosophy is entitled to be regarded as real philosophy and that the issues that concern Chinese philosophers are philosophically significant.

However, the difference in ways of doing philosophy between Chinese philosophers and Western philosophers (esp. analytic philosophers) does not exclude analytical methodology from being used in the study of Chinese philosophy. On the contrary, when analytic methodology is understood in a broad sense—namely, when it is regarded as the methodology of philosophizing that is characterized by seeking accuracy, clarity, and logical coherence in reasoning and expression—it can serve as a useful tool for studying Chinese philoso-

---

[7] This idea and a detailed discussion on it were first presented in an invited lecture, entitled "The Way Chinese Philosophers Do Philosophy," which I delivered at the University of Arkansas, Little Rock, on February 22, 1996.

[8] This point is developed from a suggestion made by Stephen Rowe in his comments on a draft of this Introduction.

[9] A similar point is made by Peimin Ni in his comments on a draft of this Introduction.

phy.[10] Although writings of ancient Chinese philosophers themselves are essentially not analytic, analytic methodology might be very helpful in understanding them and teaching them in contemporary times. Moreover, analytic methodology is indispensable for making Chinese philosophy accessible to non-Chinese readers and bringing intelligible dialogues between Western philosophers and Chinese philosophers.

To understand and appreciate Chinese philosophy, one must first try to know exactly what Chinese philosophers say and mean in their writings. To do so, one needs to analyze concepts used by Chinese philosophers and find structures of their arguments. Scholars in Chinese philosophy have attempted to do so for a long time. For example, the debate over the meaning of the concept of Dao in the *Dao De Jing* is such an attempt. When Chinese philosophy is treated as an object of scholarly study, language analysis and clarification of concepts is unavoidable. To teach or introduce Chinese philosophy also needs analytic methodology. To make Chinese philosophy understandable to students, especially Western students, one must express ideas of Chinese philosophers as clearly as possible. It might have been perfectly fine for ancient Chinese philosophers such as Confucius to teach philosophy in the way they did, i.e., to lead students to certain directions of reflection and practice and let them interpret very suggestive meanings of philosophical teachings, given the historical context of their time. But such a method is no longer feasible in contemporary times when philosophy needs to be taught to mass audiences in the university. Although writings of Chinese philosophy in general appeal to intuition and emotions of their readers, teaching them requires logical and clear presentations. Generally speaking,

---

[10] A detailed discussion about analytic methodology was presented by Bo Mou, in his paper "Analytic Methodology and Chinese Philosophy: Some Methodological Considerations," at the Meeting of the Society for Asian and Comparative Philosophy, Eastern Division meeting of the American Philosophical Association, Philadelphia, December 30, 1997. There is some overlap between what I am saying here about the analytic methodology understood in a broad sense and what Mou has said in his presentation. I was the commentator of Mou's presentation. Part of my discussion on the subject here originates from my comments on Mou's presentation. However, Mou Bo believes that analytic methodology is much more than an instrumental tool for studying Chinese philosophy. For his detail discussion on this issue, see Mou 2001.

within contemporary contexts, to study and teach Chinese philosophy well requires analytic methodology.

Certainly, analytic methodology is not the only methodology which should be employed in studying and teaching Chinese philosophy. It has its limitations. Given the way Chinese philosophers do philosophy, overemphasizing analytic methodology in studies of Chinese philosophy may lead to overlooking special merits of Chinese philosophy and make Chinese philosophy seem inferior to Western philosophy. But this does not mean that analytic methodology should be rejected in studies of Chinese philosophy. As I have argued above, analytic methodology must be taken seriously in studying and teaching Chinese philosophy.

Most essays in the volume are analytic in a broad sense. To a certain degree, all authors of these essays have attempted to clarify those concepts which are not clearly articulated by ancient Chinese philosophers and construct logical structures which are not obviously visible in ancient Chinese philosophical writings so that the philosophical significance of teachings of ancient Chinese philosophers could be clearly presented to non-Chinese readers.

II

The volume begins with Jiyuan Yu's comparative study of Confucius and Aristotle. By focusing on Aristotle's conception of virtue (*arete*) and Confucius' conception of *ren*, Yu systematically compares Aristotle's and Confucius' theories of virtue. In the last three decades' revival of virtue ethics, more and more philosophers study Aristotelian ethics not just for historical interest but more out of current theoretical considerations. For many contemporary moral philosophers, Aristotelian ethics is a better alternative to contemporary ethical theories such as utilitarianism and Kantian ethics. Meanwhile, some of them have also noticed that there is another virtue ethics which needs to be studied, namely, Confucian ethics in the Chinese tradition. Today, although it is a widely accepted view that both Aristotelian ethics and Confucian ethics are virtue-based theories, little systematic research on the similarities and differences between these two virtue theories has been done. Yu is one of a small number of philosophers beginning to engage in this comparative study system-atically. Furthermore, a distinctive characteristic of Yu's essay is that it not only praises the respective theoretical merits but also reveals weaknesses of Aristotelian and Confucian ethics. By doing so, the essay clearly shows how comparative study of ethics can contribute to the current development of ethical theories.

Chenyang Li's contribution on filial piety intends to provide a Confucian perspective on filial morality as an alternative to the main-stream Western perspective. Li argues that the Confucian tradition does make a stronger case for filial morality than a rights-centered tradition does. Although there is a large literature on filial piety, there are very few works that bring the West and the East together on filial morality and understand filial piety in cultural contexts as Li's essay does. As Li points out, filial morality is one of the areas that deeply divide the Chinese and the Western tradition. Filial piety is one of the most important concepts of Confucian ethics and a cardinal vir-tue in Chinese culture. For Confucians, filial piety in moral life is so fundamental that it is the starting point of humanity. For the Chinese, filial piety has always been one of the most basic qualities of a good person. On the contrary, in the West, filial piety is not an agreeable value to many philosophers and common people. Such an attitude seems deeply rooted in the Western culture of individual rights. Li's essay shows that a strong notion of filial morality cannot be justified from the rights perspective but it can in the Confucian framework, an alternative perspective which defines the human being in terms of social roles and relationships.

Although the Chinese tradition is not rights-centered, that does not entail that the concept of rights is completely absent in it. The belief in human rights originated in the Western tradition, but it now has been widely accepted by contemporary Chinese. However, it has been controversial whether the Chinese tradition has any idea related to human rights and if the Chinese tradition can contribute anything to the current discussion on the subject. Zijiang Ding attempts to throw some light on these issues. According to Ding, it is not the case that the thought of rights is totally absent in the Chinese tradi-tion. But it is not correct either to say that the thought of rights has played a significant role in the Chinese tradition. Ding argues that the idea of rights in Chinese culture is not a conceptualized, analyzed, rationalized, and theorized thought but a kind of vague consciousness that leads to spontaneous behavior. To support such a conclusion, Ding has made use of sources not only in Chinese philosophical writings but also in Chinese legal documents. In addition to its originality Ding's work provides rich data to the study of Chinese conception of human rights.

Xunwu Chen's essay is a comparative study of moral reason in Confucianism and contractualism. It throws new light on the current debates on moral reason. Chen argues that both Confucianism and contemporary contractualism agree to a certain degree that moral judgement is both reason-guided and feeling-laden and in our moral experience reason and emotion penetrate one another. Although contractualism elaborated by Thomas Scanlon associates justification of action with reason, as many Western ethical theories do, it does hold that moral feeling can constitute a special class of reason under some circumstances and that a moral feeling itself has a reason-giving power. For Confucians, moral feelings and moral reason are intrinsically connected with each other and are always present at the same time, as the *yin* and *yang* are always together. They are two indispensable elements of moral judgement.

Peimin Ni discusses the Confucian account of freedom. Ni offers a noteworthy new perspective on the concept of freedom in the Chinese tradition. Many scholars in Chinese philosophy hold that the concept of freedom is uniquely Western and there is no idea of freedom in Confucianism. Ni argues that Confucianism does entail a positive account of freedom. According to Ni, in the Confucian tradition the highest stage of freedom is a state of no hindrance and such a state results from long-term self-cultivation. Therefore Confucian freedom is to be free from improper desire or ill will and to act spontaneously and effortlessly in accordance with virtues. The Confucian conception of freedom is more positive than that held by some Western philosophers, such as Spinoza, in the sense that it is a cultivated spontaneity but not a state of indifference. Furthermore, such freedom is totally consistent with the Confucian emphasis on relationship with others. For Confucians, there is no individual in isolation. One's relatedness to others is a necessary condition for one to be free.

My own essay is about Mencius' view on moral responsibility. "Everyone has a share of responsibility for the fate of his/her country" is a widely known saying in China. For centuries it has inspired many, especially intellectuals, to strive for a better China. It may not be an exaggeration to say that Chinese culture is a culture of responsibility. As a result, Chinese people, historically and in the present, tend to blame themselves for their failures and rarely look for any external excuses for themselves. For example, students will blame themselves if their grades are not good, rather than rashly blaming their teachers; teachers will critically examine their teaching but not easily condemn their students if students fail to do well. Ironically, in contemporary literature on Chinese philosophy there are very few discussions on how moral responsibility is addressed in classical Chinese philosophy. Yet Mencius' example shows that responsibility is an important concept in classical Chinese thought, and that Chinese philosophers grappled with important problems about responsibility. I argue that in Mencius' ethics the sensitivity to the influence of environment on moral development and the emphasis on responsibility coexist without any contradiction.

Sin Yee Chan's essay connects Confucian and feminist ethics. Chan explicates the meaning of the Confucian concept of *shu* (reciprocity) and shows how it can be applied to the ethics of care as described by some feminist theorists. She defends and further develops Fingarette's interpretation of *shu* as identifying with another person while critically evaluating the latter's perspective based on one's own. Applying the concept of *shu* to the context of caring actions, Chan shows that it can offer a viable solution to a dilemma in the ethics of care. When caring for another person, should we go by her perspective or ours in deciding what to do on her behalf? The question poses a dilemma: if we follow our own perspective, we may be acting paternalistically without giving due regard to the autonomy of the cared-for; and if we follow the perspective of the cared-for blindly, we may not be acting upon our best judgment and really benefiting the cared-for. *Shu* can help us on this question. For *shu* implies the affirmation of both the perspective of the caring agent and that of the cared-for, but assigns a priority to the former.

Yong Huang's essay on Zhu Xi is the only one that discusses neo-Confucianism in the volume. Huang's comparative study of neo-Confucian ethics and contemporary Western ethical theories offers a new approach to the study of Zhu Xi. Huang brings the contemporary liberal-communitarian debate into dialogue with neo-Confucianism. According to Huang, the liberal-communitarian debate has entered an impasse between the liberal insistence on "the right-prior-to-the-good" and the communitarian espousal of "the good-prior-to-the-right." The Confucian discussion of *ren* and love, as represented in the neo-Confucian Zhu Xi's philosophy, can provide a way out of that impasse. Huang argues that the Confucian idea of *ren* and love is compatible with the modern Western conceptions of the good and the right and that Zhu Xi's view of *ren* and love presents an alternative to liberalism and communitarianism.

Ruiping Fan brings Confucian ethics and contemporary moral issues together in a very intriguing discussion of the relevance of Confucian ethical theory to medical ethics today. Fan argues that the Confucian tradition might offer a solution to the current difficulty in health care allocation. According to Fan, health care allocation has become a difficult issue at present, not only because our society faces constant and unbearable increases in health care costs, but also because the guiding ideology in health care allocation, either individualistic or statist, fails to provide efficient solutions to the problem. According to Fan, the Confucian emphasis on the family offers an alternative ideology that works more efficiently. Applying such a philosophy to health care issues, we will see that, families, rather the State or the individual, should be responsible for the health care of each family member. Although society should offer help to families for their health care costs under some circumstances, it should not be the main resource for covering such costs. This Confucian solution to the health care allocation problem deserves much attention. The current Singaporean health care system is a manifestation of such a Confucian familialism.

Bo Mou's essay provides us with new insights comparing pragmatist and Daoist ideas of morality. By examining metaphysical foundations of Pragmatism and Daoism, Mou argues that Dewey and Laozi share some pragmatic insights on morality, namely, that we should not take any pre-set and fixed moral rule or principle as the final and absolute moral authority, and we should pay attention to the moral agent's own moral experience that responds to the felt demands in concrete situations. Although Dewey and Laozi arrive at that insight differently, they both base this idea on their metaphysical visions of the world. Their metaphysical views could complement and enhance each other. On the one hand, Laozi's dialectical cosmology could be supplemented by Dewey's evolutionary view of the world in its more or less scientific terms; on the other hand, Dewey's evolutionary view could be enhanced by Laozi's transcendent outlook of the world.

The volume ends with Jay Goulding's "'Three Teachings are One': The Ethical Intertwinings of Buddhism, Confucianism and Daoism." Goulding argues that three great Chinese ethical traditions form a continuum and that Buddhist ethics stands in between Confucian virtuousness and Daoist cosmology. According to Goulding, Buddhism offers meditative strategies which lead to ethical conduct. By curtailing daily desires, Buddhists attempt to embrace all things with compassion (*karuna*). Wisdom (*prajña*) becomes the realization that all *dharmas* are empty. The ethics of a good life is the teaching of this wisdom of emptiness to all persons. Such "emptiness" is not simply a retreat from the world of morality but an entrance back into it in another way. Emptiness is not nothingness. It both is and is not. The dynamics of the two—being and non-being—lead to and from the middle, the in-between of heaven and earth. To a certain degree, Buddhist ethics is the undoing of ethics as simply worldly obligations (Confucianism) or celestial obligations (Daoism). Yet it draws strength from both Confucian and Daoist traditions. Its 'realization' can arise in both this world and the next. All of the above exemplify the ethical intersection of Buddhism, Confucianism and Daoism and return to the slogan, "three teachings are one."

III

All essays in this volume are explicitly philosophical in nature. That distinguishes it from those which are focused more on historical and textual aspects of classical Chinese philosophical writings. Additionally, most are comparative studies of Chinese and Western moral philosophy in one way or another. Most contributors to this volume have made full use of their familiarity with both Chinese and Western moral philosophy and attempt to make their writings serve as bridges between these different traditions. Hopefully, this volume will bring Chinese moral philosophy into a dialogue with Western mainstream moral philosophy on a new level and contribute something significant to current studies of Chinese and comparative ethics in particular and philosophy in general.[11]

Xinyan Jiang
Summer 1998
Revised October, 2001

REFERENCES:

Fung, Yu-lan. 1948. *A Short History of Chinese Philosophy.* New York: Macmillan.
Jiang, Xinyan. 1992. The Law of Non-Contradiction and Chinese Philosophy," *History and Philosophy of Logic* 13.
Mou, Bo. 2001. "An Analysis of the Structure of Philosophical Methodology—in View of Comparative Philosophy." In Bo Mou ed. *Two Roads to Wisdom?—Chinese and Analytic Philosophical Traditions.* La Salle: Open Court.
Ren, Jiyu (edited and annotated) *Laozi (Daode Jing).* Shanghai: Ancient

---

[11] I am grateful to Lawry Finsen, Chenyang Li, Peimin Ni, Stephen Rowe, and William Whit for their comments or suggestions on early drafts of this Introduction. I also would like to acknowledge the fact that my summaries of some essays included in the volume are based on the abstracts of those essays written by their authors themselves.

Books Press.

Zhang, Dongsun. 1946. *Knowledge and Culture*. Shanghai: Shangwu Press.

Zhong, Hui and Su Lei (edited and annotated). 1994. *Three Characters Classics*. Beijing: World Books Publishers Company.

Zhu Xi (edited and annotated). 1985. *Collected Commentaries on the Four Books*. Rerprint. Changsha, China: Yuelü Press.

Zhuangzi. 1987. *Zhuangzi*. Edited and Annotated by Sha Shaohai. Guiyang, China: Guizhou People's Press.

Contributors

Sin Yee Chan is Associate Professor of Philosophy at the University of Vermont. She received her B.A. from the University of Hong Kong and her Ph.D. from the University of Michigan, Ann Arbor. She has published papers on Confucianism, philosophy of emotions, and feminism.

Xunwu Chen is Assistant Professor in the Department of English, Classics, and philosophy, University of Texas at San Antonio. He received his BA in philosophy from Zhongshan University, and his Ph.D. from Fordham University. His papers have appeared in such journals as *Journal of Chinese Philosophy*, *Journal of Value Inquiry*, and *Asian Thought and Society*. He has a forthcoming book: *Being and Authenticity* (Rodopi).

Zijiang Ding is Professor of Philosophy at California State Polytechnic University at Pomona. He received his M.A. from Peking University (Beijing University) and his Ph.D. from Purdue University. He taught philosophy at Peking University and Indiana University at Indianapolis. He specializes in comparative and socio-political philosophy. He has published in the *Journal of Chinese Philosophy*, the *Journal of Interdisciplinary Studies, Modern China Studies*, and *Philosophy and Culture*, etc. He is the author or co-author of several books.

Ruiping Fan is Assistant Professor in the Department of Public and Social Administration at City University of Hong Kong. He received his Bachelor of Medicine from Baotou College of Medicine (in Inner Mongolia, China) and his Ph.D. in philosophy from Rice University. Focusing on comparative studies in bioethics and the philosophy of medicine, he has authored over forty journal articles and book chapters in both English and Chinese languages. He was the editor of an anthology entitled *Confucian Bioethics* (Kluwer, 1999). He serves as Assistant Editor of the *Journal of Medicine and Philosophy* (USA) and Co-Editor of *Chinese and International Philosophy of Medicine* (China).

Yong Huang is Associate Professor of Philosophy at Kutztown University of Pennsylvania. His interests are primarily in philosophy of religion, social and political philosophy, and Chinese and comparative philosophy. He is the author of *Religious Goodness and Political Rightness: Beyond the Liberal and Communitarian Debate* in the Harvard Theological Stduies series (2001). He has also published in *Philosophy Today*, *Philosophy and Social Criticism*, *Religious Studies*, *International Journal for Philosophy of Religion*, *Journal of Law and Religion*, *Journal of Chinese Philosophy*, and *University of Dayton Review*. He received his B.A. (1982) from East China Normal University, M.A. (1985) and Ph.D. (1988) from Fudan University, and Th.D. (1997) from Harvard University.

Jay Goulding is Lecturer in Sociology at York University, Toronto, Canada. His expertise is in ancient and medieval Chinese religion and philosophy as well as hermeneutic phenomenology. He has published in *Journal for the Scientific Study of Religion*, *Sociological Analysis: A Journal of Comparative Religion*, *Political Theory*, and *Catalyst*. As author of two previous books, he has completed a third, *Visceral Manifestation and the East Asian Communicative Body* (Hampton, forthcoming in 2002) which compares Chinese and Japanese philosophy with phenomenology and critical theory. He received a B.A. (1977) from McMaster University and M.A. (1978) and Ph.D. (1981) from York University.

Xinyan Jiang is Assistant Professor of Philosophy at the University of Redlands. Her interests are primarily in Chinese philosophy and ethics. She has published in the *History and Philosophy of Logic*, *Philosophy East and West*, *Journal of Chinese Philosophy*, *Philosophical Inquiry*, and *Hypatia: A Journal of Feminist Philosophy*. She received her B.A. (1982) and M.A. (1984) from Peking University (Beijing University) and taught there for three years. She earned her Ph.D. (1994) from the University of Cincinnati. She is currently Chair of the Committee on

Asian/Asian American Philosophers and Philosophies of the American Philosophical Association.

Chenyang Li is Professor and Chair of Department of Philosophy at Central Washington University. He earned his B.A. (1982) and M.A. (1984) in philosophy from Peking University (Beijing University), and Ph.D. (1992) in philosophy from the University of Connecticut. His recent teaching and research interest includes Chinese and comparative philosophy, ethics, and value theory. He has published two books, *The Tao Encounters the West: Explorations in Comparative Philosophy* (1999), and *The Sage and the Second Sex: Confucianism, Ethics, and Gender* (ed. 2000). His publications also include numerous articles in such journals as *International Philosophical Quarterly, Journal of Value Inquiry, Journal of Applied Philosophy, Philosophia, Philosophy East & West, Review of Metaphysics, Hypatia: A Journal of Feminist Philosophy,* and *Journal of Chinese Philosophy*. He was the first president of the Association of Chinese Philosophers in America, 1995-1997, and is currently vice executive director of the International Society for Chinese Philosophy.

Bo Mou is Assistant Professor of Philosophy at San Jose State University. After receiving his B.S. in mathematics (1982), he received his M.A. in philosophy (1987) from Graduate School of Chinese Academy of Social Sciences and his M.A. (1993) and Ph.D. in philosophy (1997) from the University of Rochester. His current research interests are primarily in metaphysics, philosophy of language, analytic philosophy, comparative philosophy, and Chinese philosophy. He has published in *Synthese, Metaphilosophy, The Southern Journal of Philosophy, Philosophical Papers, Philosophy East and West, Journal of Chinese Philosophy,* and *Polylog*. He is the editor and contributor to four volumes of anthology, *Two Roads to Wisdom?—Chinese and Analytic Philosophical Traditions* (Open Court, 2001), *Contemporary Inquiries into Fundamental Issues of Philosophy* (The Commercial Press, China, 2001), *Comparative Studies of Chinese and Western Philosophies* (The Commercial Press, China, forthcoming in 2002), and *Comparative Approaches to Chinese Philosophy* (Ashgate, forthcoming in 2002).

Peimin Ni received B. A. and M. A. from Fudan University and Ph.D. from the University of Connecticut. He is currently Professor of Philosophy at Grand Valley State University in Michigan. Ni's publications include over forty journal articles and book chapters, and four books—*On Confucius* (Wadsworth, 2002), *On Reid* (Wadsworth, 2002), *Thomas Reid* (San Min Press, in Chinese, 1996), and a forthcoming volume, co-authored with Stephen Rowe, titled *Wandering—Brush and Pen in Philosophical Reflection* (Oriental Press and Art Media, 2002). Ni is a founding member, vice President (1995-97), President (1997-99), and Secretary (1999-2001) of the Association of Chinese Philosophers in America. He is the editor of the ACPA Series of Chinese and Comparative Philosophy.

Jiyuan Yu is Assistant Professor of Philosophy at the State University of New York at Buffalo. His interests are primarily in Ancient Greek Philosophy and Greek-Chinese comparative studies. His papers have appeared in, among others, the *Oxford Studies in Ancient Philosophy*, *History of Philosophy Quarterly* (twice), *Aperion*, *The Southern Journal of Philosophy*, *International Philosophical Quarterly*, *Philosophy East and West*, *Journal of Chinese Philosophy*, and in several anthologies. He has co-authored (with Nick Bunnin) *A Dictionary of Western Philosophy: English-Chinese*, and co-edited (with Jorge Gracia) *Rationality and Happiness from the Ancients to the Early Medievals*. He received his Ph.D. (1994) from the University of Guelph, Canada, and was a Post-Doctoral research fellow in the University of Oxford, England (1994-1997).

Acknowledgements

I would like to thank Professor Robert Cummings Neville, the author of *Boston Confucianism* (2000) and many other influential works on Chinese philosophy, for his support, and especially for his foreword to this volume. I would also like to thank Professor Stephen Rowe, my friend and former colleague, for his persistent encouragement. My thanks also go to the ACPA Series Editorial Board for making this collection the first volume of the ACPA series of Chinese and Comparative Philosophy. I am very grateful to all of the authors for their contributions and for their understanding and patience.

Several articles in this volume were first published in the following journals:

Sin Yee Chan, "Can *Shu* Be the One Word that Serves as the Guiding Principle of Caring Actions?" *Philosophy East and West*, 50:4 (2000) 507-524.

Yong Huang, "Zhu Xi on *Ren* (Humanity) and Love: A Neo-Confucian Way out of the Liberal-Communitarian Impasse," *Journal of Chinese Philosophy*, 23 (1996) 213-235.

Chenyang Li, "Shifting Perspectives: Filial Morality Revisited," *Philosophy East and West*, 47:2 (1997) 211-232.

Jiyuan Yu, "Virtue: Confucius and Aristotle," *Philosophy East and West*, 48:2 (1998) 323-47.

I would like to express my appreciation to all of these publishers for their reprint permissions.

I would also like to acknowledge the following: an early and much shorter version of Bo Mou's "A Pragmatic Insight on Morality and Its Distinct Metaphysical Foundations," under the title "A Pragmatic Insight Regarding Morality: From A Comparative Perspective," was published in P. Weingartner, G. Schurz and G. Dorn eds., *The Role of Pragmatics in Contemporary Philosophy* (Kirchberg, Austria. ©1997, Bo Mou); the main ideas of Peimin Ni's "The Confucian Account of Freedom," were articulated in a much abbreviated form, in the section "Freedom" of his book, *On Confucius* (Belmont, CA: Wadsworth, 2002).

Xinyan Jiang
Redlands, California

1

Virtue: Confucius and Aristotle

Jiyuan Yu

My aim in this essay is to compare Aristotle's conception of virtue (*arete*) with Confucius' key notion *ren*—which has also been interpreted as "virtue"[1]—in order to make explicit whether and to what extent they correspond. The issue is of current interest given the distinction between ethics and morality in the contemporary revival of Aristotelian virtue ethics.[2] Confucius has been interpreted as a

---

[1] *Ren* has been translated in a variety of ways, including "humanity," "benevolence," "love," "virtue," "manhood," "authoritative person," and so forth. James Legge calls it "complete virtue," but he admits that "We cannot give a uniform rendering of this term" (see Legge, 2-3). Given this situation, I find it more convenient to keep it untranslated in discussion. *Arete* is translated as either "virtue" or "excellence," but "virtue" seems more popular. Hence I adopt this conventional translation, despite the asymmetry I might create as I keep *ren* untranslated.

[2] Cf. Williams, 1985, 6. These two terms originally mean the same thing. "Ethics" is a transliteration of the Greek word *ēthikos* and "morality" is from the Latin word *moralis*, which is the Latin translation of *ēthikos*. Currently, morality is characterized in dealing with an agent's actions and their consequences, and in attempting to formulate law-like moral principles and rules that are universally applicable to all moral actions. It emphasizes "obligation" and "moral rightness" and takes an impersonal point of view regarding moral agents. Morality in this sense denotes modern moral systems, in particular utilitarianism and Kantian deontology, and has been the target in the recent anti-theory or anti-morality movement. Williams even claims that for such a morality "we would be better off without it"(Williams, 1985, 174). Ethics, on the other hand, is believed to concern, as the word "ethics" itself suggests, an agent's character, or the kind of person an agent is, and treats the agent as culturally and traditionally embedded. Its central notion is "virtue," or the excellence of character, and it takes personal commitment, attachment and deep convictions into serious consideration. Hence the sphere of ethics is much broader

thinker concentrating on ethics or moral philosophy. Now with regard to the distinction between ethics and morality, we may ask on which side Confucius lies. Is *ren*, understood as virtue, the sort of virtue that should be treated as standing in contrast to morality? I hope that the following synoptic comparison of these two complex notions will be helpful not only in achieving a mutual illumination but also in bringing Confucius' thinking into the framework of contemporary virtue ethics.

1. A Structural Similarity

The word "virtue" is a transliteration of the Latin *virtus* (from *vir*, literally "manhood"), which was in turn employed by Latin authors to translate the Greek *arete*, originally referring to excellence of manly qualities. The word "*ren* " was employed in the *Book of Poetry* (a text earlier than Confucius) to describe noble huntsmen. Some scholars therefore speculate that the concept of *ren* means, in a sense, "manly" or "manhood" (Schwartz 1985, 75). If that is true, an etymological parallel between *ren* and virtue (*arete*) comes to the surface.

But they come to be used differently. The term *ren* consists of two components, meaning respectively "human" and "two," and points toward human relationships. It is this sense that figures in Confucius' basic teaching that by learning to be good one becomes a person of *ren*. In Athenian philosophy, the word *arete* is associated with *aristos* (excellent, best) and means the goodness of a kind of thing (It is therefore also translated "excellence"). For Aristotle, "something's virtue [or excellence] is relative to its own proper function (*ergon*)"(Aristotle, *Nicomachean Ethics* [hereafter *NE*] 1139a17),[3] that is, the characteristic activity peculiar to something or its distinctive mark.[4] A virtuous X is an X that fulfils its *ergon* well. Any kind of

---

than that of morality. This distinction is essentially a distinction between virtue and morality. An anti-morality movement seeks to replace morality with a virtue ethics, a tendency described as "from morality to virtue" (Slote, 1992).

[3] Unless otherwise specified, the quotations of the *NE* is from T.H. Irwin (Hackett, 1985). Quotations of other Aristotelian treatises are from J. Barnes, ed. 1985.

[4] For Aristotle, a function is also a thing's end (cf. *De Caelo*, 286a8-9; *De Partibus Animalium*, 694b13-15; *Eudemian Ethics*, 1219a8).

thing can be said to possess its (specific) virtue by performing its function well. As far as human beings are concerned, virtue is human excellence or goodness with regard to human function. As Aristotle says: "the virtue of a human being will likewise be the state that makes a human being good and makes him perform his function well" (*NE*, 1106a23-4). Hence philosophically, *arete* is related to human function, while *ren* to human relations.

Confucius does not furnish a unified definition of *ren*. Of various utterances recorded in his *Analects,* two remarks characterizing *ren* are fundamental: "to love humanity"(*Analects*, 12:22)[5], and "to return to *li*" (*Analects*, 12:1. The translation of *li* ranges from "rites" to "propriety," "ceremony," "decorum," and "manners"). What, then, is the relationship between *ren* as love and *ren* as returning to *li*? Which one of these two determinations should be considered as central? In the prevailing interpretation, *ren* as love is taken as the fundamental meaning, and the two aspects of the notion of *ren* in question are described as the relation between *ren* and *li*. This is certainly supported by the following remark: "what can a man do with *li* who is not *ren*?" (*Analects*, 3:3). The conformity to *li* without inner feeling can only be a formality rather than a human goodness. Nevertheless, given the fact that love is a natural property, how can that determine what moral goodness is? A man might love his parents, brothers, and his friends, but he may still be a bank-robber, a drug-smuggler, and even a brutal murderer. Confucius is not unaware of this gap between love and human good. He explicitly claims that "One who is fond of *ren* without being fond of learning is liable to lead to foolishness" (*Analects*, 17:8; cf.8:2). Learning means to learn *li*, to recognize it and embody it in behavior. Hence *ren* as love is not identical with human goodness, and needs to be constrained by *li*. "To return to *li*" turns

---

or what constitutes a thing's essence (cf. *Meteorologica*, 390a10-12; *De Partibus Animalium*, 640b33-641a6; *De Generatione Animalium*, 731a25-6; *Metaphysics*. 1045b32-4; *NE*, 1176a3-9; *Politics*, 1253a23-5).

[5] "Love" as a determination of *ren* is affection and emotional attachment that originate among family members, and are then extended to the larger society. It carries the implication of neither romantic love nor sacred love. Love in Confucius is close to "care" or "concern," and is similar to the Greek *philia* (see, below, note 26).

out to be equally fundamental for being good, that is, being a person of *ren*. If neither *ren* as love nor *ren* as returning to *li* can be a complete notion of human goodness, what is *ren* in such a sense?

Confucius sometimes views *ren* as a particular quality, along with cleverness, trustworthiness, forthrightness, courage, unbendingness, and so on. However, there are also many passages in which *ren* is described as a comprehensive virtue, including all the above and other moral characters and determining their goodness. The distinction between *ren* as an exclusive virtue and an inclusive virtue is well recognized.[6] How, then, is this distinction connected with the distinction between *ren* as returning to *li* and as love? Is there a unified notion to cover all these aspects?

While Confucius' concept of *ren* involves a tension between *ren* as returning to *li* and *ren* as love, there is also a tension at the heart of Aristotle's notion of virtue. According to his *ergon* argument, human virtue is the good performance of human function. And human function is, literally translated, "the soul's activity that expresses reason (*kata logon*) or not without the reason" *(me aneu logou)* (*NE*, 1098a5-6).[7] *Kata logon* and *me aneu logou* refer to two parts of the soul that distinguish a human being from other kinds of animals. The former is the part that has reason in itself, and the latter is the part that is nonrational but obeys reason.[8] Aristotle then divides virtue into two kinds: that which corresponds to the part of the soul that has reason in itself is intellectual virtue (*dianoetike arete*, or excellence of intelligence), and that which corresponds to the part of the soul that is nonrational but obeys reason is ethical virtue (*ethike arete*, or excellence of ethical character). "The human good," i.e. *eudaimonia* (happiness, or well-being), Aristotle concludes, "turns out to be the soul's activity that expresses virtue" (*NE*, 1098a16).

Aristotle's *ergon* argument immediately faces a challenge. Reason as a natural property may distinguish humans from other animals, but

---

[6] For a list of the texts upon which this distinction is revealed, see Chan, 1955, 297-8.

[7] Following Urmson and Irwin, I prefer to translate "*kata*" as "expressing" rather than "in accordance with."

[8] Cf. *NE*, 1102b14-1103a1, 1198a4.

does not seem to be the criterion that distinguishes human good from human evil. Acting rationally and acting well ethically do not seem to be identical. If one performs one's rational function well, we would say that one is intelligent or clever rather than that one is good in the ethical sense. For intelligence may be put to the service of evil actions. A clever bank robber or a thief with sophisticated skills of stealing is "good" as a robber or as a thief, but is unlikely accepted as being good ethically. There is a gap between rational excellence and social respect.

For Aristotle, however, there is another dimension of human nature: "Man is by nature a political [social] animal" (*Politics*, 1253a1).[9] A person cannot live in isolation from some community and must participate in and share the life of society. Ethical virtue is, in a more direct sense, concerned with character (*êthosê*) (*NE*, 1103a17), which is informed by social and cultural customs and habits (*ethos*). It is the disposition or quality to feel and act in ways admired by the society. This kind of stable, settled and long-lasting disposition forms a state (*hexis*, which is connected in Greek with "to have") (*Categories*, 8b27-8).[10] In terms of the claim that a human being is a social animal, Aristotle avoids Socrates' extreme position of intellectualism, and expands the area of ethics from the study of moral knowledge and reasoning to the study of development of good habits of feeling and action.

Aristotle's distinction between intellectual virtue and ethical virtue is hence not only based on the two parts of the soul, but corresponds to the dual dimensions of human nature as a purely rational animal and as a social animal. There are various debates regarding how to reconcile these. In Aristotle's ethics, they lead to two seemingly incompatible notions of *eudaimonia* (happiness). *Eudaimonia* is the activity that expresses virtue (*NE*, 1098a16). According to the *ergon* argument, the best life should be that which most fully exercises one's rational activity, and that is, according to Aristotle, the life of contemplation (*NE*, X. ch.7). On the other hand, *eudaimonia* as the

---

[9] Cf. *NE*, 1097b9-11, 1169b18-9.
[10] Cf. also *Categóries*, 9a8-13., *NE*, 1100b11-17, 1105a32-3, 1152a30-3.

most desirable sort of life needs to include all intrinsically worthwhile activities and, in addition, external goods (*NE*, 1099a31-b6).[11] The issue that is more essential to our current purpose is this: Is ethical virtue determined more fundamentally by the established habits and custom of the particular cultural and historical context into which one happens to be thrown, or by human rationality which belongs to any self-determining agency? Intellectual virtue includes theoretical wisdom, and practical wisdom (*phronesis*).[12] While theoretical wisdom does not involve action, practical wisdom is "concerned with action about what is good or bad for a human being" (*NE*, 1140b4-6). The question, then, is about the relation between practical wisdom and ethical virtue. On the one hand, ethical virtue must be associated with practical wisdom, and Aristotle claims that a full virtue "cannot be acquired without practical wisdom"(*NE*, 1145a16). On the other hand, he says: "practical wisdom, the eye of the soul, cannot reach its fully developed state without virtue" (*NE*, 1144a30-31); and it is his recurring remark that "virtue makes the goal correct, and practical wisdom makes what promotes the goal" (*NE*, 112b13).[13]

---

[11] There is no need in this paper to enter the long-standing dispute about whether Aristotle's notion of *eudaimonia* is intellectualist (dominant) or comprehensive (inclusive). Personally I am sympathetic with the position that the tension between these two notions is not as sharp as is generally supposed. A life of contemplation is an ideal for human being. Aristotle advises us to seek to realize completely this ideal, as he himself pursues in all his life. But he also acknowledges that it is beyond the human level. For this reason, although he remarks that the life of moral virtue "is happy only in a secondary degree" compared with contemplation, he affirms that "the activities expressing this virtue are human"(*NE*, 1178a8-10). [Since the publication of this paper, I have dealt with this issue in detail in my "Aristotle on *Eudaimonia*: After Plato's Republic," *History of Philosophy Quarterly*, Vol. 18 (2), 2001].

[12] Other translations of *phronesis* include "intelligence" (Irwin), "Prudence" (Rackham).

[13] Cf. *NE*, 1112b34-35, 1144a8-9, 1145a5-6, and 1140b 11-20, 44a34-b1, 1151a15-19, *Eudemian Ethics*, 1227b12-19). This remark leads to a reading that practical wisdom and ethical virtue are a relation between end and the means, and consequently that reason has nothing to do with ends. In opposition, many commentators tend to argue that the Greek phrase "means to the end" ("*ta pros to telos*") indicates a more wide relation than its English counterpart suggests. "Means" can be either constitutive (i.e. what pertains to the end) or instrumental (e.g. what is

We seem to be caught in a circle between ethical virtue and practical wisdom (*NE*, 1144b31-2).

In the following I argue that a complete notion of virtue in Aristotle lies in an interplay between the two determinations of intellectual virtue and ethical virtue. Similarly, a complete notion of *ren* in Confucius lies in a synthesis of the two determinations of *ren* as love and *ren* as returning to *li*. On this basis, I try to provide an answer to each of the questions raised above. Both *ren* and Aristotle's virtue are concerned with how a person should live within a society. While Aristotle's virtue hinges on practical wisdom, *ren* is contingent on filial love. This is because while Aristotle emphasizes how a person as a self-determining being can live, Confucius' *li* is an ideal social system, and hence his concern is how a person can comply with *li*, rather than what we should comply with. Finally, I will show that different conceptions of virtues also lead to different pictures of the cultivation of virtue.

2. *Li, Ethos,* and Practical Wisdom

Let us start with Confucius' remark that *ren* is to return to *li*. *Li* originally refers to the rules of rituals or ceremonies involved in religious affairs. In the *Analects* it is conceived far more broadly, containing both abstract principles and detailed forms of social regulations. It prescribes not only what the relations between rulers and the subject should be (*Analects*, 3:18, 3:19), what one ought to do in supporting one's parents, in holding a funeral, and in paying for a sacrifice (*Analects*, 2:5), but also what kind of ceremonial cap one should wear, and even when one should prostrate oneself before ascending steps in seeing a king (*Analects*, 9:3). This latter prescription is like the rule that requires one to wear black tie in the fellows' dinner at Oxford. Both are cultural norms rather than moral demands. In 12:1, Confucius claims that returning to *li* means that one should follow the guid-

---

towards the end) (Cf. *Metaphysics.*, 1032b27; *Politics.*, 1325b16, 1338b2-4, *NE*, 1144a3), and what Aristotle means is the former rather than the latter. This is certainly right. However, once we notice the circle between reason and ethical virtue, the interpretation becomes also one-sided.

ance of *li* in "looking," "listening," "speaking," and "moving." "One has no way of taking his stand unless he knows *li*"(*Analects*, 20:3). *Li* is thus the totality of socially acceptable behaviour patterns and life styles, including both moral and non-moral norms. It corresponds to Aristotle's *ethos* (social custom),[14] that is, the traditional social mores and cultural settings.

When Confucius claims that *ren* is to return to *li*, he is asking each agent to act in conformity with social values, and thereby become accepted and respected by the society or tradition he or she is in. To be a person of *ren* is first of all to be a social person, equipped with what Aristotle calls "excellence of character" or "ethical virtue."

Yet Confucius' *li* turns out immediately not to be *ethos* or custom as such (which is in Chinese *feng su*). He is not a common-sense moralist. *Li* is an object that Confucius requires us to "return to" (Chinese, *fu*) rather than simply to "conform with." The word "return" in Chinese means to go back to what we have deviated from. *Li* thus has a particular reference, the *li* of the Zhou dynasty. Confucius has a profound commitment to the Zhou *li*: "The Zhou had the advantage of surveying the two preceding dynasties. How resplendent is its culture (*wen*)! I follow Zhou" (*Analects*, 3:14). He even claims that this set of *li* would not be changed for more than a hundred of generations. "Should there be a successor to the Zhou, even a hundred generations hence can be known" (*Analects*, 2:23).

In Confucius' time, the Zhou dynasty collapsed into many small states that had been warring against each other. The Chinese society underwent a turbulent period of transition during which there was little order and stability. When the Zhou house overthrew its predecessor, the Shang dynasty, it claimed that the Shang had forfeited the *Tian Ming* ("Mandate of Heaven") or *Tian Dao* ("Way of Heaven") through its misrule, while its own social institutions conformed to the will of Heaven. Yet they were now broken. Where, then, could be found the Way of Heaven to order the state and guide people's lives? This is the basic problem for Pre-Qin Chinese philosophy. Confu-

---

[14] It also amounts to what Wittgenstein calls "form of life." For an interpretation of *li* in terms of "form of life," see Hansen, 1994, 75ff.

cius' answer is that the social turmoil was due to the loss of traditional values of the Zhou culture. He therefore requires to "return" to the social framework of that ideal state. *Ren* as returning to *li* means to be a person acceptable according to the Zhou *li*.

Although a blueprint of the Zhou *li* is not presented in the *Analects*, [15] its core turns out to be a humane social hierarchy modelled on family relationships. "Let the ruler be a ruler, the subject a subject, the father a father, the son a son" (*Analects*, 12:11). A society is governed by a network of names each of which reflects a status which has a prescribed set of duties. An ordered society is that in which names are "rectified." If each person played a role suitable for the personage he assumed in society, the society would be pacified and harmonious.

Confucius' upholding of the Zhou *li* has been interpreted as testimony to his radical conservatism or traditionalism. Hence, those scholars who would uphold Confucius generally tend not to mention clearly the fact that *li* is the Zhou *li*. However, Confucius' conservatism is not necessarily a fault. His beliefs were generated by his reflection on the brutal social reality of his time. This might be compared with Edmund Burke's conservatism, the result of his reflection on the violence of the French Revolution. It does sometimes seem that Confucius fails to distinguish clearly between fundamental principles and the trivial regulations in the Zhou *li*, and his frequent emphasis on regulatory detail conveys an impression of rigidity. Nevertheless, what he really embraces is the spirit and essence of the Zhou *li*. When he claims that the Zhou *li* will not change for a hundred generations (*Analects*, 2:23; 3:14), he is not saying that none of the detailed regulations of the Zhou *li* is changeable. As a matter of fact, he does endorse some changes. For instance, frugality is preferred to extravagance in ceremonial practice (*Analects*, 3:4), and a ceremonial cap of linen can be changed into a cap of black silk for reasons of economy (*Analects*, 9:3).

---

[15] *Analects*, book X describes in detail *li* in daily life and activities, yet it is widely regarded as "inauthentic."

Confucius fully realizes that the Zhou *li* itself is developed from the preceding two dynasties, incorporating a variety of good elements from them (*Analects*, 15:11). The idea of social development is not alien to his thinking. What should remain unchanged is, however, the deep meaning of the Zhou *li*, the radical alteration of which can only lead to calamity. As his disciple Zi Xia says: "If one does not overstep the bounds in major matters, it is of no consequence if one is not meticulous in minor matters"(*Analects*, 19:11). Confucius admires the Zhou *li* because he believes that it must be the ideal of social regulations, and this is the context within which humanity can gain its full expression. *Li* is thus the Way, or *logos*.[16] To "return" is not simply to go back, but to hold onto the authentic. A person of *ren* should embody the authentic spirit of a culture. Chinese civilisation is the longest-lived of historical traditions, and it is generally believed that Confucianism is what has generated the cohesive force behind this civilisation. And the strength of Confucianism is its insistence of traditional values.

Confucius does not present detailed justification for why the Zhou *li* is the ideal ethical and political order. He seems to believe that it has s divinity that is derived from the Heaven (*Tian*) and *Dao*. The fact that the Zhou *li* had declined in his time he ascribes to the fact that *Dao* had not prevailed in the empire (*Analects*, 16:2; 5:6). To illustrate the relation between *Tian* and *li*, we must here introduce another major notion of Confucius: *de*. While *ren* is referred to as virtue, *de* in various translations is also defined as virtue. The identical translations of these two concepts could be justified on the ground that *de* in Chinese is derived from "to get," and in Confucius can be understood as the consequence of returning to *li*. It is hence a counterpart of ethical virtue in Aristotle. If a culture gets the spirit of *Dao* (or Heavenly *Dao*), it is endowed with "*de*." It is in this sense that Confucius says that the *de* of Zhou "can be said to have been the highest" (*Analects*, 8:20). If a person lives in accordance with *li*, then he has *de*. Sometimes Confucius directly claims that Heaven is the

---

[16] In this sense Herbert Fingarette is certainly right to call it "holy rite" or "sacred ceremony" (Fingarette, 1972, 6-7).

author of *de* (*Analects*, 7:23, cf. also 9:5), and sometimes he justifies a *de* in terms of the operation of Heaven. For instance, clever talk or loquacity is not considered as a *de* (*Analects*, 15:27; 17:17). Why is this? Confucius explains: "What does Heaven ever say? Yet there are the four seasons going round and there are the hundred things coming into being. What does Heaven ever say?" (*Analects*, 17:19). Confucius takes the Zhou *li as* the full embodiment of *Dao* or *logos*.

He further distinguishes the "*de* of the gentleman" from the "*de* of the small man," but never says what the ground is for this distinction. This gives rise to some confusion in understanding this concept. Such a distinction seems to suggest precisely the distinction between the Zhou *li* (*ethos*) and *ethos* in general. If *de* is cultivated out of the Zhou *li*, it is a *de* of the gentlemen, and if it is a habitual quality out of the prevailing but non-authentic *ethos*, it is the *de* of the small man. He says: "The village worthy is the ruin of *de*" (*Analects*, 17:13). But the village worthy is no doubt a kind of traditional custom. A good person should neither be liked not disliked by all in the village, but should be liked by those who are good and disliked by those who are bad (*Analects*, 13:24).

While Confucius' ethics is confined to the sacred Zhou *li*, Aristotle's *ethos* is simply the prevailing social customs and conventions. Aristotle believes that a human being must be a social animal, and accordingly must conform to social norms. Nevertheless, like Confucius, he does not think that to cultivate ethical virtue is simply a matter of passively complying with the existing customs and rules, whatever they may be. It is possible that the existing ends are in conflict, and are not even good. Within the same social context, there are rival lists of virtues and different definitions for the same virtues. This situation is not exceptional within the *polis* of Athens in the fifth century, as Plato's early dialogues attest. In terms of this fact, Aristotle distinguishes between "a good man" and "a good citizen"(Aristotle, *NE*, 1130b28, *Politics*, 1276b34). The social norms, constitutions, and form of government change, and the meaning of a "good citizen" changes accordingly. "There is not one single virtue of the good citizen that is perfect virtue" (*Politics*, 1276b32-3). In contrast, there is a single perfect virtue for human beings as human beings, namely their reason. Aristotle's self is both a self-determining rational being and a being determined by the social norms. But since his ethics concerns more what a good man should be than what a good citizen should be, reason becomes the ultimate determinant. "For it is our decisions to do what is good or bad, not our beliefs, that make the character we have" (*NE*, 1112a4).

Hence, while one cannot live in isolation from society, one must maintain a reflective attitude towards *ethos* in order to be a good person. This reflective function is one's practical wisdom (*phronesis*). First, practical wisdom helps one to understand why the ways of behaviour that one has learned are really noble and true. One therefore proceeds from knowing "that" (*oti*) to knowing "why" (*dioti*). A person of experience sometimes can do better than a person of knowledge, but knowledge is still superior to experience because it grasps the cause, whereas experience does not (*etaphysics*, 981a29). A man of practical wisdom (*phronimos*) performs a virtuous act because it is really virtuous, rather than a simulacrum of virtue.

Second, practical wisdom does not merely provide a person with a more articulate opinion as to why the instructed behaviour is good, but is also required to compare various views of what goodness is, and then also to grasp true conceptions of what ends are really good and should be pursued in conflicting situations (*NE*, 1143b21-22).[17] This clarification of existing ends is itself also the process of achieving a new end. For Aristotle, practical wisdom is concerned with the conception of the good life in general, and the *phronimos* deliberates well "about what promotes living well in general" (*NE*, 1140a27-28).

Third, practical wisdom has a dimension of contextuality or particularity. Aristotle acknowledges that the subject of ethics is indeterminate, and that universal principles are not flexible enough to

---

[17] This is, indeed, the task Aristotle ascribes to his ethics. His dialectical ethics shows that we need to examine the *endoxa*, the received or reputed views (*NE*, 1098b23-6), at least the most influential among them (*NE*, 1095a28-30), to discover the *aporiai* these views cause, and then decide which of them should be followed or what can be preserved (*NE*, 1146b5-6, *Eudemian Ethics*, 1235b15-8). Aristotle tries to draw the whole truth that other views capture only in part.

cope with various particular situations (*NE*, 1098a26ff, 1103b34). Practical wisdom is concerned with actions, and actions are always about particulars. Hence it has a dimension of perception, i.e. practical intuition, for determining what should be done or can be done well in certain particular circumstances: "For nothing perceptible is easily defined, and [since] these [circumstances of virtuous and vicious action] are particulars, the judgment about them depends on perception" (*NE*, 1109b22-3).[18] A practical perception recognizes the salient features of the particulars and is aware of the limits of the universal principles in application. Practical wisdom thus enables one to reach an equilibrium between universal and particular and to be aware of what should be done in accordance with the good end in a concrete situation.

Aristotle then develops the topics related to practical wisdom, such as choice, deliberation, responsibility, incontinence (*akrasia*), and so on. In contrast, Confucius says little about these issues.[19] This is largely because his *li* is not something towards which we are required to maintain a critical attitude. We have a choice only between following *li* and falling into disorder. For Confucius, "a good man" and "a good citizen" should not be different, and indeed it is as a good citizen that one can be a good person. Aristotle does agree that in the best form of society, a good person and a good citizen would be the same, but the best form of society is to be found by the science of politics. Both Aristotle and Confucius are concerned with what a good person should be and connect this with social culture and tradition. However, whereas Aristotle suggests an attitude which is not one of blind compliance with tradition, Confucius insists on the continuity and authenticity of tradition. It is out of this belief that Confucius devotes much of his life to the transmission of the ancient classics, which record the *li* or civilisation of Zhou.

---

[18] Cf. also *NE*, 1110b6, 1126b4, 1141b27-8, 1142a24-7; 1143a28-5, b6, 1147a3, 25-26, b5.

[19] In this sense, Fingarette is certainly right in remarking that Confucius lacks a proper moral psychology (Fingarette, 1972, Ch 2, "A way without a crosswords").

Nevertheless, the lack of an Aristotelian notion of practical wisdom turns out to be the weakness in Confucius' thinking. Here we need to discuss another of his important notion: *yi* (which is generally translated as "righteousness," "meaning," or "morality"). In one instance, he says: "In dealing with the world the gentleman is not invariably for and against anything. He is on the side of *yi*" (*Analects*, 4:10). What, then, is *yi* and what is its relation to *li*? *Yi* appears in the *Analects* 24 times without a unified definition or elucidation. More often, this term is used in opposition to personal advantages or profit (in Chinese also *li*): "The gentleman understands *yi*, the small man understands what is profitable" (*Analects*, 4:16; cf. also 19:1; 7:15; 14:13). *Yi* in this sense means the right principle of behaviour, in contrast to egoism. It is something like the principle of justice or what action one should follow or conform to. This sense is in fact not far from *li*.[20]

The relationship between *li* and *yi* can be understood as follows. As we mentioned earlier, *li* has both its detailed forms and its spirit. Its detailed forms cannot cover all the possible and complex situations in our actual life. When such a situation occurs, we should act in accordance with the spirit of *li*, the rightness agreed to and believed by the community. *Yi* is thus close to the convention of what is moral binding.[21] Accordingly, Confucius is saying in the

---

[20] Cf., *Analects*, 1:13; 2:24; 5:16; 7:3; 12:10 and 20; 13:4; 15:16; 16:11. For the notion of "*yi*" at the passage 4:10 which is under discussion, many translators tend to view it as something external and objective, and render it as "what is moral" (Lau), "righteousness as the standard" (Chan). In other senses, *yi* is sometimes related to the regulation of the character of courage (*Analects*, 2:24, 17:23), which is again close to *li*, and is sometimes opposed to small cleverness (*Analects*, 15:17). Confucius says: "The gentleman has *yi* as his native substance (*zhi*), and by observing *li* puts it into practice" (*Analects*, 15:18). Since native substance at 4:16 is in contrast to culture (*wen*), *yi* in this context seems to refer to natural character before cultural refinement.

[21] Schwartz, 1985, 79-80 also distinguishes *li* from *yi*, but he claims that *yi* is simply what is right beyond the reach of the prescription of *li*, and thus makes *yi* an independent source of right behaviour alongside *li*. Chad Hansen also sees *the distinction between li* and *yi* as the distinction between etiquette (social mores) and real morality. Nonetheless, he also remarks: "Given the nature of Confucius' reference

passage at 4:10 (quoted above) that when a particular act lacks the guidance of the concrete form of *li*, we must follow the right (*yi*). And the source of the right is the spirit of *li*, or authentic tradition. If we should adhere to *yi* in a situation where the concrete regulations of *li* are not available, we need a way to judge and elaborate what is the right (*yi*), that is, what constitutes the deep spirit of *li* or the enduring *dao* and what is peripheral to the authentic tradition. We need to reflect upon what concrete forms of *li* embody the authentic spirit of the tradition and what should be emended, revised, and even partly rejected. We must identify when the *dao* or Way prevails or when it is hidden. Confucius' notion of *yi* seems to open the door for an Aristotelian notion of practical wisdom, but he fails to work it out. He has a major virtue called "wisdom" (*zhi*), but it must also be based on the conformity to *li*. "How can the man be considered wise who, when he has the choice, does not settle in *ren?*"(*Analects*, 9:1). Yet he says nothing further about how *zhi*, based on *ren*, can determine what *yi* is. [22]

---

to *yi* (morality), we cannot tell if he distinguished between real morality and a community's social mores," and "the discourse in the *Analects* makes no distinction between moral *dao* and conventional mores" (Hansen, 1994, 82).

[22] This account of *yi* and its relationship with *li* is in contrast to the interpretation of Hall and Ames (Hall and Ames, 1987) who claims that there is a long-ignored distinction between *li* and *yi*. While *li* is not "divinely established" (ibid. 89), the notion of *yi* reflects a capacity to import the agent's significance into the world, a "flexibility for a person to interact with and integrate into ever new situations." *Yi* is particular, creative and responsive, and it is a "central theme" in Confucius to "underscore the creative and novel dimensions of *yi*" (ibid. 95). Consequently, a person of *ren* is made by exercising his own judgment (*yi*) to adept the tradition (*li*). Although the authors do not refer to Aristotle, it is interesting that their reading of Confucius is virtually an Aristotelian one. *Li* corresponds to undogmatic *ethos*, and *yi* to practical wisdom (*phronesis*). Since I have argued that Confucius insisted on the continuity of the Zhou *li*, and that *yi* is conventional on the basis of *li* rather than personal, their interpretation seems to me to be challengeable. Nevertheless, it is insightful of the authors of this interpretation to draw our attention to the ignored notion of *yi*, which seems exactly the place for developing Confucius' thinking.

3. Filial Love and Self-love

The main problem addressed by Aristotle's ethics is how one should live. When Confucius claims that a person of *ren* is to live in accordance with *li*, he seems already to have provided an answer to this question. He then needs to deal with how it is possible for a person to "return to" or "comply with" *li*. For unlike Mencius after him, Confucius is not an utopian concerning human nature. He does not believe that human nature is innately programmed to comply with *li*. Instead, he has a deep suspicion that it is naturally attracted to *ren*.: "I have never met a man who finds *ren* attractive or a man who finds not-*ren* repulsive. A man who finds *ren* attractive cannot be surpassed" (*Analects*, 4:6). When he claims that *ren* is "to return to *li*," the more complete expression is "to overcome oneself and to return to *li*." Accordingly, in returning to *li*, one must first of all discipline the "self."

Of course, a person could be forced to accept *li*'s requirement through punishment. Yet in that case one "will stay out of trouble but will have no sense of shame" (*Analects*, 2:3). Confucius' *li* might be normative, but in contrast to both Kantian ethics and utilitarianism, it is not something external that one ought to obey without regard to one's inner motivation. For him, ethics is not a matter of how we should be bounded (*obligare*), but of how we can follow social rules willingly and naturally. It is against this background that Confucius introduces another major determination of *ren*: "*Ren* is to love humanity" (*Analects*, 12:22).

Ren as love is based on the feeling one has toward one's own parents and brothers. "Filial piety and brotherly love are the roots of *ren*" (*Analects*, 1:2).[23] In Confucius' view, these roots have the most important ethical value: "The gentleman nourishes the roots, for once the roots are established, the *dao* will grow therefrom" (*Analects*, 1:2). If family love is the ground for *dao* to prevail, given the relation between *dao* and *li*, *ren* as love becomes fundamental for *ren* as return-

---

[23] Here I follow the translation of Wing-tsit Chan (*A Source Book in Chinese Philosophy*, 20).

ing to *li*. Filial love as natural sentiment is inborn and not culturally specific. What is required is to cherish and nurture it.

Filial love is crucial because Confucius believes that the gratitude and affection toward one's parents enable one willingly to accept parental authority and the hierarchical relation between parent and child. Such an ingrained and intimate relation is given as justification for the practice of the three-year mourning period when a parent dies: "A child ceases to be nursed by his parents only when he is three years old. Three years' mourning is observed throughout the Empire" (*Analects*, 17:21). To repay three years with three years might appear too formal, but the idea here is that filial love might inspire an internal feeling that causes one willingly to carry out the responsibility toward one's parents. Kinship is a natural hierarchy and establishes natural authority relations, while its extension/expansion to other social relations naturalises the idea of hierarchy and authority in the wider society. By the same token, the feeling toward one's brothers makes one agreeably altruistic. A family may not be a democratic forum or provide a context for equality, but it is a place one loves to be in.

Ren as love is the expansion of the roots of filial love. This expansion consists in the transferring of the family's relation of hierarchy and fraternity to the larger society. As a good father makes a good ruler, a good son makes a good subject. A man of *ren* starts with loving the parents, and then gradually expands the circle of love. "The young should behave with filial piety at home, and with brotherly love abroad"(*Analects*, 1:6); eventually "All within the Four Seas are his brothers"(*Analects*, 12:5). "A man who possesses filial piety and brotherly love is unlikely to transgress against his superiors, and to incline to start a rebellion" (*Analects*, 1:2).

Hence, the determination that "*ren* is to love humanity" serves to justify the inner basis of returning to *li*. Earlier I mentioned, but without discussion, that there is a well-recognised but unspecified distinction in Confucius between *ren* as complete virtue and *ren* as particular virtue. If my argument thus far is sound, this distinction can be set on an intelligible foundation. While *ren* as love seems a particular virtue, *ren* in its complete sense is a synthesis of *ren* as love and *ren* as returning to *li*. Neither is dispensable. On the one hand, the conformity to *li* must be based on *ren* as love: "What can a man do with *li* who is not *ren*?"(*Analects*, 3:3); on the other hand, *ren* as love itself must be regulated by *li*: "one who is fond of *ren* without being fond of learning [of *li*] is liable to lead to foolishness" (*Analects*, 17:8). One can be fully good only when one conforms to *li* out of love. Although Confucius does not specify, it does not seem far from his mind that such an interplay or synthesis underlies all admirable characteristics, that is, particular virtues. For instance, courage cannot be characterized as a virtue if it does not contain this unity of *ren* as love and *ren* as returning to *li*. It will become unruly if not regulated by *li* (*Analects*, 8:2; 17:8), but if it is not motivated by love it will also lead to unruly behaviour (*Analects*, 8:10). Even filial piety as a virtue is determined by such a unity. On the one hand, filial piety needs to conform to *li*: "When your parents are alive, comply with *li* in serving them; when they die, comply with *li* in burying them and in sacrificing to them"(*Analects*, 2:5), and on the other hand it requires a feeling of love in serving the parents; otherwise, "Even hounds and horses are, in some way, provided with food. If a man shows no reverence, where is the difference?"(*Analects*, 2:7).

Ren as love not only keeps the compliance with *li* from being a matter of externally imposed limitations, but also provides an inner ground for altruism. Virtues can be either self-regarding or other regarding or both. It has been one central concern for virtue ethics to provide the rationale for altruism, that is, other-regarding virtue. Confucius' insight is that if we want to nurture altruism, then filial love serves as a root or an innate spring.[24]

Like Confucius, Aristotle fully acknowledges the intrinsic goodness of love. *Philia*, which is generally translated as "friendship" is one of the central topics in several treatises.[25] Human beings are political or social animals, "tending by nature to live together with others" (*NE*, 1169b17); and "The will to live together is friendship

---

[24] Russell seems to miss the point entirely when he says: "Filial piety, and the strength of the family generally, are perhaps the weakest point in Confucian ethics" (Russell, 1922, 40).

[25] *NE*, VII, *Rhetoric* 1380b33ff.

(philia)" (Politics, 1280b38). *Philia* includes every kind of social relation involving mutual loving and liking, and hence "love" seems a better translation.[26] It exists not only within family members and fellow-citizens, but also in various associations of individuals who share a common interest in utility, pleasure, or virtue. The former kind is natural, while the latter is voluntary.

For Aristotle, it is friendship that creates "family connexions, brotherhood, common sacrifices" *(Politics,* 1280b37), and it is "the greatest good of states" *(Politics,* 1262b8) to have and to preserve friendship. At a personal level, friendship is necessary for happiness *(eudaimonia).* It is not merely the "greatest" and "most necessary" of external goods *(NE,* 1169b10, 1154a4-5), but also intrinsic to a happy life. For one needs it in all circumstances and in every period of life. A man without friends cannot be happy *(NE,* 1155a5-6, 116968-10, 1169b16-7). It creates an arena for one to realise and express one's virtue. The natural love or friendship within the family is also highly valued by Aristotle. A parent loves his children because he regards them as "something of himself," and children love their parents because they regard them as the "source of origin" *(NE,* 1161b18-9). Brothers love each other because they are from the same parents.

The discussion of friendship or love earns Aristotle credit for putting friendship and family attachment as important, intrinsic items into the ethical sphere. This is regarded as a significant advantage of his ethics over modern moral theories that focus instead on impartiality and the impersonal point of view. Aristotle's discussion of friendship, especially of family love, corrects Plato's radical anti-family position in the *Republic.*

Both Confucius and Aristotle advocate the ethical status of love, but their discussions differ in certain significant aspects. The family love that Confucius emphasizes is filial love, the love of children toward their parents. Filial love is prior to virtue and is the root of the latter. We nurture this root to the effect that the society is seen as an enlarged family. All social sympathy or love is derived from filial love

---

[26] This is suggested by Nussbaum (1986, 354). Other translations include "social relation" (Urmson), "social sympathy" (Barker).

and can be reduced to it. On the other hand, the family love Aristotle emphasizes is parental love. He believes that the parents' love toward children is more intense than the other way round. This is because parents know children better and have a stronger sense of possessing, and also because their love toward their children starts right from their birth. "While children become fond of the parent when time has passed and they have acquired some comprehension or perception" (*NE*, 1161b27). Since a parent is an adult and has already established a stable character, parental love cannot be a starting-point for the formation of virtue and is not associated with the notion that a state is an enlarged family. Hence, when Aristotle divides natural family love and voluntary social love, he never says that the latter is derived from the former. He draws a clear-cut distinction between household and political life, and claims that it is mistaken to think that families and city-states are different only in size rather than in kind (*Politics*, 1,1). He truly acknowledges the importance of family and social sympathy in ethics, but unlike Confucius, he fails to appreciate family love as an ethical value that is the basis for other social regulations.[27] In dealing with family and emotional commitment, Confucius goes much further than Aristotle, for he not only does justice to these ethical phenomena but also considers them an Archimedean point for his ethics.

For Aristotle, social love or friendship is an extension of one's love to himself rather than an extension of filial love: "The defining features of friendship that are found in friendship to one's neighbours would seem to be derived from features of friendship toward oneself" (*NE*, 1166a1-2). All forms of love must be understood in the context of self-love. Such an analysis of the essence of friendship is associated with his view that a human being is essentially a rational being. He declares that "The good person must be a self-lover (*philautos*)"(*NE*, 1169a11).[28] He distinguishes two

---

[27] For Aristotle, the relations between father and son, between husband and wife, and between brothers are various. They can be either monarchic, aristocratic, timocratic, or tyrannical, oligarchic and democratic. Accordingly, family relation cannot be in itself a source of social justice.

[28] Cf. also *NE*, 1169b1.

kinds of self-lovers: one is a base egoist who does his best to gratify appetite and the nonrational part of the soul (*NE*, 1186b17, 1168b22-23); the other pursues the gratification of the rational part of the soul, for reason is, above all, "what each person is, and the decent person likes this most of all" (*NE*, 1169a2).[29] The good man as a self-lover is the latter kind who is obedient to the voice of reason within himself and sets his life in accordance with rationality.

We once again face the relation between Aristotle's dual dimensions of human nature. A human being as a social animal requires love, but man as a rational being explains the nature of love. The love of others is grounded in the love of self. It follows that a human being is first of all a rational being rather than a social being, albeit the latter status is indispensable.

Aristotle is charged with leaving little room for altruism in his ethics. He fails to explain consistently why a rational person needs to cultivate other-regarding virtues in the *NE*. A good person will perform actions for other people's interests, but that is for the perfection of one's own character. If so, when there is a conflict with other agents in pursuing the development of their own characters, it is rational for an agent to develop his own, rather than curtailing it. Furthermore, according to Aristotle's ethics, one should only pursue the actions that are relevant to one's development of ethical character. Aristotle's virtuous person could certainly be altruistic out of habituation, but a rational self-love account seems not to be sufficient to justify this tendency. In discussing the paradigm case of friendship, that is, the friendship based on virtue, or what Cooper called "character friendship" (Cooper, 1980, 308), Aristotle keeps remarking that those friends "wish goods to their friend for the friend's own sake" (*NE*, 1156b10-12).[30] Many commentators accordingly interpret the virtue of friendship as a supplement or modification of Aristotle egocentric ethics. But this hardly stands up under close scrutiny. Aristotle still explains this form of altruism in

---

[29] Cf. also *NE*, 1162a15, 1168b35, 1178a2-3.

[30] Cf. *NE*, 1156a17-8, 1156b10; cf., also *Eudemian Ethics*, 1244b15-22, *Rhetoric*, 1385a18-9.

terms of the rational self-love: "In loving their friend they love what is good for themselves" (*NE*, 1157b33). A virtue friend is "another me" or "another self." We care for friends because a friend is a mirror by which I can contemplate myself better.[31] What we seek in this kind of love is the friend's rationality and persistent traits of character, rather than the friend's accidental properties. By experiencing that character we enrich and develop our own ethical characters. In the final analysis the love of one's virtuous friends is still self-oriented.[32]

Confucius' *ren* as love provides a sort of justification for altruism. Nevertheless, his altruism is graded. Love is certainly universal, for we are required to treat all people under heaven as brothers. Yet this does not mean that a man of *ren* should love everyone equally. The expansion of love is hierarchical and makes distinctions. This idea is explicitly defended by Mencius in criticizing the Moist type of impartial universal love. This graded love has been accused of partiality. Nonetheless, it is intrinsic to Confucius' thinking. Love must be rooted in family love because the latter involves an inherent intimacy between affection and ethical training. Denial of this intimacy will destroy the Confucian ground of complying with *li*, in particular the inner ground of other-regarding virtue. Such a graded love seems to be echoed in contemporary socio-biology and evolutionary ethics, which suggest that we have a gene-determined altruistic tendency as a human adaptation in evolution, but, everything being equal, we are biologically determined to co-operate first of all with our close kin and others whose reciprocation is expected. It is also echoed in contemporary environmental ethics that extends the scope of moral community beyond human beings to animals and even to nature itself.

An equal and impartial universal love is definitely more desirable, but as the highest ethical virtue it requires an independent source of justification. The central concern of modern moral systems

---

[31] *Magna Moralia*, 1213a10-26, *Eudemian Ethics*, 1245a29-37. *NE*, 1170b7.

[32] Furthermore, virtue friendship exists only between good people who are similar in virtues. Hence virtue is prior to and necessary for friendship.

is to provide such a justification. But neither deontology nor utilitarianism is thought to fulfil this task satisfactorily. Both of them are accused of holding an impersonal point of view. As a matter of fact, one's affection toward other, unknown children cannot be as intense as that toward one's own. Williams' famous problem whether a rescuer is permitted to rescue his wife first[33] will present a dilemma for an advocate of impartial love, but not for Confucius.

Given its fundamental status, Confucius protects filial love strongly from any attack. This is illustrated in the case of a father who steals a sheep. The Governor of the village believes that the son who testifies against such a father is an example of a "straight" person. On the contrary, Confucius claims that "Fathers cover up for their sons, and sons cover up for their fathers. In such behaviour is straightness to be found as a matter of course" (*Analects*, 13: 18). What he is saying is that the father might be open to punishment for his wrongdoing, but it is not his son's position to take responsibility for seeing that justice is done. Family love itself is certainly subjected to the regulation of *ethos* or *yi* (rightness), but if an *ethos* encourages the disruption of filial love, it is for Confucius the greatest evil.

4. Cultivation

For Confucius, *de*, the acquired *ren*, is "to get," and for Aristotle, ethical virtue is connected with "*hexis*" (having"). Both "to get" and "to have" require a process of ethical training and cultural refinement. For Confucius, this is a process of expanding one's filial love to society so that one may willingly accept the constraints of *li*; for Aristotle, this is a process of the habituation and development of practical wisdom. But both believe that such a process of cultivation is life-long, and virtues are eventually internalised as second nature. According to Confucius, he himself set his heart on learning at fifteen, but not until seventy can he follow his heart's desire "without overstepping the line" (*Analects*, 2:4). That amounts to saying that at

---

[33] Williams, 1981, 18.

that time the disposition is well entrenched and is a *hexis* or a second nature in the Aristotelian sense (*NE*, 1103a31-b21). Confucius views the process of cultivation as mainly a matter of education. Public education is an extension of family education. The Chinese word "education" (*jiaoyu*) is composed by two words: "teaching (*jiao*) + nurturing (*yu*)," and it is not merely to convey knowledge, but also to shape correct behaviour patterns and internalise them as one's character. In Hansen's words, it is "character building."[34] Such an education is carried out through a dual dialectic. On the one hand, a person is taught by his parents, teachers, and the noble people surrounding him what should be done and how to do it. He is required to respect all those who teach him as father-like. A teacher is traditionally called "teacher-father," and the proverb goes, "A teacher of one day makes a father for all life." Government officials, as the practitioners of *li*, are called "parents officers." The head of the state is called "the state-father," and the first-lady "state-mother." On the other hand, a father supports the living, but should act more importantly as an educator, as is reflected in the proverb that "it is the fault of a father only to support but not to educate." A teacher's duty is not merely to teach, but also to serve as a model of ethical behaviour. The duty of a teacher is frequently described as "to be a teacher and model for others." Furthermore, the function of a ruler is not only to order, but also, and even more importantly, to serve as a model of behaviour for the people. The basic principle of governing is "to guide them [people] by *de*, and keep them in line with *li*" rather than "to employ punishment" (*Analects*, 2:3).[35] This is because, in a sense, they are also teachers, and are also required to love their subjects as their own children.

Hence, the hierarchical relationship is a model-copy relationship of behaviour, and each form of it can be reduced to a teacher-pupil relationship, which is in turn reduced to a father-son relationship. The persons who are superior in social status are supposed to establish themselves as the paradigm of humanity, that is, the model for

---

[34] Hansen, 1994, 78.
[35] Cf. also *Analects* 2:1

juniors and inferiors to follow and catch up with. The society is an extended school as well as an extended family.

Confucius is reported to have remarked that there is a single thread pervading his *dao* (*Analects*, 4:15), which is interpreted by his disciple as "*zhong* and *shu.*" The character "*xin*" (heart) is a component of both words. *Zhong,* traditionally rendered as "loyalty," is better translated by D. C. Lau as "doing one's best," that is, in dealing with relationships with others. *Shu,* etymologically related to "as," is explained by Confucius to mean "Do not imposes on others what you yourself do not desire" (Analects, 15:24), and its translation varies from "using oneself as a measure to gauge others" (Lau); "altruism" (Chan), "consideration" (Waley), "reciprocity" (Dawson), and so on. *Shu* is intrinsically related to *ren* in its etymologically relational sense[36], and in one place Confucius considers *ren* as the positive enunciation of the principle of *shu:* "A person of *ren* helps others to take their stand in so far as he himself wishes to take his stand, and gets others there in so far as he himself wishes to get there" (*Analects*, 6:30).

How to interpret this "single thread" has been a matter of considerable controversy. Given the relation between *shu* and *ren*, and given that the self of a *ren* person in Confucius is essentially embedded in his relations with his family members, I would like to think that the "single thread" means that one should do one's best to deal with others as one deals with one's parents and brothers. Interpreted in this way, Confucius' "single thread" indicates how one can expand filial love to society, that is, the way of cultivating virtue. This seems to be confirmed by Confucius' remark that "To be able to judge others by what is near to ourselves may be called the method of realising *ren*."[37] One's parents and brothers are certainly what are closest to a person. To make an analogy to them in deciding what one should or should not do in dealing with others is the art of the acquisition of virtues. In Chinese ethical training, a person is generally

---

[36] For a useful discussion of their relationship, see Hall and Ames, 1987, 286-287.

[37] The translation is based on that of Wing-tsit Chan whose paragraph number is 6:28, while Lau's is 6:30.

told "to think of him as your brother" or "to think of her as your sister" to decide what you should or should not do in dealing with others. Even in the training of self-regarding virtue, such as diligence, a person is taught "to work hard to earn honour for your parents". The family-centred Chinese culture is essentially indebted to Confucius' teaching.

Aristotle agrees with Confucius that human beings are not by nature ethically good. As he says: "the many, especially the young, do not find it pleasant to live in a temperate and resistant way" (*NE*, 1179b34-5). Virtue does not develop spontaneously. The cultivation of moral virtues starts with habit. A virtue is acquired by doing fine things repeatedly and thus one can fall into the habit of doing them. The process of habituation essentially involves practice and repetition. "Character (*êthos*), as the word itself indicates, is that which is developed from habit [*ethos*]" (*EE*, 1220a39-b3). It is a process of moderating one's desire and emotion and of directing them towards the appropriate objects. This requires that we should be brought up from our very youth "to find pleasure and pain as it is appropriate" (*NE*, 1104b11-13). Since a good upbringing is a matter of luck, Aristotle's cultivation of virtue is dependent to luck.

A good upbringing implies that one has a good ethical training environment, and there is correct order of some sort to follow. The good instructions can be from the father: "...a father's words and habit have influence, and all the more because of kinship and because of the benefits he does; for his children are already fond of him and naturally ready to obey" (*NE*, 1180b5-7), but the role of a father or any other individual is limited, for "a father's instruction, however, lack this influence and compelling power." It is the law that "has the power that compels" (*NE*, 1180a19-22), because many people fear penalties rather than shame. Accordingly, habituation is more an issue for the city rather than for the family. "Law must prescribe their upbringing and practices" (*NE*, 1179a35). A good upbringing mainly requires to live under correct laws and Aristotle accordingly pays more attention to the function of legislation than of the family in moral education. The standard by which a good political system is distinguished from a bad one is whether it effectively facilitates good habituation.

During the course of habituation, many people become accustomed to things that they used to find painful, and even come to take pleasure in doing such things. This kind of well brought-up person accordingly possesses "a character suitable for virtue, fond of what is fine and objecting to what is shameful"(*NE*, 1179b30-31). For Aristotle, people with such a nature are "like ground that is to nourish seed," and only they can be taught by ethical arguments and are proper students of his ethics, whereas other people without this nature continue to require brutish methods of constraint (*NE*, 1179b24-9). This is in contrast to Confucius' view of a habituation that focuses on the expansion of filial love through an emulation of the models that surround one, rather than on the role of law and punishment. In fact, Confucius always adopts a negative stance towards litigation (*Analects*, 12:13).

For Aristotle, cultivation as a process of habituation is a process of acting in accordance with the good instructions from one's father and the law of one's community, as well as a process of developing one's practical wisdom.[38] In the course of repeatedly performing actions he is told are noble and just, a person comes to realise why they are said to be good. He will diminish his dependence on other people telling him what to do, and will come to see what is right himself. He will also develop a practical perception of what should be done in a particular circumstance. The exercise of rational judgement becomes inherent in education. Confucius' picture of cultivation, in contrast, lacks the development of practical wisdom.

Earlier we mentioned that in Aristotle's concept of virtue, there is a circle between practical wisdom and ethical virtue. On the one hand, practical wisdom is not simply a matter of rational calculation. It is distinguished from such notions of capacity as deliberation

---

[38] There is indeed a traditional interpretation in Aristotle scholarship that the cultivation of ethical virtue out of habits is a purely non-cognitive process of habituation. But it has been convincingly rejected by Burnyeat, "Aristotle on Learning to be good," Richard Sorabji, "Aristotle on the Role of Intellect in virtue" (Both articles are included in Rorty 1980), and Nancy Sherman, *Fabric of Character*, Clarendon, Oxford, 1989.

(*bouleusis*) and cleverness (*deinotes*). It is not morally indifferent, but involves an essential reference to, or presupposes, ethical virtue (Aristotle, *NE*, 1143b11-14, 1144a30-31). Aristotle explicitly declares that "we cannot be a person of practical wisdom without being good" (*NE*, 1144a36), and he therefore rejects that an incontinent person has practical wisdom. Practical wisdom is inseparable from ethical virtue and is embedded in the tradition. On the other hand, practical wisdom also reflects and criticises the tradition, as we indicate in the second section of this essay. Viewed from the standpoint of the dynamic process of cultivation, this circle is not vicious. It is inherent in this process and promotes the fabric of character as well as the reformation of the tradition itself. The ethical virtue that provides the goal for practical wisdom is not the full virtue, for the goal it teaches derives from experience rather than from clear knowledge and a critical attitude. A human being as a rational animal cannot be merely a creature of habit. Without exercising rational activity a man cannot be a human being in the fullest sense. Only when one develops one's own practical wisdom, can one fully enjoy doing noble things. A full moral virtue, that is a person's second nature, cannot be acquired until one exercises one's own reason.

A state of character can be good because it aims at the mean state of feeling and actions (*NE*, 1106b28, 1109a20-30). This notion of a mean is not one of quantity, but one of correctness.[39] The mean is a state that "enables one to act at the right time, about the right things, towards the right people, for the right end, and in the right way" (*NE*, 1109a20-23). This rightness is determined by correct reason (*orthos logos*), that is, practical wisdom (*NE*, 1144b28). Reason determines rightness differently in different situations. On such a basis Aristotle derives his complete definition of ethical virtue:

---

[39] The traditional discussion of Aristotle's doctrine of the mean focuses on its quantitative determination, and the doctrine is accordingly not highly valued. But this traditional approach has been rejected by Urmson who argues convincingly that the mean refers to the mean disposition towards to action, rather than a disposition towards the mean action. See Urmson, "Aristotle's Doctrine of the Mean," *American Philosophical Quarterly* (1973), 223-230, reprinted in Rorty 1980.

"virtue is a state (*hexis*) concerned that decides, consisting in a mean, the mean relative to us, which is defined by reference to reason, i.e., to the reason by reference to which the person of practical wisdom would define it" (*NE*, 1107a1-3).

We now see that while for Confucius a complete notion of *ren* is a synthesis of *ren* as love and *ren* as conforming to *li*, for Aristotle a full notion of virtue comprises virtue as state of character as well as virtue as exercising practical rationality, and is an organic synthesis of them. It is the synthesis of these two determinations that determines the mean state. Virtue as mean in turn determines the nature of all other ethical virtues.

It is interesting to note that with regard to the concept of virtue, neither Confucius' synthesis nor Aristotle's synthesis is fully respected historically. In the West, Aristotle's practical wisdom and ethical virtue have been separated since the Enlightenment. Philosophers contrast the authority of reason to tradition, and then try to establish universal and trans-cultural principles of morality in which virtue does not have any significant place. The current revival of virtue ethics is in a sense to "return" to Aristotle's interplay between reason and virtue, although with significant alterations.[40] Correspondingly, in the East, Confucian' synthesis of *ren* as love and *ren* as returning to *li* is also severed in the later development of Confucianism. *Ren* as observing *li* comes to be more and more rigid and inflexible, and moves far from *ren* as love. *Li* was eventually accused in the May Fourth movement of "eating man."[41] The basic spirit of the May Fourth movement is to set a sharp contrast between Chinese tradition and Western science and democracy, and then uphold the latter while rejecting the former. But the recent resurgence of Confucianism in East Asia emphasizes the value of Chinese tradition and criticises Western individualist morality. This sounds like a tendency to "return" to Confucius' notion of *ren*. If the

---

[40] MacIntyre asks "Whose justice? Which rationality?" (Duckworth, 1988), and Williams attempts to replace both theory and prejudice with "reflection"(Williams, 1985, 112).

[41] The remark is from Lu Xun's *Diary of the Madman*.

comparison of this paper is sound, we would like to suggest that while an Aristotelian revival would do well to borrow the Confucian insight of filial love, a Confucian revival could hardly be constructive without developing an Aristotelian function of rationality in weighing and reanimating the tradition.[42]

REFERENCES

Aristotle. 1985. *Nicomachean Ethics*. Trans. Irwin. Indianapolis: Hackett.

Barnes, J. ed. *The Revised Oxford Translation of The Complete Works of Aristotle*, Princeton, NJ: Princeton University Press, 1984.

Burnyeat, M. F. 1980. "Aristotle on Learning to be good." In Rorty 1980.

Chan, Wing-tsit (trans.). 1963. *A Source Book in Chinese Philosophy*. Princeton, NJ: Princeton University Press.

————. 1955. "The Evolution of the Confucian Concept *Ren*," *Philosophy East and West*, 4, 295-315.

Confucius. 1979. *Analects*. Trans by D. C. Lau. Hong Kong: The Chinese University Press.

Cooper, J. M. 1980. "Aristotle on Friendship." In Rorty 1980.

Fingarette, Herbert. 1972. *Confucius—The Secular as Sacred*. New York: Harper Torchbooks.

Hall, David L. and Ames, Roger T. 1987. *Thinking Through Confucius*. Albany: State University of New York Press.

Hansen, C. 1994. *A Daoist Theory of Chinese Thought*. Oxford: Oxford University Press.

Legge, James (trans.). 1966. *The Four Books*. Paragon Book Reprint Corp.

---

[42]An early version of this paper was presented at the Chinese Philosophy Symposium of November 1995 held at the Centre for Modern Chinese Studies, University of Oxford. Thereafter it was circulated in the Center's working paper series (edited by Nicholas Bunnin). I wish to thank Nick Bunnin for his helpful advice and generous support. I am also grateful to Roger Ames, Roger Crisp, Kenneth Dorter, Matthew Liao, James McMullen, Christopher Taylor, and the referees for *Philosophy East and West* for valuable comments on the earlier versions.

MacIntyre, Alasdair. 1988. *Whose Justice? Which Rationality?* Notre Dame: University of Notre Dame Press.

Nussbaum, Martha C. 1986. *Fragility of Goodness.* Cambridge: Cambridge University Press.

Rorty, Amélie O. (ed.). 1980. *Essays on Aristotle's Ethics.* Berkeley: University of California Press.

Russell, Bertrand. 1922. *The Problem of China.* London: George Allen & Unwin.

Schwartz, Benjamin 1985. *The World of Thought in Ancient China.* Cambridge: Harvard University Press.

Sherman, Nancy. 1989. *Fabric of Character.* Oxford: Clarendon Press.

Slote, Michael. 1992. *From Morality to Virtue.* Oxford: Oxford University Press.

Sorabji, Richard. "Aristotle on the Role of Intellect in virtue" In *Essays on Aristotle's Ethics,* edited by Rorty.

Urmson. J. O. 1973. "Aristotle's Doctrine of the Mean," *American Philosophical Quarterly* 10, 223-230.

Williams, Bernard. 1981. "Persons, Character, and Morality," *Moral Luck.* Cambridge: Cambridge University Press.

—————. 1985. *Ethics and the Limits of Philosophy.* London: Fontana Press.

2

Shifting Perspectives: Filial Morality Revisited

Chenyang Li

Does morality require filial obligation of grown children towards their aged parents? If the answer is negative, then why is this so? If the answer is affirmative, then on what basis is this obligation founded? People of different cultures have different views on this issue. Perhaps the justification of filial morality, or the lack of it, is deeply rooted in the culture. Perhaps something that is easily justified in one culture may be hard to justify in another. If this is true, the only way to resolve the matter is to look into the culture itself. In this essay I will first examine some problems with five accounts of filial morality that have been put forth in recent years, and then turn to Confucianism and show how it provides a sensible alternative perspective.

1. Critiques of Some Recent Theories

It appears that today's American culture generally does not favor the notion of filial obligation, or at least not a strong notion of it. Arguments pro and con have been put forth on both sides, but none of them seems to have been successful in either undermining or establishing filial morality.

1.1   English's *Friendship Model*

Jane English is probably the most representative of those Westerners who deny or doubt the existence of filial obligation.[1] In her article "What Do Grown Children Owe Their Parents?" Jane English proposes a theory based on the concept of friendship (1979). According to English, grown children have no more filial obligation toward their parents than the kind of obligation one has toward friends or the people whom one loves. Accordingly, if parents' earlier sacrifices for their children have resulted in friendship and love in their children, parents may have the good fortune to be honored and served by their children when the latter have grown; if parents' earlier sacrifices have failed to produce friendship and love in their children, then the children have no filial obligation to serve and honor the parents. "After a friendship ends, the duties of friendship end," she writes (353).

English distinguishes two kinds of relationships, indebtedness and friendship. Here "indebtedness" is not limited to literal debts, but is understood broadly to include all situations where a favor has been done. "Favors create debts," English writes (352). If person *B* has done a favor for person *A*, then *A* is indebted to *B*. *A* ought to do something to reciprocate the favor. She maintains that friendship, unlike indebtedness, is characterized by mutuality rather than reciprocity; in friendship, a person can benefit from what her friend has done for her out of friendship, but she is not thereby indebted to him. She does not "owe" him anything.

Then why is the typical relationship between children and parents not characterized as "indebtedness"? Because, English argues, parents' earlier voluntary sacrifices for their children are not favors to their children, and therefore these sacrifices do not render their children "indebted" to the parents. When the children grow up and the parents need help, the children may lend a helping hand out of friendship and love—if parents' earlier sacrifices have resulted in friendship and love. There is no filial obligation beyond that.

But why are parents' earlier sacrifices for their children not favors, which should be reciprocated? English argues that parents' earlier sacrifices are not favors because their children did not request

---

[1] Some of these views can be found in A. John Simmons 1979 and Michael Slote 1979.

them. Obviously, the children were too young to request favors from anyone, including their parents. Therefore the children are not obliged to repay them when the parents are in need.

It may be debatable whether small children make requests. It can be argued that requests do not have to be verbal ones, which infants are certainly incapable of, and that requests can be made through gestures, eye contacts, and so forth. Many pet owners think their pets do make requests in many ways. Therefore in a broad sense of the word, from the mother's point of view, a crying baby is making a request for help. For the sake of argument, however, let us grant English that small children cannot and do not make requests for their needs. Now, does it follow from this that parental care is not a favor to their children?

A favor results, according to English, when person *A*, at person *B*'s request, bears some burden for *B*, and consequently, *B* incurs an obligation to reciprocate. If Max asks Nina, his new neighbor he barely knows, whether she will take in his mail while he is gone for a month's vacation. Nina agrees and does it. If, subsequently, Nina asks Max to do the same for her, then Max has a moral obligation to agree. This is so because, English maintains, Nina has done a favor for Max and, therefore, Max owes a favor to Nina. But consider what happens when "Max simply goes on vacation and, to his surprise, finds upon his return that his neighbor has mowed his grass twice weekly in his absence. [Then] This is a voluntary sacrifice rather than a favor, and Max has no duty to reciprocate" (352). In the latter case no favor has been done because, as English indicates, Max did not request the service from his neighbor.

But is a request necessary for a favor to take place? I do not think so. Whether a favor is done has more to do with whether a person being benefited would like the thing done for him or her. In English's case, imagine that, due to unusual weather Max's grass grew much faster than normal during his absence and without his neighbor's voluntary help Max would have received a substantial fine for breaking a city ordinance. Shouldn't Max consider his neighbor's voluntary help a favor?

Suppose that Nina's house is accidentally on fire, and Max happens to pass by and sees it. He manages to put out the fire and thereby suffers a financial loss due to missing a business appointment at the time of the fire. Even though she did not request his help, it would be outrageous if Nina does not consider Max's sacrifice a great favor. It would be indecent if Nina does not think she has a moral obligation to lend a hand when Max later needs some help from her.[2] Under these circumstances, whether a request has been made is irrelevant to whether a favor has been done.

Since English does not deny that a person is morally obliged to return a favor, her entire friendship model depends on the argument that parents' earlier sacrifices are not favors to their children. And her argument in turn relies on the claim that a request is a necessary condition for a favor to occur. This claim is unwarranted, and therefore so is her conclusion that parents' earlier sacrifices are not favors to their children.

1.2   Belliotti's *Contribution to Self Principle*

Against English, Raymond Belliotti argues for filial obligation. He proposes an argument based on personal identity that he characterizes as the "Contribution to Self Principle." According to this view, "we have moral requirements of a special sort to those who contribute to and help nurture our identities, and those whose attachment is essential for our self-understanding" (1986, 152). Belliotti believes that, in addition to her failure to recognize unrequested favors, English has assumed an atomistic notion of self. He criticizes English's position for ignoring "the way our parents affect directly our very identities, how we have moral requirements to them and in fulfilling these requirements we are, in a literal way, being true to our 'selves'" (1986, 152).

Belliotti's identity thesis bears some similarities to Confucianism, which I will discuss in the second part of this essay. But it is also different from Confucianism in an essential way. In brief, while Con-

---

2. Needless to say, Nina's obligation to Max is not unlimited.

fucianism is both backward- and forward-looking, that is, it looks at what one has become and at what one will or ought to become to determine one's moral duty—Belliotti's thesis appears solely backward-looking; it relies solely on what parents have done to shape a person's identity. Therefore it is not unfair when Jan Narverson summarizes Belliotti's principle as follows:

> Premise: Person A contributed factor X to the "identity" of another person, B.
> Conclusion: B morally *owes* something to A. (1987, 66)

One problem with this thesis concerns the negative contribution. In a person's life there are countless factors that have directly or indirectly contributed to her identity. If Belliotti's thesis is to be taken as a general one, as it appears to be, it would follow that a person has moral obligations to those who have made whatever contributions, both positive and negative, to her identity. One should love her father for having taught her to be a good fisherwoman and hate him for the scar he has caused to be left her on her arm during a fishing accident. However, the notion of negative contribution to self and hence negative moral obligation seems inappropriate here because Belliotti was discussing what moral duties grown children have toward their parents, by which he evidently means what good grown children ought to do for their parents. It is unclear what Belliotti would say on this problem.

Perhaps Belliotti's thesis can be modified to state that we have moral obligations only to those who have contributed something *positive* to our identities. But then there is the question of what counts as a positive contribution. Suppose someone's father contributed a great deal to her being a fine fisherwoman and she hates her profession; should she be grateful for his contribution? Also, positive contributions may come from different directions. We need not be grateful to all whose actions have resulted in positive contributions to us. Suppose someone grew up in an orphanage, and a vicious man in the orphanage caused her all kinds of hardship, but as a result she has developed a strong character, which has enables her to endure future hardships on the way to a highly successful future. Should she be grateful for the man's *positive* contribution to her identity? Probably not. So, contributions to our identities alone, even if limited to positive contributions, cannot serve as a foundation for filial morality.

1.3 Narveson's *Prudent Investor Thesis*

Jan Narveson favors filial obligations on the part of grown children by arguing that "parents do put themselves to much trouble to benefit their children, and if the children in question agree that the effects of those efforts really have been beneficial, then they should see to it that they are benefited in turn to at least the degree that renders it non-irrational for the parents to have done this" (1987, 74). Belliotti calls this the "prudent investor thesis" (1988, 288).

Narveson believes that one rational motive for people to do good to others is that it is an investment (1987, 72). According to this conception, people tend to do good to one another "because they see the potential benefits of having everyone so disposed, and if we are to secure such a general disposition, we must instantiate it ourselves" (73).

One difficulty with Narveson's thesis lies in the clause "if the children in question agree that the effects of those [parental] efforts really have been beneficial." Belliotti remarks that this clause "holds the existence of the moral requirements hostage to the child's judgment that she has been benefited by her parents' efforts" (1988, 288). Under this condition, a child can easily let herself off the ethical hook by simply denying that her parents' past efforts were beneficial. "Given human proclivities for rationalization and good faith errors of judgment, this is dangerous" (289).

Although a grown child should have love and friendship toward her parents, and acknowledge that she has benefited from her parents' earlier sacrifices, even if she does not acknowledge this, she is not thereby exempt from her filial obligation (if there is one). A person may not feel grateful for her parents giving her a life and bringing her up. But that only shows that she is ungrateful. The lack of love and friendship on her part does not exempt her from her filial obligation to serve her aged parents. Morality demands that one fulfill one's obligation regardless of whether or not one acknowledges it.

However, the requirement that the child agrees that her parents' sacrifices have been beneficial to her does not seem indispensable to Narveson's thesis. For he could simply delete the phrase "the children in question agree that" and let the clause read "if the effects of those efforts really have been beneficial, then..." By doing so, Narveson could easily get himself off Belliotti's hook.

There is another problem, however, which in my view is more serious than the first one. It is the question of whether parents need a rational motivation for having children. Perhaps we can provide a rational justification for having children, but it seems to me that parents do not have to have one. The desire to have offspring, whether conscious or not, is rooted deeply in every species; otherwise the species would cease to exist. In this regard, humans are not different from animals. Regardless of whether we have any rational justification, humans will continue to have offspring. It is a law of nature, and a law of nature does not need a rational justification. Therefore, Narveson's notion that a child has filial obligation toward her parents because she should see that it is not irrational for parents to have children is itself unjustified and perhaps unjustifiable.

1.4 Sommers' *Conventional Expectation Thesis*

Christina Sommers proposes a theory of ethical duties which she calls "the thesis of differential pull." It is the thesis that "the ethical pull of a moral patient will always partly depend on how the moral patient is related to the moral agent on whom the pull is exerted" (1987, 74). Based on this thesis, Sommers argues that children have special moral obligations toward their parents because of their special relationship with their parents. She attempts to justify this special relationship as follows:

> The presumption of a special positive obligation arises for a moral agent when two conditions obtain: (1) In a given social arrangement (or practice), there is a specific interaction or transaction between moral agent and patient such as promising and being promised, nurturing and being nurtured, befriending and being befriended. (2) The interaction in that context gives rise to

certain conventional expectations (e.g., that a promise will be kept, that a marital partner will be faithful, that a child will respect the parent). (1987, 75)

Sommers argues that because of the existence of this parental conventional expectation of the children, children's failure to perform their expected behavior will cause unwarranted interference with the rights of the parents. I will call this "the Conventional Expectation Thesis." Much of Sommers' argument for filial morality is dependent on it. Although I agree with Sommers on her thesis of "differential pull," which is similar to the Confucian notion of graded love, I do not think Sommers' Conventional Expectation Thesis is valid.

By justifying moral obligations on the basis of conventional expectations, Sommer seems to have confused morality with mores. Simply put, the conventional is not tantamount to the moral. Good performance of conventionally expected behavior is not necessarily moral; and failure to perform such behavior is not necessarily immoral. Much conventionally expected behavior is actually immoral and should be avoided. At times in some parts of the world it has been conventionally expected that, if a man could not repay his debts, he should give away his wife or daughter to his creditor, or offer himself as a slave to the creditor. Yet this is not a moral practice. If I cannot repay my debts and refuse to offer my wife or myself to my creditor, he may feel that his right has been violated. But the fact of the matter may be that he has never had such a right, even though it may be a conventional practice. Under these circumstances, a breach of conventional expectations would be a morally justifiable behavior and should be encouraged and praised. Therefore, one cannot successfully argue for what ought to be the case merely from what is conventionally expected to be the case; one cannot argue for filial obligation by simply stating that it is conventionally expected.

Sommers' thesis also relies on the concept of rights, which, as I will show next, has an even deeper problem in connection to the notion of filial obligation, and this may undermine her thesis.

1.5   Blustein's *Gratitude Theory*

Jeffrey Blustein's thesis is that grown children owe their parents many things and yet are not indebted to them. He distinguishes between two kinds of duties, duties of gratitude and duties of indebtedness.

> Duties of gratitude are owed only to those who have helped or benefitted us freely, without thought of personal gain, simply out of a desire to protect or promote our well-being. ... Duties of indebtedness, in contrast, can be owed to those who were motivated primarily by self-interest or by the desire to help only insofar as this was believed to involve no risk or loss to themselves. (1982, 177)

A person with duties of indebtedness is subject to claims for repayment, while a person with duties of gratitude is not. Grown children's duties to their parents are typically duties of gratitude. With such duties, grown children ought "to express their gratitude in words or deeds or both" (176), but the parents do not have claims for repayment from their children.

Blustein suggests that the occurrence of duties of indebtedness requires two conditions. First, the giver does not have a duty to benefit the receiver; second, the receiver not only receives, but also accepts, the benefit (183). In order for claims to repayment to have any moral force, Blustein writes, "it must first be established that what parents claim repayment for is something that they were morally at liberty to give to or withhold from their children" (182). But a lot of things that parents do for their children are things required by their parental duty and demanded by the children's rights. "Children's claim rights," as Blustein writes, "correlate with the obligations of their parents" (164). Mere fulfillment of duties does not create indebtedness. When person A owes person B money, B has a claim right to get the money back. If A pays B the money, A only fulfills his obligation, and B is not thereby indebted to A.

Moreover, Blustein maintains that one cannot become indebted if one does not *accept* the benefit that one receives. If you, under no obligation, offer to maintain my lawn while I go on vacation and I accept your offer and benefit from the service, then I am indebted to you. But if I refuse your offer, then you cannot make me indebted to you by maintaining my lawn. In the latter case I only receive, not accept, the benefit.

Blustein argues that, within the family, the parents do have a duty to provide care for their young children, and the children, while young, "cannot exercise genuine choice with respect to the benefits of early care" (183). Therefore, unless the parents have done something good for their children that is not required by parental duty, and the children accept it (or would have accepted if they could exercise genuine choice), the children will not have duties of indebtedness to their parents.

One objection to Blustein might be that parental duty cannot be clearly defined. For example, is it a parental duty that the parents should get up in the middle of a cold night to check and see if their child is sleeping well when they hear some small, unidentifiable noise? Would it be supererogatory if the parents feed their children expensive fish instead of chicken on weekends? Would it be a supererogatory act if the parents spend two hours playing with their kids instead of one hour? If a couple does more for their children than average parents, and if their children appreciate it, would that entitle the parents to some claims over the children for repayment? Social conventions cannot help much to resolve these issues. As soon as one starts drawing the line between what belongs and what does not belong to parental duty, one is treating the family as a group of self-interested strangers. Family members are not strangers.

However, this objection may be trivial. For Blustein can say that the main issue here concerns the large portion of parental sacrifices clearly required by parental duty; if parents cannot claim repayment for these services required by parental duty, then there is no base for demanding that the children reciprocate for these services. One cannot deny that parents do have a duty to care for their children. If fulfillment of duties does not create indebtedness, then it follows that children are not indebted by benefiting from their parents' service, which is required by parental duty. If this is the case, Blustein's goal is achieved.

I agree with Blustein that what parents do for their children should not be considered merely and literally as a loan to be repaid later. I also agree with him that children owe duties of gratitude to their parents for their earlier sacrifices. But I am convinced that grown children "owe" their parents many things in a much stronger sense. The sense is so strong that grown children can be said to be "indebted" to their parents and, that from their grown children parents are entitled to and can, with full moral force, *claim* "repayment," in terms of financial assistance, physical attendance, personal care, etc.

I think Blustein, within his theoretical framework of rights, has presented a strong negative case that cannot be easily dismissed. And his argument may be used against some of the above-mentioned authors, who are in favor of a stronger notion of filial obligation. Perhaps Blustein is right that, from the rights perspective, a strong notion of filial morality cannot be justified. Perhaps this partly explains why so many people in this culture of individual rights do not accept filial morality. I will, instead of arguing against Blustein within his framework of rights, turn to an alternative framework, Confucianism, and see what light it can shed on this important issue.

2. The Confucian Alternative

The Chinese newspaper *People's Daily* (overseas edition) of August 25, 1993, reported that in Shandong province of China a ninety-year-old woman sued her two sons for failing in their filial duty. The woman's husband died young and left her with two sons, one and three years old, respectively. Through countless hardships she brought them both up. Now she had become old and could not work. Neither of her two sons wanted to take care of her. The court intervened in her favor, and the sons agreed to take full responsibility for her living and medical expenses. In China the law requires that parents have a legal obligation to rear their young, and grown children have a duty to support their aged parents.[3] This reflects a Chinese social value that is deeply rooted in a mainly Confucian culture.

Unlike in the West, where filial morality is rarely a philosophical topic, in China it has long been at the center of philosophical discourse. Renowned scholars like Chien Mu and Hsieh Yu-wei have described the Chinese culture as "the culture of filial morality (*xiao de wenhua*)."[4] One cannot understand traditional Chinese culture without understanding the role of filial morality.[5]

2.1   What Confucian Filial Piety Means

The Chinese word "*xiao*" is usually rendered in English as "filial piety" or "filiality." It can also be rendered as "filial ethics" or "filial morality." It is one of the most important concepts of Confucian ethics and a cardinal virtue in Confucian tradition. This can be seen in the fact that the *Classic of Filial Piety* (*Xiao Jing*) and the *Analects* were the two most widely read among the Confucian Classics.[6] The *Classic of Filial Piety* makes filial piety a cardinal virtue by stating that "filial piety is the unchanging truth of Heaven, the unfailing equity of Earth, the [universal] practice of man (ch. 7)."[7]

Filial morality is one of the areas that deeply divide traditional China from the contemporary West. Many Westerners have found this Confucian value hard to accept. For example, Bertrand Russell

---

[3.] The Marriage Law, Section 3, Article 15.

[4.] See Liang Shu-ming 1990, 28. Chien's remark originally appeared in his "Weekly Article" in *Da Gong Bao*, Chong Qing, November 1942, and Hsieh's is from his *Filiality and Chinese Culture* (*Xiao yu Zhongguo Wenhua*), Young Army's Publisher, no year was given.

[5.] For the relation of filial piety to the Chinese society as a whole, see Hsieh Yu-Wei 1986, 167-187.

[6] See Huang Junlang 1992, "Sketching on the Classic of Filial Piety," 10. Some think the Classic of Filial Piety was compiled by Han Confucians. But Huang argues that the fact that the Spring and Autumn Annuals of Master Lü (compiled in the third century B.C.) quoted it indicates that it was before Han dynasty. See Huang, 4-5.

[7] Translations of Confucian classics are either my own or from Arthur Waley's Analects of Confucius, (1989) and D. C. Lau's Mencius (1970) with my own revisions where it is appropriate.

commented: "Filial piety, and the strength of the family generally, are perhaps the weakest point in Confucian ethics, the only point where the system departs seriously from common sense" (1922, 40). Undoubtedly, in this regard, Russell, Jane English, and many others in the West will find themselves on the same side in opposition to the Confucians.

But what does filial piety mean in Confucianism? The Chinese character "*xiao*" consists of two components, one standing for child and the other meaning the old. The word has the part symbolizing the old above the part symbolizing child, meaning that the child supports and/or succeeds the parent. A dictionary of ancient Chinese, the *Shuo Wen Jie Zi*, defines "*xiao*" as "one being good at serving one's parents (*shan shi fu mu zhe*)."

In ancient China, filial piety included five types of behavior.[8] First, one must support one's parents. The *Classic of Filial Piety* states that "supporting one's parents is the filial piety (*xiao*) in common people" (ch. 6). Second, one must honor, revere, and obey one's parents. Confucius said, "Filial piety nowadays means to be able to support one's parents. But we support even dogs and horses. If there is no feeling of reverence, wherein lies the difference? " (*Analects*, 2:7). Mencius said "the greatest thing a filial son can do is to honor his parents" (*Mencius*, 5A:4). The *Book of Rites* (*Li Ji*) lists honoring one's parents at a higher order of filiality than merely supporting them (ch. 6). The third type of filial behavior is producing heirs. Mencius said "There are three ways of being unfilial. The worst is to have no heir" (*Mencius*, 4A:26). The fourth is to bring honor and glory to one's ancestors. The *Classic of Filial Piety* states that "to establish oneself, to enhance the Way, and to leave a good fame behind, in order to make one's parents illustrious, are the ultimate goal of filiality" (ch. 1). Finally, after the death of one's parents, one must be able to mourn and offer a memorial service and sacrifice to them. The *Classic of Filial Piety* has ample discussion of this, particularly in Chapters 10 and 18.

Among these five types of ancient filial behaviors, the one that appears most incomprehensible to many Westerners is the third.

---

[8] See Ping Cheung Lo 1993, 38-41.

What does producing heirs have to do with filial piety? After all, filial piety has to do with treating one's parents well; one can certainly do this without producing heirs. People who think along this line, however, have overlooked the religious dimension of Confucianism. It should be noted that in Confucianism there is no Heaven to ensure an eternal life as is the case in Christianity. The Confucians have to look elsewhere for the meaning of life, and to satisfy the almost universal human desire for immortality. The place to find it, for the Confucians, is human-relatedness, which has many dimensions. One primary dimension involves continuing the family line. Through reproduction, one can pass along not only one's family name but also one's blood, and hence life, to later generations. Also, the meaning of life is realized when one is loved by the members of one's family and, after death, remembered by family members later to come. Therefore, one of the most important things to avoid is to "discontinue the sacrificial burning of incense" (*duan le xiang huo*) by not providing for later generations. The continuation of the family line is a necessary way to achieve this purpose. Not having heirs means cutting off the family line that has been passed down by the earlier generations, and it is therefore unfilial.

This line of thinking also explains the fourth and fifth types of filial behaviors listed above. One would feel life is (more) meaningful if one believes that one will be remembered and honored and even glorified by later generations.

Another often neglected implication of having children is that, without raising children of one's own, one cannot fully appreciate the efforts of one's parents in raising their children. There is a Chinese saying that "we do not really know our parents' kindness until we raise our own children" (*yang er fang zhi fumu en*). Having one's own children gives one the necessary experience to appreciate fully one's parents' love and care, and is therefore instrumental in helping to make a person filial toward one's parents.

The most fundamental among the five behaviors have been the first two—and this is increasingly so today, with the contemporary trend of fading religious convictions and the felt need by society for a strong family structure. Of these first two, many Westerners probably have more difficulty with the second: honoring, revering, and obeying one's parents. Many people are under the impression that Confucianism demands a son's absolute obedience, but this notion may have been exaggerated. Tu Wei-ming has argued that Confucianism does not demand a son's absolute obedience (1985, 113-130, 1989, 42). According to the *Classic of Filial Piety*, Confucius explicitly said: When [the father] is not right, the son can*not not* contend with (*zheng*) the father... Hence, if the son follows the father without contending with him when the father is not right, how can this be filial? " (ch. 15).

Mencius also defended Zhangzi, who offended his father by asking his father to do the right thing (*Mencius*, 4B:30). Xun Zi even went as far as to say that following one's father is merely a small virtue, compared with the great virtue of following righteousness, which sometimes may require one not to follow one's father, and he gave specific examples of occasions when the son must not follow the wish of his parents (*Xun Zi*, ch. 29). Fung Yu-lan was right in summarizing Confucian filial piety as follows:

> On the spiritual side, filial piety consists, during the lifetime of our parents, in conforming ourselves to their wishes, and giving them not only physical care and nourishment, but also nourishing their wills; while should they fall into error, it consists in reproving them and leading them back to what is right. After the death of our parents, furthermore, one aspect of it consists in offering sacrifices to them and thinking about them, so as to keep their memory fresh in our minds. (1952, 359)

For our purpose in this essay we follow this mainstream view on filial piety, and particularly focus on filiality as the supporting and honoring of one's parents.

It should be noted without further delay that the Confucians would agree with Raymond Belliotti that parental care and nurture are reasons for filial obligation of the child, and they would agree with Jan Narveson and Christina Sommers that the child should not let his parents down after they have devoted ("invested") so much effort in nurturing him. As a matter of fact, the concept of reciprocity is of extreme importance in Confucian culture, and Chinese culture in general. But, for the Confucians, there is a lot more to it.

What kind of justification do the Confucians give for filial piety? Although filial piety is a cardinal virtue in Confucianism and there is plentiful discussion of it by the writers of the Confucian Classics, one can hardly find its well-formed, systematic statement of justification among them. This is so, perhaps, because in the old days there was such overwhelming support for filial piety and it did not need philosophical argument to support it. The Chinese did not distinguish reason from feeling; Mencius, for example, appealed directly to human feelings to justify moral virtues. When there was already a strong feeling for something, there was hardly any need for philosophical justification to convince people of its value. For our purpose, however, an appeal to feelings is not enough.

On the subject of justification, I agree with John Rawls:

> What justifies a conception of justice is not its being true to an order antecedent to and given to us, but its congruence with our deeper understanding of ourselves and our aspirations, and our realization that, given our history and the traditions embedded in our public life, it is the most reasonable doctrine. (1980, 519)

The issue of filial piety may be seen as part of the larger issue of justice. To see how the Confucians justify the doctrine of filial piety, we need to see how this doctrine is congruent with their deeper understanding of themselves, and we need to understand this doctrine as one deeply embedded in their tradition. Specifically, we need to look into the central concept of Confucianism, the concept of *Ren*, and its place in Confucian ethics. In what follows, I will look into *Ren* in general, then examine this concept in light of two important aspects of Confucianism, self-realization and duty ethics.

2.2   Filial Piety as a Requirement for *Ren*

The concept of *Ren* occupies a central place in Confucian philosophy. Confucius said, "*Ren* is (the distinguishing characteristic of) man"(*Doctrine of the Mean*, ch. 20). The concept of *Ren* defines humanity and the destiny of a person. In the English-speaking world, "*Ren*" has been rendered as benevolence, love, altruism, kindness, charity, compassion, human-heartedness, humanity, and so on. These words, though individually inadequate in rendering the meaning of *Ren,* collectively offer a good clue to understanding this concept. Ideally or theoretically, a person of *Ren* must love all people (*Analects,* 1:6, *Mencius,* 7A:46). But Confucius and Mencius believed that persons practicing *Ren* should start with their parents and siblings and then extend it to other people. Confucius said that "the greatest application of *Ren* is in being affectionate toward relatives" (*Doctrine of the Mean,* ch. 20), and "filial piety and brotherly respect are the root of *Ren*" (*Analects,* 1:2). A person of *Ren* must love first his parents and elder siblings and then, by extension, other people. Mencius said, "Treat with respect the elders in my family, and then by extension, also the elders in other families" (*Mencius,* 1A:7). He believed that a person of *Ren* should be *Ren* to all people but attached affectionately only to his parents (*Mencius,* 7A:45). This means that one's parents exert a greater ethical pull on him or her. Therefore, filial piety is one's primary duty.

Why must a person of *Ren* start with loving one's parents? The Confucians observe the following line of reasoning. From childhood a person must begin moral cultivation. The first social environment in which one finds oneself is the family. The first people with whom a person is acquainted are, naturally, one's parents. Therefore, in order for one to become *Ren,* one must first learn to be *Ren* with one's parents; and *Ren* in that aspect is filial piety.

The *Doctrine of the Mean* states that the way to becoming a virtuous person may be compared to what takes place during travel, when, to go to a distance, we must first traverse the space that is near, and to ascend a height, we must begin start from the lower ground (ch. 15). Confucius stated the "way" of the good person in the following order: filial when at home, respectful to elders when away from home, becoming earnest and faithful, loving all extensively, and being close to people of *Ren* (*Analects,* 1:6). Similarly, Mencius believes that if one loves one's parents, one will, by extension, be *Ren* to people in general; and if one is *Ren* to people in general, one will be caring to everything in the world (*Mencius,* 7A:45). If one fails to learn to be *Ren* at home, namely to be filial to one's parents while young, it would be difficult to be *Ren* to others after he grows up. Therefore, filial piety is the fountainhead of *Ren*, and the morality of *Ren* first of all demands filial piety.

The *Classic of Filial Piety* states that filial piety forms the root of all virtues, and with it, enlightened learning comes into existence (ch.1). The *Book of Rites* states,

> As the people are taught filial piety and brotherly love at home, with reverence toward the elder and diligent care for the aged in the community, they constitute the way of a great king; and it is along this line that states as well as families will become peaceful. (10:45)

The great king is a moral role model for the people. The way of the great king is also the way of a morally superior person. In order to be a moral person, one must fulfill one's filial duty.

2.3 Filial Piety as a Requirement for Self-Realization

The Confucian self has a spatial as well as a temporal existence. Diachronically speaking, the self is a process of realization and transformation. Synchronically, the self extends beyond the individual point in space that we ordinarily think a person occupies. One important way to understand the Confucian notion of filial piety is through understanding this diachronical dimension of the Confucian self.

Confucians do not regard the self as a ready-made soul or entity. The self is a process of realizing one's Heaven-endowed potential. All of us were born with the potential to be fully human, but realizing it takes lifelong effort. For the Confucian, the realization of this potential is one's Heaven-imposed duty and one's ultimate goal. In this view, the life process is not merely a biological growing up and becoming older; it is, most importantly, a process of moral improvement and development. It is a process of the unfolding of our Heaven-endowed nature. Our ultimate destiny is to become *Ren*, or to achieve full humanity. We can only reach this goal through self-cultivation and self-transformation. We cultivate ourselves through reinforcing and expanding our human-relatedness,[9] and our human-relatedness starts with our relationship with our parents. Therefore, becoming a filial son or daughter is a necessary part of the process of achieving humanity.

In this sense, one endeavors to develop both physically and morally for the sake of oneself (*"wei ji"*). In urging their children to study, Chinese parents often remind them of this notion by asking: "Are you learning for someone else?" The answer is, of course, "no." One learns and grows for the sake of oneself. This also extends to filial piety.

Mencius maintained that it is human nature that we love our parents (*Mencius*, 3A:5). Since the Mencian school of Confucianism believes that human original nature is good, it follows that we ought to retain our original nature. Mencius believed that it belongs to our original heart to love our parents and that developing this original heart will directly lead to filial piety. Whether human nature is good, bad, or neutral is as subject to dispute today as it was in Mencius' time. But Confucians in general hold a person-making, not rule-following, ethics. In order to become a good person, one must develop good character. It is hard to imagine someone who treats his or her parents badly to be a good person (with good character). If self-realization is the way to develop into a good person, as the Confucians believe, then filial piety is a requirement for our self-realization. Since filial piety is a step in our self-realization, being filial is not only for the sake of our parents; it is also for our own sake.

Speaking of our relationship with our fathers, Tu Wei-ming writes:

> For their own sake as well as ours, we must appeal to our Heaven-endowed nature, our conscience, for guidance. After all, it is for the ultimate purpose of self-realization that we honor our fathers as the source of the meaningful life that we have been pursuing. (1985, 127)

---

[9] This leads to the "synchronical" dimension of Confucian self, which we will discuss in the following section.

According to Tu, in Confucianism we can never realize ourselves as isolated individuals. We must recognize our personal locus as a starting point of self-realization, with reference to our fathers among other relationships. Therefore, we must honor and respect our fathers (and mothers, it should perhaps be added), not because they dominate us or because we dare not disobey them; in a strong sense, we honor and respect them for our own sake, namely for our self-cultivation and self-realization.

Lin Yutang writes: "The greatest regret a Chinese gentleman could have was the eternally lost opportunity of serving his old parents with medicine and soup on their deathbed, or not to be present when they died" (1993, 751-7). In a person's life there are many things that one must be able to do in order to live a fulfilled life. Serving one's aged parents is one of them. Without such an experience there is an irremediable lacking in one's life, which is a cause for lifelong regret. This is so because, for the Confucians, filial piety is a main road to become *Ren* and a requirement for self-realization. The loss of the opportunity of being a filial son or daughter is at the same time a loss of opportunity to live a wholesome life, to make progress in achieving the goal of *Ren* and in developing into a fully cultivated human being.

For the Confucians, therefore, filial morality is an essential element for our self-realization and self-transformation in becoming fully human. From this perspective, one's filial duty is by no means supererogatory. And it is even not merely a duty for the benefit of other people (i.e., one's parents). It is, in a deeper sense, a duty one owes to oneself for the sake of oneself. Becoming fully human is one's ultimate destiny, and therefore the development of one's own morality is in one's highest self-interest.

2.4   Filial Piety as a Requirement for Confucian Duty Ethics

Those who believe in the existence of filial obligations usually draw (partly) on the fact that parents do make a significant sacrifice in raising children. Confucians share this view. Thus, can they counter Blustein's argument that parental non-supererogatory sacrifices are merely discharging their duties and therefore do not generate indebtedness? The answer lies in another dimension of the Confucian understanding of the self.

Synchronically, the Confucian self is not an atomic individual that happens to exist in a nexus of relationships. To use Roger Ames's metaphor, the Confucian self is a "focus-field." In Ames's focus-field model, the self is a center or focus that fades off into a ritually ordered society (1994, 187-212). The focus, of course, exists only in the field and exists only as long as the field exists. In other words, the existence and identity of the focus depends on the field. It is from this focus, this center, that one gradually reaches out to form one's identity.

In the eyes of the Confucians, each of us perform certain social roles, and our being is realized in these roles, as son or daughter, brother or sister, father or mother, and so on. The relationships in which one finds oneself constitute the field in which the self is located as the focus. In this view, these roles are not something into which we as atomistic individuals have accidentally fallen. They constitute our identity. They define who we are and what we are, what duties we have, and consequently what behaviors we ought to express.

Based on this Confucian view of self, we are in a better position to understand the Confucian ethics as a duty ethics in contrast to the rights ethics of the contemporary West; this is another key perspective from which to understand Confucian filial morality. Whereas in the rights ethics individual rights receive primary importance, in a duty ethics the primary concern is one's duties and responsibilities.

Unlike the Contractarian, for whom the society is formed on the premise of a contract among rational self-interested individuals, the Confucians view society as an extended family. The family has been at the center of traditional Chinese life. Within the family, members see each other as part of their own selves, and they nurture and care for each other without negotiating reciprocity as a precondition. The Confucian ideal is to build a society after the model of the family. To view society as an extended family is to view it as, in Tu Wei-ming's words, "not an adversary system consisting of pressure groups but a fiduciary community based on mutual trust" (1989, 48). In such a human community the primary relationship between its members is that of benefactor and beneficiary—a relationship that is not maintained on a contractual basis. According to this view, as descendants from the same ancestors living together under Heaven, all of us are, some of the time and in some way, benefactors and beneficiaries. In Confucian duty ethics the morality of *Ren* demands that, within such a fiduciary community, those who have resources, spiritual as well as material, ought to be the benefactors, and those who are in need are entitled to be beneficiaries. In this view, from the fact that one has received benefits because he was entitled to them it does not follow that he will not be obligated to benefit his former benefactors when later they are in need and he in turn has the resources to be a benefactor. The Chinese phrase "being rich but failing to be *Ren*" (*wei fu bu ren*) condemns those with resources who fail to help those in need. In a sense, possessing resources implies social responsibilities.

In Chinese culture, people in need are usually unwilling to ask favors; it is up to those who are capable of offering favors to come forward to do so, if they have a good sense of *Ren*. In other words, it is the moral requirement of *Ren* that compels the capable to offer benefits or favors to those in need. The person being offered a favor would show reluctance to accept it and decline out of modesty by saying things like, "I would not want to burden you with that ... ;" unless he is sure that the offering party is sincere, he would not accept the offer. Hence, for the Chinese, request has little to do with the generation of favors. If Jane English were right in holding that a request is a necessary condition for a favor, she would have to rule as non-favor a great proportion of favors given out in the Chinese cultural context.

An often cited Chinese proverb says, "An earlier generation plants trees under whose shade later generations rest." This short sentence has a rather profound significance. Traditionally, Chinese peasants would take a rest under a shade tree while they worked in the fields under the burning midsummer sun. When people doing things beneficial to late-comers cite this proverb, they mean that if nobody had planted the trees, later-comers would not be able to rest under the shade; therefore, in order for their descendants to enjoy some sort of benefits, the benefactors feel a need to do things even though they themselves may not benefit from them. When later-comers received the benefits "planted" by their forebears, they would cite the proverb, meaning that they appreciated their forebears' efforts in "planting the seed" for later beneficiaries. There is also the proverb, "When you drink the water you must not forget those who dug the well for you." In this kind of culture, the relationship of benefactors and beneficiaries is expressed in terms not of rights but of duties and benefits that we owe each other.

Based on this duty ethics, there is a mutual obligation between parents and children. When children are little, the parents have a duty to take care of the children; in turn, when children have grown and their parents are in need, the children have a duty to take care of the parents. In this duty ethics, from the premise that parental care is a discharge of parental duty it does not follow that the child does not owe his or her parents anything when they grow old and are in need.

Confucius's teachings can be summarized in two words, *zhong* and *shu* (*Analects*, 4:15). *Zhong* implies conscientiousness. One should be conscientious in developing one's virtuous character. *Shu* means extending one's own mind to others. This is the golden rule that you should not do to others what you do not wish others to do to you (*Analects*, 5:11); by extension, you *should* do to others what you *wish* others to do to your (*Analects*, 6:28). The idea of *shu* enforces the duty ethics on filial piety. Confucius himself specifically applied the concept of *shu* to filial piety by including the following in the Way of the morally superior person: "to serve my father as I would expect my son to serve me" (*Doctrine of the Mean*, ch. 13). Would not every one of us wish that our children accompany us when we are old and lonely, or serve us at our bedside when we are sick and infirm? The Confucians would say, then, that we ourselves must start serving our own parents.

2.5   A Confucian Response

So, what can be learned from this Confucian filial morality? Confucianism states that humans are not atomistic, self-serving, rights-laden individuals coming to construct a society out of self-interests. We are defined by the social roles that we take on, and these social roles define our humanity. Humanity or *Ren* morality demands filial piety. In such a human society, each of us is benefited some of the time and in some way, and we should feel grateful and show our gratitude for the benefits that we receive. This includes our relationship with our parents.

It is assumed here that a normal person appreciates the fact that he or she is alive, and that his or her parents have endured hardship and sacrifice to bring up their children. It is also assumed that given the choice between having been born and not having been born, the normal person would strongly prefer the former, and between being well cared for and not well cared for as a child, the normal person would strongly prefer the former. Then this person "owes" his parents a great favor for giving him life and bringing him up, even though he did not request either. And this person is under moral obligation to reciprocate the favor he has received; when his parents are old and in need of assistance, he is obliged to help. Although how much help he can offer depends on circumstances (just as how much benefit his parents were able to offer depended on the circumstances), his moral obligation to help his aged parents is greater than his general duty to help other people in need. This, then, is a Confucian response to a position like the one offered by Jane English.

Gratitude, however, is not the sole grounds for filial morality. The morality of *Ren* demands that, within a community, those who have resources, spiritual as well as material, should be benefactors, and those who are in need are entitled to be beneficiaries. In this view, when person B does good to person A, A should be grateful to B even if B is simply discharging his or her duty, and from the fact that A has received benefits from B because B had a duty to be beneficial it does not follow that A will not be obligated to benefit his former benefactor when B is in need and A in turn has the resources to be a benefactor.

When one is a child, her parents have the duty to benefit her. From that it does not follow that when her parents grow old and are in need she would not have a duty to be a benefactor to them. Therefore, even though Jeffrey Blustein is right that parents do have a duty to care for their children, it does not follow that this would not result in children's obligation, when they are grown, to care for their aged and infirm parents. This, then, is a Confucian response to philosophers with Blustein's view.

3. Why Shift Perspectives?

The primary purpose of this essay is to provide a Confucian perspective on filial morality as an alternative to the mainstream Western perspective, namely to show that the Confucian perspective is plausible on its own account. I, however, do not pretend to have found an over-arching framework in which one can demonstrate that one tradition on the whole is superior to the other. I agree with Alasdair MacIntyre that the moral good can only be vindicated within a tradition (1984). I submit, again without an overarching framework, that the attempt to demonstrate that one tradition is superior to another would be futile. For example, there are people who reject outright the Confucian ontology of humanity. Some are convinced that we humans are indeed atomistic individuals who enter society with a contract. For them, the question of filial morality is linked to the concept of personhood; to debate this topic is beyond the scope of this essay.

Nevertheless, one may be able to compare aspects of two traditions to see how each deals with some problems of shared interest. Through comparison one may be able to show that one tradition has a stronger and more plausible view in some particular areas. I hope I have shown that the Confucian tradition does make a stronger case for filial morality than a rights-centered tradition does. Therefore, proponents of filial morality may have good reasons to shift to the Confucian perspective. As a matter of fact, it appears that some authors I have cited in this essay have, wittingly or unwittingly, thought along the Confucian lines. We need to make this alternative explicitly available and clear to all. For people who do not believe in filial morality, by shifting to a new perspective, I hope I have shown them that there is a sensible way to vindicate filial morality. It would appear that, to the extent that developing one's humanity is important, the world would be a better place if something like Confucian filial morality were widely practiced.

REFERENCES

Ames, Roger. 1994. "The Focus-Field Self in Classical Confucianism." In *Self as Person in Asian Theory and Practice*, edited by Roger Ames with W. Dissanayake and T. Kasulis, Albany: State University of New York Press.

Belliotti, Raymond A. 1986. "Honor Thy Father and Thy Mother and To Thine Own self Be True," *The Southern Journal of Philosophy*, 24 (2).

──────. 1988. "Parents and Children: A Reply to Narveson," *The Southern Journal of Philosophy*, 26(2).

Blustein, Jeffrey. 1982. *Parents and Children: The Ethics of the Family*. New York and Oxford: Oxford University Press.

Confucius. 1989 *The Analects*. Trans by Arthur Waley. New York: Vintage Books.

English, Jane. 1979. "What Do Grown Children Owe Their Parents?" In O'Neill, Onora and W. Ruddick.

Fung Yu-lan. 1952. *A History of Chinese Philosophy*, vol. 1. Trans. Derk Bodde Princeton: Princeton University Press.

Hsieh Yu-Wei. 1986. "Filial Piety and Chinese Society." In *The Chinese Mind: Essentials of Chinese Philosophy and Culture*, edited by Charles A. Moore. Honolulu: University of Hawaii Press.

Huang Junlang. 1992. "Sketching on *the Classic of Filial Piety*." In *Reading the Classic of Filial Piety: New Interpretation*, edited by Lai Yanyuan and Huang Junlang. Taipei: Sanmin Books.

Kittay, Eva F. and Diana T. Meyers (ed.). 1987. *Women and Moral theory*. Totowa. NJ: Rowman & Littlefield Publishers.

Liang Shu-ming. 1990. "The Elements of Chinese Culture (*Zhongguo Wenhua Yaoyi*)." In *Collected Works of Liang Shu-ming*, vol. 3, edited by the Academic Committee of China's Cultural Academy. Jinan, China: Shandong People's Publisher.

Lin Yutang. 1993. "On Growing Old Gracefully." In *Vice & Virtue in Everyday Life*, the third edition, edited by Christina Sommers and Fred Sommers. Fort Worth, TX: Harcourt Brace Jovanovich.

Lo Ping Cheung. 1993. "Philosophical Reflections on Filial Piety (*Xiao zhi Zhexue Fanxing*)," *Legein Monthly*, No. 218.

MacIntyre, A. 1984. *After Virtue*, the second edition. Notre Dame: University of Notre Dame Press.

Mencius. 1970. *Mencius*. Trans. D. C. Lau. Penguin Books.

Narveson, Jan. 1987. "On Honoring Our Parents," *The Southern Journal of Philosophy*, 25(1).

O'Neill, Onora and W. Ruddick (ed.). 1979. *Having Children*. New York: Oxford University Press.

The People's Daily (Chinese overseas edition). 1993. Beijing, August 25.

Rawls, John. 1980. "Kantian Constructivism in Moral Theory: The John Dewey Lectures 1980," *Journal of Philosophy* 77.

Russell, Bertrand. 1922. *The Problem of China*. London: George Allen & Unwin..

Simmons, John. 1979. *Moral Principles and Political Obligations*. Princeton: Princeton University Press.

Slote, Michael. 1979. "Obedience and Illusion." In O'Neill and Ruddick.

Sommers, Christina H. 1987. "Filial Morality," in Kittay and Meyers.

Tu Wei-ming. 1985. "Selfhood and Otherness: The Father-Son Relationship in Confucian Thought" In his *Confucian Thought: Selfhood as Creative Transformation*. Albany: State University of New York Press.

—————. 1989. *Centrality and Commonality*. Albany: State University of New York Press.

3

"Rights"
In Traditional Chinese Anthropocentrism[1]

Zijiang Ding

The concept of "rights"[2] has gradually emerged as the subject of a particular academic field of study—a complex one, involving three aspects: conceptual approaches, theoretical orientation and practical development. The study of Chinese "rights" should be involved in the fundamental interrelation of all forms of Chinese human values and social behavior. This study will generalize about the ways in which certain naïve, vague and implied consciousness and spontaneous and haphazard actions of Chinese rights have affected the processes of Chinese social changes and human development. A convergence of goals of "rights" means that an essential restructuring of basic research and its cross-cultural comparisons must be accomplished. The study's central theme is that questions and analytical modes of "rights" in Chinese human development are rapidly being challenged as a fundamental framework for philosophical criticism, and in its place will come new research from more investigators with interdisciplinary, multi-methodological approaches and analytical examination.

I. Chinese "Rights": Controversial Perspectives

Since scholars began to think about the existence of "rights" in Chi-

---

[1] This paper was presented at the Sixty-eighth Annual Meeting of American Philosophic Association, Pacific Division, 1994.
[2] Due to the various debates, I will use quotation marks for the word *rights* in Chinese perspective.

nese cultural development, the debate over Chinese traditional human values has bounced between two emphases.

At one emphasis are those who consider "rights" as totally non-existent from a kind of absolute nihilistic viewpoint, regarding "rights" as "only an outcome of Western culture." As Wm. Theodore de Bary points out: "To many contemporary observers Confucianism and Human rights would seem to be an unlikely combination ..." (de Bary 1998, 1).

In Chung-sho Lo's viewpoint, there was no explicit concept of human rights in East Asian culture before Western political ideas arrived at the end of the nineteenth century. For example, Confucianism laid the foundations of ethics in certain social relations and the mutual obligations that were inherent in them (Lo 1949, 187). According to Henry Rosemont, Jr., clearly the concept of rights, and of human beings as autonomous, freely choosing right-bearing individuals, is identified with one major culture, Western civilization (Rosemont 1991, 60).

Julia Ching finds "two opposing interpretations" for the topic of human rights and Chinese culture and both of them concur that human rights are not historically a Chinese concept, but a Western import: one is to introduce human rights into China as an unnecessary cultural intrusion into a culture and society quite self-sufficient in its own pursuit of humane values and social harmony; the other is to maintain that Chinese civilization has nurtured for millennia a brutal political culture that has only commanded passive obedience without permitting the development of any real idea of civil rights and liberties (Ching 1998, 70).

Irene Bloom agrees that lately in China and the West there have been those who, for different reasons, have voiced the concern that "human rights" is a Western idea without relevance to or resonance in the Chinese tradition (Bloom 1998, 95). Randall Peerenboom suggests that those contemporary advocates of Confucianism must respond to the challenge of rights, and in particular to the charges that Confucianism not only failed to develop a theory of rights but that it is in some fundamental sense incompatible with rights (Peerenboom 1998, 247).

Conversely, at the other emphasis are those who stress that "rights" has affected Chinese human development in it own way. Among those holding that view, D. W. Y. Kwok strongly believes that the literature on human rights in traditional Chinese culture is legion and already highly sophisticated (Kwok 1998, 83). However, for Kenneth K. Inada, it is incorrect to assume that the concept of human rights is readily identifiable in all societies of the world. The concept may perhaps be clear and distinct in legal quarters, but in actual practice it suffers greatly from lack of clarity and gray areas due to impositions by different cultures. This is especially true in Asia, where the two great civilizations of India and China have spawned such outstanding systems as Hinduism, Buddhism, Jainism, Confucianism, Daoism, and Chinese Buddhism (Inada 1990, 91).

As a result, these two emphases might lead to a different understanding of Chinese civilization—its spirituality, value system and actual socio-political mechanism. The study of "rights" in the Chinese context has probably faced more difficulties in limiting its concern to conceptualization and theorization of "rights" than the other analytic terms in socio-political philosophy. We must trace its intellectual origins and concerns to literatures and documents that may imply a certain possible consciousness of "rights" in the history of Chinese political and legal thought.

In recent years, more and more scholars have planed to build a positive dialogue on human rights between Western and Eastern cultures. Among them, the most leading one is Wm. Theodore de Bary. In 1994, he appealed for more conferences on human rights with a comparative Confucian-Western perspective to promote unconfrontational, multicultural dialogue on the basic value issues underlying human rights concepts and practices. Some possible topics to be discussed included: (1) Confucian concepts of self, person and individual in relation to state and society and self-discipline as the key to governance; (2) "Rights" protected in Confucian ritual and Chinese law, the relation between rights, responsibilities, and duties; and (3) Human rights in the perspective of Confucian concepts of social justice (de Bary 1998, xvii-xviii).

Later, to advance future dialogue, de Bary proposed more points for discussion as follows: (1) Confucian values and discourse

for centuries have concerned many of the same issues that have occupied Western human rights thinkers, though in somewhat different
language; (2) Thinking about human rights is a relatively recent development and has diverse roots in the West; (3) It is significant that
several East Asian countries have not found their Confucian past an
obstacle to the acceptance of Western-style constitutions and guaran-
tees of human rights; (4) Although Confucianism has had a great emphasis on social and communitarian values, a respect for the dignity
of the self and person has been central from its inception; (5) In the
long-term evolution of Confucian thinking there is an increasing consciousness of the need for law in constitutional and due process
senses; (6) Individual rights, social duties or communitarian needs
should be mutually implicated and equally necessary; (7) There are
two questions that can not be in equal measure today for East and
West: the first is whether human rights could be effective in the absence of a civil political infrastructure, the second is whether the
various social and economic problems that confront us today do not
demand new human rights conceptions and practices, with a humane
concern extending beyond the human to the earth and all forms of
life (de Bary 1998, 24-25). Many Western and Eastern scholars believe that a significant compatibility should exist between Confucianism and human rights.

Jeremy T. Paltiel emphasizes that Confucian Chinese values and
Western liberal values are not mutually exclusive, but they are different. He wrote, "To view cultures in dichotomous terms exaggerates
these differences and destroys points of tangency. Intercultural encounters can recognize common attributes of humanity" (Paltiel
1998, 270-271).

Sumner B. Twiss describes his goal as "to develop a constructive framework for intercultural human rights dialogue and to illustrate its utility with respect to the Confucian tradition." To realize this
goal, he offers a sketch of how human rights under his revised understanding can fit within the Confucian tradition: (1) to outline his general understanding of those parameters of Confucian tradition that
may have a particular bearing on human rights; (2) to mention a historical contribution of Confucian tradition to the Universal Declaration of Human Rights; (3) to propose that all three generations of

human rights can be compatible with Confucian moral and political thought; (4) to suggest that it is fully open to the Confucian tradition to justify on its own terms, to its own participants, its agreement to participate in human rights consensus at the international level. Twiss proposes that the two-level approach permits us to chart interactions in the future between the Confucian tradition and the international human rights community (Twiss 1998, 27).

Tu Weiming, one of the most important contemporary leaders for reviving Confucianism,[3] asserts that Confucian "core values" are not only compatible with the implementation of human rights but they can enhance the universal appeal of human rights that includes the perception of the person as a center of relationships rather than simply as an isolated individual, the idea of society as a community of trust rather than merely a system of adversarial relationships, and the belief that human beings are duty-bound to respect their family, society, and nation. According to Tu, the danger of using Confucian values as a cover for authoritarian practices must be fully explored. Many of those values, however, such as duty, harmony, consensus, network, ritual, trust, and sympathy, need not be a threat to rights-consciousness at all. Clearly, Confucian values as richly textured ideas of human flourishing can serve as a source of inspiration for representing human rights as the common language of humanity. The challenge is how to fruitfully introduce a Confucian perspective on evolving human rights discourse without diffusing the focused energy of the national and international instruments that have been promoting political rights with telling effectiveness in some selected areas of the world (Tu 1998, 287-305).

In his comments on Tu Weiming's arguments, Joshua Cohen positively emphasizes that Confucian humanism offers an account of the reason for supporting basic human rights, but this account operates from within an ethical outlook dominated by notions of persons as embedded in social relations and subject to the obligations associ-

---

[3] Jeremy T. Paltiel says, "By and large they (Chinese intellectuals) seem to reject Professor Tu Weiming's efforts to revive Confucianism with new meaning for the contemporary age." See Paltiel, 270.

ated with those relationships, rather than depending on a Western-ized liberal conception of persons (Cohen 1996, 8).

Chung-ying Cheng puts forward an argument for "transforming Confucian virtues into human rights." In his view, the rights of human beings have never occupied a prominent place in Chinese thinking, because the Chinese and Western conceptions of the rise of government differ. However, this is not because there is nothing whatever like human rights in the Chinese tradition. For example, the natural right to change a government for the well being of the people was conceived by Mencius. It was based on his view of human nature as an embodiment of the Mandate of Heaven from which people are entitled to claim what is originally intended for them by Heaven. The Confucian social duty of mutual respect and mutual help between friends may be a native source for an ethics of equal human rights with Chinese characteristics. For this reason, even in Confucianism there is this dimension of human rights. Besides, many other Confucian virtues are compatible with human rights, such as the Confucian aspiration to secure a proper place in society according to one's ability and merit (Cheng 1998, 144-51).

II. Chinese "Rights": Conceptual Perspectives

Since the discussion of rights is an important concern of political philosophers, it is necessary for us to define this concept analytically and critically. Rights can be considered an explanatory variable, a reference parameter, a conceptual framework or an analytical mode, which will be examined on its possible grounds and according to its characteristics—the objects, the subjects, the motivations, the sources and the extent.[4]

---

[4] The following books may help us to understand the conception of rights: Bendiff, Theodore M.. *Rights*, Totowa, NJ: Rowman and Littlefield, 1982; Bilancia, Philip R., *Dictionary of Chinese Law and Government (Chinese-English)*, Stanford University Press, 1981; Bodde, Derk, and Clarence Morris, *Law in Imperial China Exemplified by 190 Ching Dynasty Cases*, Cambridge: Harvard University Press, 1967; Bodde, Derk, *China's Cultural Tradition: What and Whither?* New York: Holt, Rinehart and Winston 1966; Bridge, J. W. (ed.), *Fundamental Rights*, London, 1973; Chen, Philip M., *Law*

There are differences as well as similarities between Eastern and Western human cultural developments. Chinese "rights" can be found even through certain "universal" ways. For most scholars: (1) "rights" should be a kind of claim, demand, justification, protestation, declaration, assertion, affirmation, pretension, title, license, perquisite or appanage; (2) "rights" should be just, fair, appropriate, proper, lawful, impartial, reasonable, legitimate or equitable; (3) rights should be moral, legal or political; (4) rights should be applied or exercised by a holder; (5) rights should be based on human nature, a value system, spirituality, a legal system or a traditional culture; and (6) rights should be for something, such as power, interests, benefits, advantages, welfare, privileges, prerogatives, enjoyments, unity, happiness, titles or reputations, and so on. I will try to adopt these six viewpoints in examining the what, why, how, and who questions regarding "rights" in traditional Chinese culture.

For study purposes, "rights" can be discussed or examined according to five analytical modes or theoretical assumptions and explanatory variables as follows:

"Rights to" Mode: the possible objects of rights. This mode is about some direct objects for its realization, actualization or materialization. First, it shows us a Being Status (Right-To-Be-Something), such as the right "to be a congressperson," "to be a professor," "to be a pilot," "to be a voter" or "to be a employee," etc. Second, it

and Justice: The Legal System in China 2400 B. C. to 1960 A. D., New York: Duhellen Publishing Company, 1973; Coleman, Jules, *Philosophy and Law*, Basil Blackwell In., 1987; Edwards, R. Randle, *Human Rights in Contemporary China*, New York: Columbia University Press, 1986; Frey, R. G., *Interests and Rights*, Oxford: Clarendon Press, 1980; Hsiung, James C. (ed.), *Human Rights in East Asia*, New York: Paragon Houn Publishes, 1984; Lin, Fu-shun. *Chinese Law, Past and Present*, New York: Columbia University, 1966; Martin, Rex, *Rawls and Rights*, University Press of Kansas, 1985; Melden, A. I., *Rights in Moral Lives: A Historical-Philosophical Essay*, Berkeley: University of California Press, 1988; Moore, Charles (ed.), *The Status of the Individual in East and West*, Honolulu: University of Hawaii Press, 1968; Ritchie, David G., *Natural Rights*, London: George Allen and Union Ltd., 1952; Shue, Henry, *Basic Rights*, Princeton, NJ: Princeton University Press, 1980; Thomson, Judith Jarvis, *The Realm of Rights*, Cambridge, Massachusetts: Harvard University Press, 1990; White, Alan Q. *Rights*, Oxford: Clarendon Press, 1984; Wu, Yuan-li, *Human Rights in the P. R. China*, Boulder, Colorado: Westview Press, 1988.

shows us a Doing Status (Right-To-Do-Something), such as the right "to educate or to be educated," "to run a business," "to speak," "to participate in politics," "to immigrate," "to make an association," "to know something," "to avoid danger" or "to initiate a lawsuit," etc. Third, it shows us a Having Status (Right-To-Have-Something), such as the right "to own property," "to own a gun," "to hold a religious belief," "to work under good conditions" or "to have a fair salary," etc.[5] In general, the object of a right can be a material thing, human behavior or spiritual value. The object of a right is determined by different cultures, social systems and historical periods. For instance, in a slave-owning system, the slaves are not the subjects, but the objects of right. In a feudalistic system, some persons, such as serfs, are semi-subjects as well as semi-objects of right. But in the modern social system, all people are equal and cannot be treated as an object of right at any time and in any place.[6] In the traditional Chinese social system, a part of the population, such as *"jianmin"* 賤民 (servants), was a kind of semi-object of right.

"Rights by" Mode: the possible subjects of rights. This mode is about some holders, possessors or exercisers who practice and realize the rights. From today's point of view, so-called subjects can be divided into three groups which have a capacity for rights: (a) any natural persons or individuals, such as citizens, minorities, females, disabled persons, parents, children, employees, patients, workers, consumers or criminals; (b) any legal persons or organizations, such as nations, races, governments, institutions, businesses, classes, interest groups or religious groups; and (c) any animals.[7] A subject of rights

---

[5] Those types are little different from Alan R. White's. For White, one's right may be (1) a right to do something, (2) a right to have something done to one, (3) a right to be in a certain state, (4) a right to feel something, (5) a right to take a certain attitude. See White, 13-15.

[6] According to Marxism, in a modern capitalist system, because of commercialization of the labor force, even workers become some kind of "commodity," actually a kind of "object of rights." Therefore, there are no real equal rights in a capitalist society.

[7] Some very radical viewpoints broaden "the holder of rights" to any kind of life forms, such as plants and other organisms, and even to any lifeless forms and

must have the capacity for rights. A subject of rights is also determined by different cultures, social systems and historical periods. For example, in a slave-owning society, only masters and freemen are subjects of rights. In a feudal society landlords have full capacity for rights, but peasants have only a very limited capacity. In the modern society, every person must be a subject of right. In the traditional Chinese social system, there were seven possible subjects of right—but with a difference of degree (we will discuss this later).

"Rights for" Mode: the possible motivation of rights. This mode is about some kind of intention, direction, and purpose for rights. Different holders of rights have different motivations. Politically, those motivations could be for liberty, equality, individuality, legality, security, safety, survival, democracy, development, enjoyment or happiness. Economically speaking, they could be for interests, benefits, profits, advantages, beneficence or compensation. In Chinese traditional culture, different holders or subjects of rights had different motivations.

"Rights of" Mode: the possible extent or content of rights. This mode is about topologies, classifications or categories or some kind of range, field, or domain for rights. Generally speaking, rights can be divided into three basic types: natural rights (fundamental rights, universal rights or human rights), legal rights (including political rights, economic rights, and religious rights in a broader sense), and moral rights. Natural rights are a kind of "rights" defined and recognized through human nature, a social ideal or internal need. From today's point of view, the concept of "natural rights" can be replaced by "human rights" or "fundamental rights." The term "human rights" has not been adopted with precise definition or with absolute agreement. For most Western scholars, so-called "human rights" should apply to all human beings at any time and in any place, and to any thing, regardless of blood, race, class, gender, property, religion, occupation, ideology, talent, merit, age, physical condition, sociopolitical system or other background and commitment. Generally speaking, human rights cannot be waived, changed or transferred.

---

whole-nature beings. For example, C. D. Stone argues that we should extend legal rights to forests, oceans, rivers and other natural objects. See Stone, 45.

Moral rights are a kind of rights defined and recognized through a value system, an ethical framework, human conscience, social responsibility or public opinion (Gastil 1976, 231-40). Legal rights are a kind of rights defined and recognized by an external authority, sovereign or state law.

The theory of natural rights has been one of the most important socio-political theories for human development. This theory asserts that people are created equal and that governments derive their just powers from the consent of the governed. There have been various debates about "natural rights." For example, Rousseau criticized Hobbes' and Locke's points of view. For Rousseau, indeed every person has a natural right to preserve himself and to act in accordance with this right. Civil society has no natural ground to issue a command that contradicts the natural rights. But all civil societies issue such commands; natural rights cannot be their legitimization. Humankind is naturally free and civil society takes his freedom away from him; he is dependent on the law, and the law is made in favor of the rich—or at least in its origin it was meant to favor them. For Bentham, human happiness could not be determined by reference to an objective good or to natural rights such as were proclaimed in the American Declaration of Independence or in the French Declaration of the Rights of Man and Citizen, because natural rights were selfish interests well or ill disguised (See Rousseaus 1994). A classical formulation of natural rights is presented as follows:

> Seeing any men are by nature those sons of Adam, and from him have legitimately derived a natural propriety, right, and freedom, therefore England and all other nations, and all particular persons in every nation, notwithstanding the difference of laws and governments, ranks and degrees, right to be alike free and estate in their natural liberties, and to enjoy the just rights and prerogative of mankind whereunto they are heirs apparent; and thus the commoners by right, are equal with the lords. For by natural birth all men are equally and alike born to like propriety, liberty, and freedom; and as we are delivered of God by the hand of nature into this world, every one with a natural innate freedom, and propriety, even so are we to live, every one equally and alike to enjoy his birthright and privilege. (T. Edwards 1965, 17)

Obviously, in ancient China, there existed some moral claims (rights) for social responsibility, life styles, and modes of behavior. There had also been some legal claims (rights), such as equality in initiating a lawsuit. Some great Chinese thinkers advocated certain claims corresponding to the so-called natural right—for example, the claims for life, liberty, equality, and resistance to oppression, property, beneficence, survival, subsistence, security, self-protection, interactive duties, and happiness.

"Rights from" Mode: the possible origin of rights. This mode is about some roots, sources or causes for rights. The idea of rights might come from human nature; cultural tradition and value systems; historical process and social progress, spiritual and material needs, revolutions and mass movements, organized and institutionalized activities; and most important, individuals' claims, interests and advantages. Undoubtedly, at least some of these sources for rights can also be found in Chinese history.

Is any Chinese term conceptually compatible with "rights"? In ancient Chinese documents or classical Chinese literatures, there is no special term that corresponds precisely to the Western word "rights." In modern Chinese, the term rights is translated into the Chinese word *quanli* 權利, which originally is formed by the two Chinese characters *quan* 權 and *li* 利.[8] The first means power, authority, sovereignty, mastery, supremacy, influence, competence, function, force or jurisdiction; the second means interests, benefits, advantages, profits, welfare or utilities.

In Irene Bloom's opinion, although *quanli* was not part of Mencian vocabulary, but in a deeper sense many of his concerns seem related to Westerners'. These Mencian concerns include: his sense of

---

[8] In Chinese, *li* can be represented by several different Chinese characters with the same pronunciation—all of which have certain important philosophical meanings: (1) one character *li* 禮 can be defined as "principles," "rules," "laws," "propriety," "rites," or "rituals," etc.; (2) another character *li* 理 can be interpreted as "reason," "logic," "truth," "idea," "argument," "intellect," "understanding" or "universal spiritual power;" and (3) the third character *li* 利 means "interests," "benefits," "advantages," "profits," "welfare" or "utility."

common humanity, his discovery of a moral potential common to all human beings, his devotion to the idea of "nobility," his concern with the responsibilities rulers have for the well-being of the people, his insistence on the limits of power—with what rulers should decline to do out of respect and compassion for the people (Bloom 1998, 94).

The contemporary Chinese dictionary defines the holder of *quanli* is defined as a natural person (or citizen) or legal person (or organization) who exercises the powers belonging to himself or herself and enjoys the interests according to the law.

For our inquiry, in addition to *quanli*, we may find some other Chinese characters or words, which correspond or relate to the Western term rights in the ancient or classic Chinese vocabulary. For example, *yao* 要, *qiu* 求 and *xu* 需 mean claims, demands, needs, requirements or declarations; *zheng* 正 as an adjective means just, legitimate, proper, fair, appropriate, righteous, reasonable, lawful or equitable; *que* 確 and *ding* 定 mean asserting, affirming, confirming, defining, determining, delimiting, setting, fixing, establishing or forming; *bao* 保 and *hu* 護 mean to protect, to ensure, to guarantee, to safeguard, to defend, to preserve or to maintain; *pei* 賠 and *chang* 償 mean compensation; *you* 有 and *ju* 據 mean to own or to possess. Mencius discussed "*you*" in a moral and also a legal sense. He says: "Indeed, to call everyone who takes what is not properly possessed (*you*) by him a robber, is pushing a point of resemblance to the utmost, and insisting on the most refined idea of righteousness" (Mencius 5B:4).

Indeed, this kind of reconceptualization can really help us to characterize our study. In attempting to spell out the essential conceptualizations of the Chinese concept of rights, we may use the following three basic standards for any proper, just and fair human behavior or activity according to the Chinese traditional value system: (1) *Heqing* 合情. *He* means according to, conforming to, being in line with, tallying with or square with; but *qing* means human nature, environment, social conditions, actual situations, common good, compassion or sympathy. (2) *Heli* 合理. *Li* means reasons, truth, logic, principles, theories, moral standards, rational decisions, intellectual approaches or the real ways of the world. (3). *Hefa* 合法. *Fa* 法 can be defined as laws, rules, commands or social political orders, but as

Julia Ching says, the concept of law (*fa*) is understood differently in the Chinese cultural context, such as customs that became a penal code (Ching 1998, 74).

III. Chinese "Rights": Anthropocentric perspectives

It must be emphasized with reference to all of the above definitions and modes to the theory of rights that "rights" from the Chinese perspective are inspired and derived from a totally different source and by a completely independent path—traditional Chinese anthropocentrism.[9]

In the Western sense, "rights" has three basic preconditions: the human being as the center of the earth, individuals as the starting point, and the social contract as secured guarantee. Perhaps it is superfluous to note that these features may, or may not, be unified. However, it is more creative to examine six possible ways of analyzing the issue of "rights" from the perspective of so-called Chinese anthropocentrism. So-called Chinese anthropocentrism (or, in another word, humanism) did not come from a single, unique or pure philosophic source. Actually, it was unified by Confucianism (or Neo-Confucianism), Legalism, Taoism, Moism and other Chinese cultural or spiritual roots (even Buddhism).

What is humanity? Confucius and Mencius interpreted and explained it in different terms and contexts. The first is *airen* 愛人 (love all human beings) (*Analects*, 12:22); the second is *keji fuli* 克己複禮 (disciplining oneself and restoring rites)(ibid. 5:12); the third is *jisuo buyu wushi yuren* 己所不欲，勿施與人 (do not do to others what we would not want others to do to us) (ibid. 5:11. and 12:2); the fourth is *tianren heyi* 天人合一 (the unity of heaven and humanity); the fifth is *renzheng* 仁政 (rule by humaneness) (Mencius 3A:3).

Tu Weiming believes that the Confucian perception of human self-development is based upon the dignity of the person, in terms of

---

[9] Tu Weiming refuses to use the concept "anthropocentrism." He says: "The full meaning of humanity is anthropocosmic rather than anthropocentric." See Tu 1998, 302. For me, the important issue is how to define this term.

a series of concentric circles: self, family, community, society, nation, world, and cosmos (Tu 1998, 302). For Louis Henkin human rights are rooted in a conception of human dignity that determines and defines rights and requires that they be recognized and realized. Confucian teachings encouraged civility, and inspired humane concern and mutual respect (Henkin 1998, 309). From Tu's and Henkin's views, we may find out same source—"human dignity" for both of Confucian humaneness and Western rights.

What is the traditional Chinese anthropocentrism? We may characterize it as follows: (a) Human beings, their powers and their affairs are more significant than divine beings. (b) There should be some conflicts and interactions between different kinds of human beings, such as in the five basic social relationships. (c) Balance, equilibrium and harmony among human beings are the most important social purposes, tasks and ideals. (d) For this reason, some necessary social norms, principles, rules, laws, orders, systems, values, and moral standards must be formed, organized and institutionalized. (e) Good rulers should take care of the interests of the people and bestow some benefits to them through rule by virtue and the principles of justice. (f) Governments or authority figures also must be strict and fair in meting out rewards and punishments, offering "the carrot and the stick" judiciously.

The most important principle of Confucius for an individual person to be self-realized as an ideal human being in the social life is *ren* (humanity or humaneness), from which all socio-political norms and moral standards are developed. If this "basic line" were implemented thoroughly and completely, the various human needs, claims, interests, dignity, self-esteem could be recognized, guaranteed and satisfied.

1. Ideological Sources of Chinese "Rights" Consciousness

To borrow some concepts from Western value system, the initial picture in the Chinese perspective of rights is an enormous multiplicity of spiritual sources, namely the influence and effects of five sources—individualism, liberalism, egalitarianism, legalism and democratism through integration, combination and unification. While everyone asserts that the five sources were interdependent and interactive, and attempts to build connecting bridges across the various boundaries, clearly the effort of constructing certain specialization among them should be also necessary and workable. In a sense, the above five sources have also been functional in Chinese human development, but all of them worked in some very passive, negative, naive or subordinate ways. Having placed the issue under examination, the main question is: how are we to draw the dividing lines between (1) negative individualism vs. positive communitarianism; (2) passive liberalism vs. active conservatism; (3) naive egalitarianism vs. refined discriminativism; (4) subordinate legalism vs. dominate moralism; (5) implied democratism vs. overall despotism?

Negative Individualism vs. Positive Communitarianism

With reference to this point, the performance of so-called individualism may be contrasted with the overall performance of positive communitarianism (or universalism). The following two issues are very significant on the Chinese perspective of rights. First, although taking the rights as its central focus, the liberal individualism acknowledges that the existence of human rights cannot be demonstrated. If the Chinese have a theory of rights, how do they demonstrate the existence of these rights? Second, for communitarianism, the liberalists' emphasis on rights will cause many problems. Chinese ethics in general is akin to communitarianism rather than to individualism. Therefore, if Chinese ethics has a theory of rights, what is the connection between this theory and its central claim that a person is socially embedded and locked in a network of relations?

Louis Henkin argues that in Chinese tradition the individual was not central, and no conception of individual rights existed in the sense known in the United States. The individual's participation in society was not voluntary, and the legitimacy of government did not depend on his consent or the consent of the whole people or individuals. Individuals were not equal, and society was not egalitarian but hierarchical (See Henkin 1986). In Tao Julia's opinion, the conception of individual rights is commonly contrasted with non-Western conceptions of the collective good to show not only that the

Western conception of rights is culturally peculiar to the West but also that it is morally inferior in privileging individual self-interest over the common good (see Tao 1990). But, according to A. J. Nathan, Chinese philosophy still assigned a great role to individuals; however, this was a political individualism of a very different kind from that which the term calls to mind in the modern West (Nathan 1986, 138). For Hsieh Yu-Wei, Confucianism "regarded individuals as roots, and communities as leaves—individuals as foundations and communities as roots" (Hsieh 1968, 280). In the words of Derk Bodde, "Confucian individualism" means that the individual must develop his creative potential so that he can fulfil that particular role which is his within the social nexus (Bodde 1966, 66).

On one hand, for the Chinese ruling classes, the Great Unity, the Great Entirety, the Great Integrity, the Great Centrality and the Great Universality had been their most important social ideal; as a result, dehumanization, deindividualization and depersonalization were a basic characteristic of Chinese social life;[10] on the other hand, for the Chinese masses, decentralization, deunification and deuniversalization were also important characteristics of Chinese social life. There have been very sharp conflicts between the hypocritical moral sermon, such as "to show loyalty for one's country," and "actual and realistic immoral practice," such as "Human beings die in pursuit of wealth, and birds die in pursuit of food," or "Unless a man looks out for himself, heaven and earth will destroy him."

Passive Liberalism vs. Active Conservatism

Accordingly, emphasis should be placed on inquiry into the conflicts between the institutionalized ruling mechanism and loose or unorganized anarchical disobedience. In principle, some great Chinese thinkers, such as Zhuangzi, advocated some absolute and unlimited spiritual freedom, and attempted to withdraw themselves from poli-

---

[10] Sun Yat-sen had figuratively described Chinese people as "a sheet of loose sand." For him, the negative individualism was a serious barrier for Chinese social progress.

tics and social activities, or adopted an unconventional and unrestrained lifestyle.[11] According to Yu Fen, Confucianism, Daoism, and Buddhism all have their own view on human freedom (Yu 1998, 154).

For many scholars, the anti-majoritarian function is the most leading function of rights. In Chinese culture, this anti-majoritarianism also has been popularized for many intellectuals and ordinary people.

In practice—as the Chinese saying goes, "the mountain is high, the emperor is far away"—the people who either belonged to the lowest class or to higher classes often wanted to cast off the yoke of social control to pursue their own needs and interests.

Naive Egalitarianism vs. Refined Discriminativism

This demarcation between two extremes at the level of their respective conceptual frameworks will be helpful to understand the paradoxical gap between the social ideal and reality. Equality has been one of the most important social ideals in the whole of Chinese human development. *Datong shijie* 大同世界 (The Great Universal Harmony and Perfection in the World) has been a final dreamland for many honest, upright and fair-minded ancient intellectuals.[12] In the Chinese history of thought, many great thinkers had advocated some kind of equality.

Donald Munro suggests that Confucius and Mencius demonstrate a belief in natural equality along with a moral perspective that entails evaluative inequality.[13] More significantly, Mencius deepened

---

[11] For example, many ancient scholars or poets such as Li Bai 李白 (Li Po) and Tao Yuanming 陶淵明 adopted a kind of independent thinking, a personal attitude toward life and characteristic style of literary and artistic creation.

[12] Some scholars think that "egalitarianism" or "equalitarianism" has been the leading characteristic of Chinese peasant mentality, such as "to share weal and woe." There was a very famous slogan: "to share out equality without regarding the rich and the power, to live together without regarding the noble and the ignoble."

[13] See Munro, 1969, esp. chs. 1 and 4.

the egalitarian theme. He assumes that human nature is good and that one can find norms of behavior in one's own heart, which implies that human beings are morally equal. Ideally, for him, everyone could become a Yao 堯 or Shun 舜 (Mencius 6B:2). In other words, the potential for moral development was the same for all. Wejen Chang points out that Mencius attempted to solve a problem: the idea of human equality seems to be in conflict with the fact that in any society some have to rule while others are to be ruled (Chang 1998, 124).

Confucius created a private school, and struggled for classless education and selection of officials based on equality, because "In education there should be no class distinctions" (*Analects* 15:38). The master also says: "By nature close together; through practice set apart" (ibid. 17:2). This statement seemed aptly to express a modern sense of human equality and relatedness—one that allows for both similarities and differences (Bloom 1998, 96). Following Confucian thought, later imperial governments (Sui and Tang Dynasties) created the "*keju* 科舉" system—to hold open examinations to the public to select officials by equal opportunity and free competition. Although this system had both advantages and disadvantages, it was much better than the selection of officials by blood inheritance, or family, political, economic, religious and other backgrounds.[14] Objectively speaking, Confucius' and Mencius' affirmations of human equality are not direct human rights thinking, but they can be considered a potential source of the implied human rights consciousness.

For Laozi 老子 (580-500 B.C.) and his Daoism, any conflicts, struggles or fights were based on some inequality; in other words, harmony must be based on equality.[15] Following Laozi, Zhuangzi 莊子 (355-275 B.C.) said, "There should be no inequality among natural things from the view of Dao."[16] Daoism wanted to have a claim for "equal survivorship."

For Mozi 墨子 (468-390 B.C.), there should be no inequalities among nations and human beings in this world. He emphasized *jianai*

---

[14] See *Tangshu: Xuanjuzhi* (*Annuals of Examination of Tang History*).

[15] See Laozi, *Dao De Jing* (道德經).

[16] *Zhuangzi: Qiushui* (莊子：秋水).

兼愛—universal love based on equality; *huli* 互利—mutual benefit based on equality; *shangxian* 尚賢—selection of officials by their capacities based on equality; and *shangtong* 尚同—harmony based on equality.[17] Guanzi 管子 (?-645 B.C.), an important legalist, stressed classless equality for the law and equality before awards and punishment.[18] Zi Chan 子產 (?-522 B.C.), Shang Yang 商鞅 (390-338 B.C.) and Han Fei 韓非 (280-233 B.C.) also emphasized equality before the law.

Subordinate Legalism vs. Dominate Moralism

Chinese Legalism really had a very strong influence on the Chinese political and legal system. In fact, all Chinese political theory and practice had been a mixture of Confucianism, Legalism and Daoism. Generally speaking, Confucianism was a leading ideology or value system; Legalism, a method of high-handed measures or coercive methods and artifices; and Daoism, a thought pattern or mode of thinking. There are two famous slogans used in Confucian moralism and legalism: "The penal code is invalid for literati and officialdom 刑不上大夫;" and "If a prince breaks the law, he must be punished by the same penal code 王子犯法與庶民同罪."[19]

This raises the question: What were the distinction, the relationship and the interaction between the Chinese legalism and moralism. Jeremy T. Paltiel believes that China has never known the significance of rights discourse in the context of a legal discourse that privileges legal texts and constrains the exercise of authority by reference to these (Paltiel 1998, 271). According to Andrew J. Nathan, two ancient schools, Legalism and Confucianism, shaped Chinese

---

[17]See the *Book of Mozi*, "Fayi," "Jianai," "Shangxian" and "Shangtong" (墨子：法意，兼愛，尚賢和尚同).

[18] See the *Book of Guanzi*, "Zhongling" and "Jincang."

[19] "Bao Gong" (包公) is a house word in China. It refers to Bao Zheng 包拯 (999-1062 A.D.). In a widely known story, Bao Gong, an idealistic legalist official, sentenced a *fuma* 駙馬 (the son-in-law of the emperor) to death in the Song dynasty.

thinking about the law. Both accepted the ruler's right to make law. The legalists viewed this right as unconstrained by any higher moral order. They held that the ruler could and should create any laws necessary to strengthen his state, and that harsh laws worked better than soft ones. The Confucians argued that, to be effective, the laws must comply with the moral order inherent in society. The laws and the ruler must be fair and just and must encourage the virtues of filial piety, loyalty, and social compassion. This Confucian view was parallel in a broad sense to the Western concept of natural law in that it believed in a moral order independent of the laws of the state (Nathan 1986, 127).

In Chung-ying Cheng's arguments, Confucian moralism implicitly defined the sense of human rights in terms of self in relation to virtues, rather than a sense of freestanding (Cheng 1998, 145). In a sense, for Chinese legalism, the implied sense of "human rights" was implicitly defined in terms of political control in relation to punishments, because a society must keep a good balance between different individual interests. For example, one must be punished for stealing somebody's property. Cheng characterizes transformation of Confucian virtues into modern human rights as follows: (1) One's internal ability and the external needs of other people; (2) A duty of the self to the community and a duty of community to the self; (3) The duty consciousness of virtues and an expectation of the public utility; (4) The virtuous action of an individual and of any other individuals; and (5) The public interests and the private interests of ruler (ibid. 1998, 148-49).

Peerenboom compares the rites (*li* 禮) with rights through both of the moral and legal perspectives. For him, there are similarities and differences as well as interactions between Confucian rites and Western rights. Both rites and rights are "claims," but the former are moral claims while the latter seem to be legal claims. "Rites" can complement rights, providing a moral dimension to interpersonal actions, suggesting additional possibilities above and beyond the legal relations defined by rights (Peerenboom 1998, 248-51). Normally, "rites" are "moral duties" or "social responsibilities." However, if "rites" are "claims," they can also be treated as a kind of "rights"— "moral rights."

In general, Chinese legalism emphasizes: (1) Rule by person with the emperor's law; (2) Strict material or physical rewards and punishments; (3) Powerful Political and military forces; (4) Theory of bad human nature; (5) Tactical social control; (6) Realistic attitude toward material interests; (7) Defined criteria to the public; (8) General "equality" before the emperor's law; and (9) Applying limitation, centralization and intimidation to *xiaoren* 小人 (mean man).

On the contrary, Chinese moralism, such as Zhu Xi's 朱熹 theory, emphasizes: (1) Rule by person with Confucian virtue; (2) Spiritual or ideological advice and encouragement; (3) Educational or ethical teaching and persuasion; (4) Theory of good human nature; (5) Strategic social control; (6) Critical, even nihilistic attitude toward material interests; (7) Flexible criteria for individuals; (8) Special treatment before law; and (9) Self-perfection, self-purification and self-realization for *junzi* 君子 (superior man).

Actually, in Chinese history, the rulers always applied both legalism and moralism for social control.

Implied Democratism vs. Overall Despotism

There was an implied or passive democratism and constitutionalism[20] in pre-modern China, as seen in "the system for selecting officials" and "the system for remonstrating with the emperor." Since the Ming Dynasty (1368-1644), some enlightenment thinkers, such as Huang Zongxi 黃宗羲 (1610-1695), Wang Fuzhi 王夫之 (1619-1692), Gu Yanwu 顧炎武 (1613-1682), Tang Zhen 唐甄 (1630-1704), and Yan Yuan 顏元 1635-1704), as Confucian reformers, harbored certain democratic ideas. For example, they attempted to substitute *tianxia zhifa* 天下之法 (law by all people) for *yijia zhifa* 一家之法 (law only by the emperor).[21]

---

[20] See Max Weber's discussion on "Chinese passive democratization" in his *Economy and Society*.

[21] Later, Gong Zizhen 龔自珍, Weiyuan 魏源, Lin Zexu 林則徐, Hong Xiuquan 洪秀全, Kang Youwei 康有爲, Yan Fu 嚴複, Sun Yat-Sen 孫中山 and many other

Accordingly, Huang Zongxi as well as Gu Yanwu and other thinkers made progress in their critique of dynastic rule, emphasized the political participation of the common people, and addressed renewed interest in broad constitutional issues (Hou 1957). Huang even put forward a systemic constitutional plan for a balancing of powers, because he found that Confucian values and Legalist systems were entwined, and also coexisted in some degree of tension with one another. As de Bary says: "Individually impressive as were these heroic of Confucian ministers, they were more the exception than the rule, and while they testify to moral culture compatible with human rights sentiments, something more was needed. That 'something more' as perceived by Huang Zongxi in the seventeenth century was what might be called a civil society protective of political freedom and public discussion at the Chinese court" (de Bary 1998, 16-18).

2. The Holders of "Rights"—Traditional Socio-Cultural Circles

We may have theoretical assumption of the possible existence of holders of rights in Chinese history. In ancient China, the entire society could be divided into seven basic cultural circles as follows.

Rights and the "Tianzi" Cultural Circle

Tianzi 天子 means the Son of Heaven—the Chinese emperor. The emperor was the unique and highest human ruler. He and his entire imperial and royal family (including the nobility) formed a supreme cultural circle. Chinese emperors claimed to be the unique representative of Heaven and the only direct exerciser of its mandates. They truly believed that they had divine right, divine appointment and divine arrangement according to traditional political theology (a methodically and religiously formulated political theory). Therefore, absolute obedience and blind loyalty must be the main duty or obligation for the governed. From the divine legitimacy, Chinese rulers

---

thinkers advocated the democratic ideal, and pushed forward Chinese human development.

emphasized a kind of hereditary right to transfer the political power from one generation to the next. On one hand, *tianzi* advocated that Heaven bestowed divine rights on them; on the other hand, only they could bestow the limited right to the subjects and the people by their will.

There are some similarities and differences between the divine right doctrine of Chinese emperors and that of European kings. Similarities were their "divine rights" served as an instrument or spiritual weapon of propaganda for ruling society and both were based upon the belief that dynasty or monarchy as a divinely ordained institution. Differences included the Chinese belief that emperors were responsible to an impersonal Heaven while European kings were accountable to a personal God. In the Chinese view, Heaven could withdraw the divine right from bad emperors, and people also had the "right" to change rulers and to end the imperial inheritance. People were not required to observe absolute obedience to a bad ruler. But in the European view, obedience was due to the office of king, irrespective of who occupied the office or how he had acquired his rank; or obedience was due to the person of the king and to his legitimate heirs, according to the law of primogeniture (See Figgis 1922).

"Rights" and The "Shidaifu" Cultural Circle

Shidaifu 士大夫 means literati and officialdom—the whole scholarly bureaucratic mechanism. Max Weber examined Chinese imperial administration in his theoretical formulation of bureaucracy. Accordingly, the Chinese traditional administrative system constituted a pattern somewhat closer to the bureaucratic ideal type. The higher officials in imperial China were "literati," as products of an intensive education in religion, ethical tradition, literature, and art. Selection and recruitment were carried out in large part through a very rigorous system of written examinations. But the Chinese imperial administration system emphasized the literary rather than the legal, the ethical rather than the scientific. Although Chinese society is one of humanity's highest achievements, it did not develop significantly from the imperial period to the modern, rational-scientific model that provides the framework for ideal-typical formulation of bureaucracy.[22]

In a sense, *shidaifu* represented the mainstream of the Chinese traditional culture. Generally, all the members of this circle were educated and selected by the imperial examination system. *Shidaifu* as a main part of the giant state apparatus were bestowed legitimate power from the emperors to control society. *Shidaifu* had a twofold personality: they were subjects with regard to emperors, and rulers with regard to the people. For their interests, *shidaifu* attempted to have claims or rights as follows: (1) claims or rights for rewards and punishment in the official career—so-called *shitu* 仕途; (2) claims or rights for participating in decision making—so-called *mouzheng* 謀政; (3) claims or rights for giving advice or suggestions, even warning, to the emperor—so-called *shangjian* 上諫; (4) the claims or rights for writing books to expound a doctrine; (5) the claims or rights for forming their own characteristic style of philosophy and literature.

"Rights" and The "Xiangshen" Cultural Circle

Xiangshen 鄉紳 means country gentry and squires, such as the landlords, the local despots (tyrants), the elders or leaders of patriarchal clans, owners of big manors, the heads of villages and small towns, and the heads of the neighborhood. *Xiangshen* were the main representatives of local culture and possessed certain properties, reputations, titles, good birth and social standards, and local powers. *Xiangshen* attempted to hold the basic claims or rights for local moral orders, local or clan interests, benefits, advantages or natural resources.[23] In general, *Xiangshen* emphasized some moral claims or moral rights to normalize, define and regulate local residents' conduct.

---

[22] See Max Weber's *The Theory of Social and Economic Organization, Economy and Society* and *The Religion of China: Confucianism and Taoism.*

[23] Unlike the British gentry, which was the class between the nobility and yeomanry, the "*xiangshen*" was the class between the "*shidaifu*" and "*shumin.*"

"Rights" and The "Shumin" Cultural Circle

Shumin 庶民 means the populace and the multitude or the freemen and common people, such as peasants, businessmen (traders and peddlers), petty townspeople (philistines), villains, physical workers and servants. *Shumin* were the majority of the ancient Chinese population. *Shumin* had the claims or rights for passive equality, survivorship, existence and *Shenyuan* 申冤 (to initiate lawsuits against others).[24]

"Rights" and The "Jianghu" Cultural Circle

Jianghu 江湖 literally means rivers and lakes, and actually means vagrants and itinerants—the persons who were living an unsettled life, wandering from place to place—such as chevaliers, charlatans, entertainers, martial arts players, mountebanks, quacks, beggars and temporary workers. Basically, *jianghu* attempted to have claims or rights for passive or negative freedom.[25]

"Rights" and the "Zaofan" Cultural Circle

Zaofan 造反 means rebellion, uprising or insurrection, such as revolting peasants,[26] insurrectionary armies, rioting groups, the rebelling masses, anarchists, robbers, bandits, brigands, sinister gang members[27] and other criminals. The *zaofan* circle attempted to have the

---

[24] In a sense, *"shumin"* was similar to "yeomanry" in the British history. The *"shumin,"* who were members of a class below the *"xiangshen,"* possessed small estates or had the professional skills to run a small business, or work for a limited salary.

[25] The *"jianghu"* circle has provided some of the most attractive source material in traditional Chinese literature.

[26] Even some Chinese scholars argue that the *"zaofan"*—peasant uprising—has been the real dynamics of Chinese historical progress. Indeed, the peasant uprising has been at least one of the major reasons for dynasties' changing.

[27] Chinese secret society or underworld gang. For instance, *qingbang* 青幫 and *hongbang* 紅幫 really have had a very important influence on social life.

claims or rights for survivorship and existence through overthrowing rulers and changing social orders with the mentality of anti-authority, anti-tradition, and even anti-society.

"Rights" and The "Huidaomen" Cultural Circle

Huidaomen 會道門 means sectarians and superstitious persons, such as professional Buddhists, Daoists, folk religious believers, cult or shrine members, minority groups, martial arts organizations, and other superstitious sects and secret societies. *Huidaomen* attempted to have claims or rights for religious or superstitious propaganda, and organizational expanding and development.[28]

Logically, there was a very fundamental and profound conflict of rights within the above seven cultural circles. For John Rawls, the conflict of rights might be avoided by well-drafted rights, and through the working of the institutional processes of a well-ordered society. Rey Martin thinks that the issue addressed on the "conflict of rights" is crucial to Rawls's overall theory of justice.[29] In Chinese history, if the conflict of rights was reduced, lightened and diminished, then social harmony, balance or equilibrium would appear, and *vice versa*.

3. "Rights" as Combination of Vague Consciousness and Spontaneous Behavior

Due to its different natures, qualities and functions, the concept of rights can be divided into two kinds of antithetical categories— "hard" and "soft." This division may help us understand the issue of rights in Chinese cultural tradition. So-called hard rights are defined, formalized, recognized, substantive, actualized and inalienable, but

---

[28] Unlike the church in the Europe's Middle Ages, Chinese religions have never been a dominant social power, but they have had the most influence on Chinese social spirituality and its value system. In my opinion, "*wu* 巫"—witchcraft or sorcery—was one of the most original Chinese cultural sources or roots.

[29] See Martin 1985.

so-called soft rights are undefined, unformalized, unrecognized, nominal, potential and alienable. Traditional Chinese "rights" can be considered "soft" ones.

In Chinese traditional culture, "rights" was only a combination of "naïve, vague or implied consciousness" and "spontaneous or blind behavior." As Chung-ying Cheng says, Chinese culture has had a sense of human rights implicitly defined in terms of the self in relation to virtues (Cheng 1998, 145). Like Westerners, ancient Chinese people had certain moral, legal or socio-political claims, demands, protestations or declarations for their own interests. Unlike Westerners, ancient Chinese people did not build any clear and obvious concept and theory of "rights," nor did they launch any significant struggle for "rights." "Rights" in traditional Chinese culture appear only in a passive, implied, subordinate, intuitive, irrational, and bestowed way.

IV. Chinese "Rights": Legally Practical Perspectives

Despite the long and obvious arguments and interactions between moralism and legalism, it is fair to declare that the function of *wangfa* 王法 (the imperial law) has never been properly examined and analyzed, or at least not to the extent that a reasonable conclusion emerged.[30] A task of our study will be to pursue some causative inquiry into why this is so, and to disclose certain factual processes as well as to suggest possible pioneering and productive exploration of rights in the Chinese traditional legal system.

Among all causes that may lead to the failure of Chinese political philosophers to respond to the function of *wangfa*, three in particular stand out. The first is a prejudice that considered Confucian

---

[30] *Falü* 法律 is the Chinese translation of the Western term "law." *Fa* 法 means legality, general legal system and the whole statute code *lü* 律 means the concrete provisions, clauses or articles of law and other specific degrees, rules, precedents, regulations, discipline and restraints. *Wang* 王 is emperor or imperial power. *Wangfa* 王法 can be translated "imperial law or legality." Another popular term in the Chinese legal system was *xing* or *hsing* 刑, which means "punishment" or "penal code."

moralism the only official ideology and the sum and essence of socio-political entities in the Chinese historical process. The second is a misunderstanding from which the rule by will or person was considered the government's only practice in ancient Chinese social control. The third is a distorted view that the criminal lawsuit was considered the only lawsuit in ancient Chinese legal action.

In more than two thousand years, there were many codified and written laws in China.[31] The ancients constructed a very institutionalized legal system. According to Philip M. Chen, there were four striking characteristics of the Chinese law tradition. First, more than twenty-one hundred years ago China was a bureaucratic state that had already begun to use law as an instrument for maintaining the social order. Second, even the well-organized legal system had relative insignificance in the life of the country, due in large part to the Confucian values and heritage that put law in a secondary, undesirable position. Also, because of China's vastness and the difficulty in communication, in practice, law did not reach below the country government. Third, corruption, irregularity, and other unattractive features were prominent in the administration of justice under the formal legal system. Fourth, there is no tradition of an adversary system by which an individual can defend himself against charges made by the state (Chen 1975, 7-8). This section traces the significant advancement of a probable important contributor to the ancient Chinese civilization, and its legalized human interests—the protection of life, property and dignity. We will not focus on the hypotheses generated to interpret or explain theories of rights, but rather on the factual practice of the relevant legalized claims and needs.[32]

---

[31] The earliest systematic written law was *Fajing* 法經 (*The Book of Law*) by Li Kui 李悝(?-395 B.C.). The most profound long-run impact on legality in Chinese history emerged in *Tanglu Shuyi* 唐律疏義 (*Tang Code*, 737 A.D.), which was much earlier than Constitution Criminals Carolina (1532 A.D.)). Later, *Song Xing Tong* 宋刑統 (*The Complete Books of Song Dynasty Penal Law*), *Daming Lü* 大明律 (*The Great Ming Code*) and *Daqing Lüli* 大清律例 (*The Great Qing Code*) were all complete and systematic, and had a very important influence on the ancient Chinese legal system.

[32] For better understanding, the following Chinese books are very useful: Chang, Weiren, *An Annotated Bibliography of Chinese Legal History*, Taipei: Institute of History

The Mixture of Criminal Law and Civil Law[33]

Like most nations, in ancient China, criminal law and law of tort originated from acts of personal or organizational infringement and revenge. After the establishment of political authority, compensation was, in the beginning, adopted as an efficient way to achieve certain mediation and reconciliation agreements for social balance; later, following social development, the society's members felt that acts of infringement would not only harm the personal interests, but also would destroy the social order. So, public law was developed to prevent and punish acts of infringement. To some extent, the law in the Tang dynasty had already distinguished civil liability from criminal responsibility, such as compensation and non-imprisonment or imprisonment and non-compensation for some civil dispute or negligence. But in many situations, the offense against the law of marriage, of adoption, of good quality, and debts would be punished by criminal law. On the whole, there was no distinction between civil and criminal lawsuits in the legal proceedings or contention procedures. Actually, any matter of civil lawsuits, civil abilities, civil compensation and civil mediation would be involved finally in some matter of rights. D. Bodde and C. Morris translated 190 actual cases from *Xingan Huilan* 刑案彙覽 (*Conspectus of Penal Cases*) of the Qing Dynasty (1644-1911). These case histories cover cases of civil law, such as the family and corvee services, landed property, marriage, taxes and tar-

---

and Language Press, 1976; Chen, Guyuan, *History of Chinese Legal System*, Shanghai: Shangwu Press, 1930; Dai, Yanhui, *History of Chinese Legal System*, Taiwan: Sunmin Press, 1984 ; Fazhiju, *A Short Bibliography of Chinese Legal History*, Beijing: Law Press, 1957 ; Hou, Wailu, *History of Chinese Thought*, Beijing: Renmin Press, 1957; Li, Jing, *History of Chinese Legal Thought*, Heilongjiang Press, 1983; Lu, Simian, *History of Chinese Political and Legal System*, Shanghai: Jiao Yu Press, 1982; Lu, Zhen Yu, *History of Chinese Political Thought*, Beijing: Renmin Press, 1962; Wang, Jieqin, *Chinese Legal Thought*, Taiwan: Sanmin Press, 1983; Xu, Dafong, *History of Ancient Chinese Political Thought*, Jilin Press, 1981; Xu, Zhaoyang, *The Origin of Chinese Criminal Law*, Taiwan: Sanmin Press, 1980; Yang, Shufan, *History of Political System of the Tang Dynasty*, Taiwan: Zheng Zhong Press, 1967.

[33] In ancient China, public law, private law and other laws were all mixed.

iffs, money lending, and public markets (Bodde and Morris 1967, 240-71).

Equality for Taking Legal Proceedings

Although in ancient China, people were classified as either *liangmin* 良民 (a good person) or *jianmin* (賤民 a despicable person),[34] in general, both liangmin and jianmin had equality in legal proceedings. According to the law, both had an equal capacity for duties and an equal capacity for litigation.[35] For example, if a liangmin injured a jianmin, or harmed a jianmin's property, or made a false charge against a jianmin, then he or she would be equally punished by the relevant laws.[36] Normally, both plaintiff and defendant had equality in the lawsuit according to Tang law. Significantly, a pregnant female had the right to have a baby before being executed, according to Han, Tang, Ming and Qing laws. There were also some special defined rights, such as release on bail for some suspects, punishment without involving an innocent family.

Legalized Interests and Protection in Marriage

To a considerable extent, what relates personal interests to the system of marriage is precisely what makes it intriguing. Much of the study has direct or indirect roots in the still-plausible examination or problematic theorization. As a consequence, anyone interested in attempting to formalize and reconstruct the issues raised in the traditional marriage would be bound to find himself or herself dealing with certain problems that fall under the heading of legalization. In suggesting methodological standards for this purpose, we will encounter the question of how to distinguish legal female interests from the large

---

[34] "*Liangmin*" included all free persons; "*jianmin*" included different kinds of servants or some kinds of "mean men."

[35] See *Tanglü Shuyi* 唐律疏義 (*Tang Code*).

[36] A typical case in the Tang dynasty involved the famous female poet, Yu Xuanji 魚玄機, who was executed for killing her servant girl.

quantity of non-legal interests in the traditional value system of the marriage. One possible approach is to consider some facts and evidence from historical documents of Chinese law and its legal system: (1) Marriage by cheating or coercion is illegal; (2) Generally, a husband cannot sell his wife or concubines;[37] (3) After a spouse's death, the widower or widow can remarry someone else freely;[38] (4) A husband will be punished if he beats and injures his wife;[39] (5) A wife shares ownership of property with her husband (If the husband divorces his wife without proper reason, he must return the part of the property that originally belonged to his wife, such as the dowry or trousseau); (6) A widow has the right of ownership of the property after her husband's death; (7) A married woman's parents cannot get the dowry or trousseau back after her husband's death; (8) Nobody can force a widow to remarry anyone; (9) After divorce, the relationship between a mother and her children will still exist, and the children who were born within the marriage should belong to husband, but those born after divorce should belong to the mother or her new husband (In most cases, "guardianship" of children should follow the divorce agreement); (10) Bastards or illegitimate children can be recognized by their biological father, and have certain legal rights to property;[40] and (11) The posthumous child has equal claim to property with other, elder children.

---

[37] Except in the following cases: the wife or concubines commit adultery, or run away from the husband.

[38] In ancient Chinese, *jie* 節 means female integrity, chastity, virginity or loyalty. For example, remaining chaste and faithful to one's betrothal or husband, even after his death, was demanded by the traditional moral code. But in the Chinese traditional legal system, a woman could not be forced to *shoujie* 守節—to preserve chastity after the death of her husband.

[39] "Duties" and "rights" are a unity of two opposites; husband's "duties" are wife's "rights."

[40] In the moral sense, ancient Chinese values rejected illegitimate sex between males and females, but it was more tolerant of bastards than Christian countries. In the Yuan Dynasty, division of property was such: (a). the wife's sons got 40%; (b). concubines' sons, 30%; (c). servants' sons or bastards, 10%. Later, in the Ming and Qing Dynasties, in the principle, the wife's sons, the concubine's sons and servants' sons had equal division; but the bastard had only half of each of those sons' divi-

A systematic and complete answer to why legalized Chinese female interests were not well developed, but rather in debatable repute, could be found in some synthetic and interdisciplinary cultural studies. But it is impossible and also unnecessary to achieve this difficult goal in such a brief article.

Legalized Claims for Property

In a final analysis, for any society the matter of property has been the most fundamental issue in human development. The right to property has been considered one of the basic natural rights. Locke asserted that in the state of nature, property was common in the sense that everyone has a right to draw subsistence from whatever nature offers; a man has a natural right to that with which he has "mixed" labor of his body, as for example, by enclosing and tilling land. So property and all other natural rights can be considered attributes of the individual person born with him and hence as indefeasible claims upon both society and government.[41]

To understand Chinese property rights, it is necessary to examine the sharp distinction between inalienable and alienable "rights" to property, the interactions or interconnections among legal claims for property and ownership, inheritance, division of property, and distinctions among types of ownership and possession processes that are relatively flexible and changeable. Consequently, we find that legalization of property in China was incomplete and very limited.

Perhaps the antithetical category between so-called inalienable and alienable rights is where the most important difference between Western and Chinese "rights" lies. An inalienable right is defined as "one that may never be waived or transferred by its possessor" (McConnell 1987, 43). Clearly, to characterize a right as inalienable is to claim that the consent of the right-holder is insufficient to extin-

---

sion. If there were no other sons, then the bastard could get equal division with the adopted children. If there were no other adopted sons, then the bastard could inherit all of the property.

[41] See Locke, *The Second Treatise.*

guish the right or to transfer it to another.[42] Unlike the modern Western viewpoint, the claims or rights to property in traditional China were not inalienable, and could be changed by the will of rulers or influenced by other political and economic needs and interests. For example, the government could confiscate people's private property by using any excuse as justification. But in order to secure social control, order, and stability, the dynasty governments had to define and legalize some claims and interests for private property to a certain extent.

Accordingly, the property was divided into *caiwu* 財物 (personal belongings or movable property) and *tianzhai* 田宅 (land and homes, real estate or unmovable property). The authorities legalized the claims or rights for ownership, selling, buying, renting, transferring, mortgaging, income, and profit from both of these kinds of property. The authorities also legalized the claims or rights for primitive possession of movable and unmovable properties *xianzhan* (先占), and for the inheritance of those properties. According to the Tang, Ming and Qing (Dynasty) laws, original wild lands and things (such as animals, fish, plants, and mineral resources) belonged to those who first used the manpower and labor to cultivate them. As well, lost articles, floating articles and buried articles belonged to the persons who actually found them, with certain legal limitations.

Law of Tort

On the whole, the law of tort did not have a profound impact on Chinese life; it was merely implied in some articles of law. Since the Tang Dynasty, corresponding to the Western law of tort, some claims for protection of people had been legalized, defined and formalized such as: (1) compensation for some injury to the human body, such as medical, living and funeral expenses; (2) compensation for some

---

[42] Randy E. Barnett gives us some useful analyses of inalienable rights. See his "Contract Remedies and Inalienable Rights." In Coleman and Frankel 1987.

damage to private property, such as repair expenses; (3) compensation for infringement of personal dignity and reputation, such as paying legal fees in trumped-up cases.

The purpose of comparing rights in the actual laws to the whole history of Chinese political and legal thought can be roughly classified under the headings of "rights" as legal implication and "rights" as legal practice. In terms of legal implication, "rights" were hinted at or suggested though not plainly expressed or definitely stated. We should seek the most efficient analytical and speculative formulation tool possible for intensively exploring "rights." Depending as it does on examining techniques that require thoughtful interpretative or explanatory skills on the part of the investigator, the possible analytical formulation has not been fully exploited by political philosophers interested in the study of Chinese "rights." Related to the analytical formulation are redescription, resummarization, regeneralization or reconstruction of the blind, irrational, and spontaneous Chinese legal practices for "rights." So far as is known, no attempt has been made to recollect, reinterpret, and reexplain the cases, facts, evidences, data, and various original materials in ancient Chinese legal documents. No doubt this is due in part to the fact that many scholars pay attention only to Confucian moralism and political idealism rather than legalism and legal factualism. But it is also true that new and special tools are required for the organization of collected information as contrasted with those that have been traditional *xungu* 訓詁 (literalism—literal interpretation of ancient texts) or *kaoju* 考據 (textualism—textual explanation of ancient literatures).

There was a vast accumulation of ancient legal literature in Chinese cultural development. Originally, such literature was designed to meet rulers' political needs; but now it could provide a tremendous source for our analysis of "rights" in depth. Broadly speaking, the history of Chinese legal literature is a history of changing times, interests, norms, actual practices, conceptual frameworks, thought patterns, and intellectual styles. Different stages of the legal conscious process can be distinguished from the legal practical process. But antinomies such as those between the theoretical and the practical, the active and the passive, and the substantive and the nominal should be clarified by objective and serious examination.

V. Conclusion

Whether such examination is "justified" and "reasonable" or not is not as significant as the fact that the problematic nature of "rights" exists; and socio-political philosophy does not have a simple solution already worked out. Most of what I have discussed can be summarized in a few brief propositions. "Rights" in Chinese historical perspectives can be viewed, not as a logically conceptualized, analyzed, rationalized and theorized thought, or a completely legalized, systematized, and institutionalized human behavior of critical importance in its own demand, but as two phrases in our hypotheses concerning "rights": "vague consciousness" and "spontaneous behavior."

There is a need for systematic inquiry into the ways "vague consciousness" of rights affected "spontaneous behavior" of "rights," and *vice versa*. But a satisfactory and in-depth literature has not been developed. However, a better answer might be added: "Rights" in a Chinese historical perspective that need study by political philosophers are enormously complicated and not easily observed. What has proceeded is a beginning sketch of a project designed to provide possible approaches for discussion of "rights" in traditional China on a sounder methodological basis.

In order to realize the theoretical formulation, a conceptual and analytical destination appropriate for reasoning and explaining "rights" should be reconstructed in ways that point to the strategies appropriate for establishing a more complete literature in this area. For this purpose, five standard kinds of academic tasks for the Chinese "rights" researchers might be suggested: (1) to have more case studies within the Chinese historical process; (2) to have more comparative studies between Western and Chinese cultural value systems; (3) to have more theoretical modes or assumptions built up from sufficient data of Chinese historical documents and literature; (4) to have more interdisciplinary studies involved in various fields, such as political, economical, legal, moral, literary, sociological, anthropological, psychological, and many other socio-cultural or academic fields; and

(5) to have more analytical critiques of all of the existing frameworks for evaluation of Chinese political and legal thought. Actually, the five above-mentioned tasks relate to one another, and each of them can be considered an integral part of the whole.

If these tasks could be pursued in a more satisfactory manner, our research would contribute creatively to increase substantive understanding of "rights" at a much higher level. Obviously, the progress that can be made in this direction is limited and not immediately productive. It is naive to imagine that we can find a kind of panacea for dealing with all that hitherto has been puzzling about the problem of Chinese "rights." However, our inquiring efforts should stimulate and legitimize further work.

REFERENCES

Barnett, Randy E. 1987. "Contract Remedies and Inalienable Rights." In Coleman and Frankel.

Bloom, Irone. 1998. "Fundamental Intuitions and Consensus Statement: Mencian Confucianism and Human Rights." In de Bary and Tu.

Bodde, Derk. 1966. *China's Cultural Tradition: What and Whither?* New York: Holt, Rinehart and Winston.

Bodde, Derk and Morris, Clarence. 1967. *Law in Imperial China Exemplified by 190 Ching Dynasty Cases.* Cambridge: Harvard University Press.

Chang, Wejen. 1998. "Confucian Theories of Norms and Human Rights." In de Bary and Tu.

Chen, P. M. 1973. *Law and Justice the Legal System in China 2400 B.C. to 1960 A. D.* New York: Duhellen Publishing Company.

Cheng, Chuang-ying. 1998. "Transforming Confucian Virtues into Human Rights." In de Bary and Tu.

Ching, Julia. 1998. "Human Rights: A Valid Chinese Concept?" In de Bary and Tu.

Cohen, Joshua. 1996. "Comments on Tu Weiming, 'A Confucian Perspective of Human Rights'," at the China Forum sponsored by the MIT International Science and Technology Initiative, April 29.

Coleman, J. and E. Frankel Paul Frankel (ed.). 1987. *Philosophy and Law*. Oxford: Basil Blackwell Inc.

Confucius. 1979. *Confucius: The Analects*. Trans D. C. Lau. New York: Penguin Books

de Bary, Wm Theodore and Tu, Weiming (eds.). 1998. *Confucianism and Human Rights*. New York: Columbia University Press.

de Bary, Wm Theodore. 1998. "Introduction." In de Bary and Tu.

Edwards, Thomas. 1965. *Gangraen*. In *Tracts on Liberty in the Puritan Revolution, 1638-1647*, Vol. III, edited by William Haller. New York: Octagon Books, 351

Figgis, John Neville. 1965. *The Divine Right of Kings*, New York: Harper & Row.

Gastil, Raymond D. 1976. "The Moral Right of the Majority to Restrict Obscenity and Pornography Through Law," *Ethics*, 83, 231-240.

Guanzi. 1985. *Kuan-tzu*. Trans. by Allyn Richett. Princeton: Princeton University Press.

Henkin, Louis. 1998. "Confucianism, Human Rights, and 'Cultural Relativism.'" In de Bary and Tu.

————. 1986. "The Human Rights Idea in China." In *Human Rights in Contemporary China*. Edited by R. R. Edwards, L. Henkin, and A. J. Nathan. New York: Columbia University Press.

Hou, Wailu. 1957. *History of Ancient Chinese Thought*. Beijing: People's Press.

Hsieh, Yu-Wei. 1968. "The Status of the Individual in Chinese Ethics." In *The Status of the Individual in East and West*, edited by C. A. Moore. Honolulu: University of Hawaii Press.

Inada, Kenneth K. 1990. "A Buddhist Response to the Nature of Human Rights." In *Asian Perspectives on Human Rights*, edited by Claude E. Welch, Jr, and Virgiinia A. Leary. Boulder: Westview Press.

Kwok, D. W. Y. 1998. "On the Rites and Rights of Being Human." In de Bary and Tu.

Laozi. 1990. *Tao Te Ching*. Translated and Annotated by V. Mair. New York: Bantam Books.

Lo, Chung-sho. 1949. "Human Rights in the Chinese Tradition." In *Human Rights: Comments and Interpretations*, edited by UNESCO. New York: Columbia University Press.

Locke, John. 1982. *The Second Treatise of Government: An Essay Concerning the True Original, Extent and End of Civil Government*. Edited by Richard H. Cox. Arlington Heights, Ill: H. Davidson.

Martin, Rex. 1985. *Rawls and Rights*, University Press of Kansas.

McConnell, Terrance. 1987. "The Nature and Basis of Inalienable Rights" in Coleman and Frankel.

Mencius. 1984. *The Works of Mencius*. Annotated and Trans. by Yang, Bojun. Hong Kong: Zhonghua Shuju, Hong Kong Ltd

Mozi. 1963. *Basic Writings of Mo Tzu, Hsün Tzu, and Han Fei Tzu*. Translated by B. Watson. New York: Columbia University Press.

Munro, Donald J. 1969. *The Concept of Man in Early China*. Stanford: Stanford University Press.

Nathan, Andrew J. 1986. "Sources of Chinese Rights Thinking." In *Human Rights in Contemporary China*, edited by R. Randle Edwards. New York: Columbia University Press.

Paltiel, Jeremy T. 1998. "Confucianism Contested: Human Rights and the Chinese Tradition in Contemporary Chinese Political Discourse." In de Bary and Tu.

Peerenboom, Randall. 1998. "Confucian Harmony and Freedom of Thought." In de Bary and Tu.

Rousseau, Jean-Jacques. 1994. The *Discourse on the Origin and Foundations of Inequality*. Trans. By Patrick Coleman. Oxford and New York: Oxford University Press.

Rosemont, Henry, Jr. 1991. *A Chinese Mirror*. La Salle, Illinois: Open Court.

Stone, C. D. 1972. "Should Trees Have Standing?—Toward Legal Rights for Natural Objects," *Southern California Law Review*, 45.

Tao, Julia. 1990. "The Chinese Moral Ethos and the Concept of individual Rights," *Journal of Applied Philosophy*, vol. 7.

Tu, Weiming. 1998. "Epilogue: Human Rights as a Confucian Discourse." In de Bary and Tu.

Twiss, Sumner B. "A Constructive Framework for Discussing Confucianism and Human Rights." In de Bary and Tu.

Weber, Max. 1978. *Economy and Society*. Edited by G. Roth and C. Wittich. Berkeley: University of California Press.

————. 1946. *>From Max Weber: Essays in Sociology*. Edited by H. H. Gerth and C. W. Mills. New York: Oxford University Press.

White, Alan R. 1984. *Rights*. Oxford: Clarendon Press.

Yu, Fen. 1998. "Might and Right: the 'Yellow Emperor' Tradition as Compared with Confucianism." In de Bary and Tu.

Zhuangzi. 1987. *Zhuangzi*. Edited *and* Annotated by Sha, Shaohai. Guiyang, China: Guizhou People's Press.

4

Moral Reason and Feeling: Confucianism and Contractualism

Xunwu Chen

Philosophers nowadays often ask, when we claim that an action is wrong, what kind of judgment are we making (Scanlon 1998, 1). The question is something like this: when we say that an action is morally wrong, does our statement actually express our judgment of moral truth or does it merely express our emotion about a given action? This question brings us to the deep difference between moral formalism and moral emotivism. According to moral formalism, as it is represented by Kant and many contemporary philosophers, moral judgment of right and wrong is merely a judgment of practical reason.[1] Philosophers in this tradition have argued that moral feeling has very little, if anything at all, to do with the rightness or wrongness of an action. On the contrary, according to moral emotivism,[2] as it is repre-

---

[1] Kant does not believe that moral feelings can furnish a basis for universal laws; he therefore insists that morality is not grounded in moral feeling, though "moral feeling is close to morality," in Kant's own words. See Kant, 6.

[2] As MacIntyre puts it, "emotivism is the doctrine that all evaluative judgments and more specifically moral judgments are nothing but expressions of preference, expressions of attitude or feeling, in so far as they are moral or evaluative in character... moral judgments, being expressions of attitude or feeling, are neither true nor false; and agreement in moral judgment is not to be secured by any rational method, for are none. It is to be secured, if at all, by producing certain non-rational effects on the emotions or rather attitudes of those who disagree with one. We use moral judgments not only to express our own feelings and attitudes, but also precisely to produce such effects in others." See MacIntyre, 11-12.

sented by Hume and some other contemporary philosophers, morality is more properly felt than judged of (Hume, 1888, 470). In other words, moral judgment expresses nothing but our sentiment. Partially acknowledging the argument of emotivism, Bernard Williams talks about the limit of philosophy in dealing with morality (Williams 1985).

However, the question about whether moral judgment expresses reason or feeling can be misleading. It suggests that in moral experience moral reason and feeling are separable and, in a final analysis, moral judgment expresses only one of them, not both. This suggestion is wrong. In this paper, I argue that in our ordinary moral experience reason and feeling are inseparable; any adequate account of morality, in particular moral right and wrong, must take both of them into full consideration, or otherwise the account would not be adequately compatible with our ordinary experience. I will argue that morality is about what kind of good person we should become; whatever kind of good person we will become, such a good person lives with both moral reasons and feelings. To argue for the above, I will first explore the views of contractualism and Confucianism. In both philosophies, the unity of moral reason and feeling are explicitly suggested. I then proceed to analyze the kind of substantive moral reason that we appeal to and the kind of moral feeling that we value in ordinary moral life and thus demonstrate their inseparability. In the end, I suggest that both moral formalism and emotivism are one-sided.

I. Moral Contractualism

Moral contractualism has become very influential in the West today. Its treatment of what is morally right and wrong has a wide appeal. It is one of the few moral philosophies that give moral feelings their due credits while explaining morality in terms of moral reason. According to moral contractualism, when we claim that an action is morally wrong, we claim that we have reasons to believe it to be so. When we ask what we ought to do or ought not to do, we are asking about what we have the most reasons to do or to abstain from action. At first glance, this may not sound much different from utilitarianism in which justification of action is also based upon reasons.[3] However, there is an important difference between contractualism and utilitarianism. The utilitarian concept of reason is centered on the idea of greater amount of good or happiness. The contratualist concept of reason is centered on the idea of obligation as what we owe to each other and the idea of justice. Yes, Scanlon indeed says that in contractualism, "what is special about reasons is not the ontological category of things that can be reasons, but rather the status of being a reason, that is to say, of counting in favor of some judgment-sensitive attitude" (Scanlon 1998, 56). He says that "it [contractualism] involves no specific claims as to which principles could be argued to or even whether there is a unique set of principles which could be the basis of agreement" (Scanlon 1982, 112). However, in the end, what he emphasizes, as do other contractarians, is not reasons in general, but a specific category of reasons centered on what we owe to each other in particular.

In his paper entitled "Contractualism and Utilitarianism," Scanlon defines the basic notion of contractualism as follows:

> An act is wrong if its performance under the circumstances would be disallowed by any system of rules for the general regulation of behavior which no one could reasonably reject as a basis for informed, unforced general agreement. (Scanlon 1982, 110).

In his book, *What We Owe To Each Other*, Scanlon again defends this conception of moral right and wrong (Scanlon 1998). According to him, what can be counted as reasons for us to accept or reject an action are a set of principles for the general regulation of behavior, principles that no one can reasonably reject as a basis for informed, unforced general agreement. The best archetype of principles of this kind is, of course, the principle of justice as fairness.[4] Scanlon calls

---

[3] For a good utilitarian account of reasons in ethical life, see Parfit 1984.

[4] John Rawls claims that "all obligations arise from the principle of fairness." See Rawls, 1971, 342. Scanlon agrees with this. The only difference is that Scanlon focuses on only moral obligation in this respect, which we calls obligation in terms of what we owe to each other.

this view of morality contractualism because at the core of it is an idea of morality that is based upon a shared willingness to modify our private demands in order to find a basis of justification that others also have reason to accept, an idea that "is the central element in the social contract tradition going back to Rousseau" (Scanlon 1998, 5). However, in the Scanlonian contractualism, the motivational basis for an informed and unforced agreement is not self-interest or greater amount of good for a greater number of people, but the response to the distinction between right and wrong in accordance with a set of rules that no one can reasonably reject as regulating rules of behavior.

Therefore, contractualism differs from utilitarianism in two important accounts. First, contractualism appeals to one's sensitivity to what is fair and obligated, instead of the idea of interest or the idea of greater amount of happiness. Indeed, Scanlon insists that self-interested bargaining is foreign to his account of morality (ibid.). Thus the contractualist account of morality is compatible with the idea of moral truth. It returns us back to the kind of normative moral thinking where what is right is not defined in terms of what is advantageous and profitable. Second, in contractualism, the utilitarian conception of calculative rationality is replaced by the contractualist conception of normative reasonableness as the basis for moral reasoning. As a result, moral feeling has its say in moral consideration. In both Scanlon and Rawls, moral feelings such as honor, indignation and so on can constitute reasons to act or refrain from action. Indeed, the inclusion of moral feeling in moral consideration not only demarcates contractualism from utilitarianism, but also makes it more appealing than the latter.

Contractualism also differs from Habermasian discourse ethics in several important ways. By emphasizing that moral reasons are centered around principles that no one can reasonably reject, contractualism shares many common points with discourse ethics developed by Jürgen Habermas. However, there are a number of important differences between them. First, while discourse ethics appeals to principles that can be consented to by all participants in a practical discourse of a given moral community, contractualism appeals to principles that no participant in a practical discourse of a moral community can reasonably reject. Scanlon points out the difference:

Consider a principle under which some people will suffer severe hardships, and suppose that these hardships are avoidable. That is, there are alternative principles under which no one would have to bear comparable burdens. It might happen, however, that the people on whom these hardships fall are particularly self-sacrificing, and are willing to accept these burdens for the sake of what they see as the greater good of all. We would not say, I think, that it would be unreasonable of them to do this. On the other hand, it might not be unreasonable for them to refuse these burdens, and, hence, not unreasonable for someone to reject a principle requiring him to bear them. If this rejection would be reasonable, then the principle imposing these burdens is put under doubt, despite the fact that some particularly self-sacrificing people could (reasonably) accept it. Thus it is the reasonableness of rejecting a principle, rather than the reasonableness of accepting it, on which moral argument turns. (Scanlon 1982, 111-112)

This leads to the second difference. Contractualism does not require that the epistemic validity of reasonable principles must be proven before we can endorse them as reasonable principles.[5] In discourse ethics, this is the very emphasis. As Habermas says, "its principle [the principle of discourse ethics postulates, only those norms may claim to be valid that could meet the consent of all affected in their role as participants in a practical discourse" (Habermas 1996, 305). The difference here is not about whether a reasonable principle has moral truth. Instead it is about whether a reasonable principle is reasonable if and only if its truth is made evident. It is about whether or not being reasonable always means being motivated to endorse a unified conception of moral truth.

Third, while discourse ethics grounds itself in a formal conception of rationality, viz., communicative rationality, contractualism

---

[5] Scanlon indeed says: "a philosophical theory of morality must offer an account of these reasons that is, on the one hand, compatible with its account of moral truth and moral reasoning and, on the other, supported by a plausible analysis of moral experience" (Scanlon 1982, 106). However, Scanlon is talking about the importance of the coherence of a moral theory, not that reasonable principles must prove their epistemic validity before they are considered to be reasonably irrejectable.

grounds itself in a substantive conception of moral reason (Scanlon 1998, 150). That is, in discourse ethics, a moral judgment is justified or unjustified by communicative rationality. In comparison, contractualism explains "the reason-giving force of moral judgment by characterizing fully, substantive terms, the particular form of value that we respond by acting rightly and violate by doing what is wrong" (ibid.). In contractualism, response to certain moral feelings can be a part of our response to a particular form of value.

This points to the important distinction between morality in terms of a reasonable agent and morality in terms of a rational agent (ibid. 192). True, for contractualism, reasonableness suggests rationality. Being rational, according to Scanlon, means being able to recognize, assess, and be moved by reasons for beliefs and action. As he says: "A rational creature is, first of all, a reasoning creature—one that has the capacity to recognize, assess, and be moved by reasons, and hence to have judgment-sensitive-attitude" (ibid. 23). Yet, there are a number of important differences between being rational and being reasonable. Being reasonable is, as Rawls puts it, (1) to have "the willingness to propose and honor fair terms of cooperation," and (2) to have "the willingness to recognize the burdens of judgment and to accept their consequences" (Rawls 1993, 49). Scanlon calls this having a "judgment-sensitive attitude." On the contrary, "what rational agents lack is the particular form of moral sensibility that underlies the desire to engage in fair cooperation as such, and to do so on terms, that others as equals might reasonably be expected to endorse" (ibid. 51). For example, a utilitarian who cares for his own interest first and is thus rational might not be, or needs not to be, reasonable.

Equally important is that being rational means not listening to the voice of feeling while being reasonable means also listening to the voice of feeling. In other words, while moral feeling plays absolutely no role in being rational, it plays an important role in being reasonable. Thus, for example, Scanlon says,

> The reasons provided by one's sense of honor can also have a moral character in several different ways, of which I will mention only two. These reasons can be moral in a broad sense in so far as integrity, understood as steadfastness to one's value (even

one's nonvalues), is thought of as a moral virtue. In addition, they can be moral in a narrower sense, ... if the personal value at stake is one's regard for what is morally right. (Scanlon 1998, 324)

Here, Scanlon speaks of reasons provided by a person's sense of honor. In other words, a person's feeling of honor has reason-giving force. Elsewhere, Scanlon also mentions reasons provided by a person's sense of shame or other moral feelings. It is true that Scanlon has never explained what is the relationship between reason and feeling, in particular in moral motivation. Yet, by explicitly suggesting the role of moral feeling in morality, Scanlon again reminds us of the one-sidedness of moral formalism.

If my reading of contractualism as described above is correct, then the most important insight of contractualism in the Sacnlonian sense is not its connection of moral motivation with practical reason, though this is undeniably one of its important features. Rather, it is its concept of morality in terms of a reasonable agent, different from a concept of morality in terms of a rational agent. It is its suggestion that a reasonable agent is an ordinary reflective individual who has the judgment-sensitive attitude and who listens to both the voice of moral reason and moral feeling. Such an agent is neither an artificially imagined *formal* person nor an unreflective and not judgment-sensitive emotivist. I will leave contractualism here now and turn to Confucianism.

II. Moral Confucianism

Like contractarians, Confucians also believe that morality evokes reason. To be moral in a truly Confucian sense is to act in accordance with moral reason and principles. It is to exercise reason and to act on principles that constitute the common basis for enlightened social consensus. Like contractarians, Confucians insist upon the distinction between what is right and what is profitable and the priority of the former over the latter. Confucius thus claimed that a moral person acts in accordance with the principle of righteousness while an immoral person acts on the idea of profit (*Analects*, 4:16). For Confucians, when we claim that an action is morally wrong, we are claiming that it is wrong according to a set of moral principles. Confucians believe that moral principles such as duty, justice and good have reason-giving forces. The emphasis on moral principles as the normative basis for morality is epitomized in the notion of righteousness. Mencius asked, "What is common to all human minds? It is that all human minds possess reason and think in terms of righteousness. ... Righteousness pleases a person's mind as beef and pork please a person's mouth" (*Mencius*, 6A:7).[6] Indeed, Confucian moral thinking is an obligation-centered thinking. Its central moral precept is that a person is under obligation to do the person's part as specified by the concept of righteousness in terms of the universal *dao*.

But Confucian moral philosophy is also a humanity-centered philosophy. One of the important features of its humanity-centered thinking is its emphasis on the importance of moral feelings in moral consideration. This is epitomized by the following claim in the *Analects*:

> To guide a society by laws and to keep people in line by punishment, one can expect people to stay out of trouble, but not to have a sense of shame; to guide a society by morality and virtue, to keep people in line by rites, one can expect that people not only will stay out of trouble, but also have a sense of shame and transform themselves. (*Analects*, 2:3)

In these words, Confucius emphasized not only the importance of morality to the society and people, but also the centrality of the moral feeling of shame to morality. Elsewhere, he also emphasized the feelings of love, respect, self-respect, and so on. Mencius' emphasis on the four feelings as the sentimental basis for the four moral principles is another good example to the point.

For Confucians, moral feelings themselves constitute a unique category of reasons (grounds) to act or abstain from action. Mencius claimed: "Great is the use of the feeling of shame by man. ... If a person is not ashamed of being inferior to other persons, how will the

---

[6] Unless otherwise specified, the translations of the quotations of *Mencius* are mine from the *Four Books and Five Classics*, edited by Yang (ed.). 1998. I have referred to some other translations.

person ever become their equal?" (*Mencius*, 7A:7). He thus insisted, "a person must not be without the feeling of shame" (ibid., 7A:6). He not only held that the feeling of shame could be a source of reasons to act or abstain from action, but also insisted that a person should appeal to this feeling as a reason in moral life. Elsewhere, both Confucius and Mencius emphasized that the moral feelings of compassion, piety, respect and self-respect, and right and wrong could and should constitute unique moral grounds for action or abstaining from action.

Furthermore, for Confucians, moral feelings such as shame, compassion, right and wrong, and respect and self-respect are universal and inherent in our human nature. And, as claimed in the *Doctrine of Mean*, to follow our human nature is to follow the *dao*, the universal Way (ch. 1). The Confucian view can be understood as follows. First, the moral feelings mentioned above are inherent in the original human nature of a moral agent and they are the defining features of the authentic or original human nature (Mencius, 2A:6, 6A:6). They constitute "what Mencius calls *liang-neng* and *liang-zhi* or innate capacity of being good as well as innate capacity of good" (Cheng 1991, 239). Accordingly, refusing to be instructed by them means acting not as a human. As Mencius insisted,

> ... whoever is devoid of the feeling of compassion is not human, whoever is devoid of the feeling of shame is not human, whoever is devoid of the feeling of courtesy and modesty is not human, and whoever is devoid of the feeling of right and wrong is not human.[7] (*Mencius*, 2A:6)

Second, these feelings are what we all are capable of in real life. Loss of them makes a person morally bad. In real life, there are indeed people who are ruthless and shameless. However, this should indicate that their human natures have been distorted, at least seriously corrupted, and not that they are born incapable of compassion and shame (ibid. 6A:7). Third, these feelings are the sentimental sources of the moral principles of humanity, righteousness, propriety, and

---

[7] This translation is based on Lau's with my alterations. See Lau 1970, 82-83.

wisdom (ibid., 2A:6, 6A:6). Fourth, these feelings constitute the sentimental basis of one's motivation to morality and self-improvement (ibid. 6A:12, 7A:7).

At any rate, for Confucians, sentimental attachment and response are not something alien to moral experience, but something constitutive of it. Moral feeling is not something external to a moral agent and the agent's reason, but constitutive of the agent. A person's relation to the world and to the moral community is partially given by his or her moral feelings and sense of what he or she can or cannot "live with," and what he or she ought or ought not to "live with." For Confucians, morality is not only about moral beliefs, truths, rules, and principles, but also about what we are, what we care deeply about and what we hold dear. Thus, morality involves moral feelings. Moral consideration involves consideration of moral feelings because not only a person's authentic being, but also the person's integrity depends upon being in touch with these feelings. Morality also matters to us because we want to and feel good to live in a certain way and to be a certain kind of person. For Confucians, morality matters because we want to be human beings in the full sense. A part of being a human being in the full sense is to be in touch with our innate moral feelings. It is to be able to feel as a human. Thus, for example, the feeling of shame indicates that a person does not want to be below the person's self or to be associated with action that will put the person below the person's self (Shun 1997, 59). Therefore, for Confucians, *he li* (being rational) and *he qing* (conforming to feeling) are emphasized together.

This means that the Confucian emphasis on moral feelings is not meant to dethrone reason, but to enrich reason. What Confucians advocate is a more substantial conception of morality that differs from both formalism—viz., Kantian ethics—and emotivism, viz., Humean moral philosophy. What Confucians insist is that morality also has a great deal to do with a moral agent as a reasonable human being. To such a human being, moral right and wrong is defined not only in terms of principles, but also in terms of moral feelings that informs an agent what the agent owes to the agent himself or herself and what the agent as a moral being does not want to "live with," and ought not to "live with." Accordingly, as mentioned above, for

Confucians, moral enterprise is meant to transform people, not just to hold people in line. It is to refine people. Therefore, for Confucians, a moral judgment of a moral agent expresses not only what the agent believes to be morally true and reasonable, but also what the agent feels morally about what is judged.

III. A Rethinking of Moral Reason and Feeling

In light of the above, we should now proceed to analyze further the unity and inseparability of moral reason and feeling. Indeed, moral reason and feeling are quite different. Not only what can be ontologically counted as reason differs from what can be ontologically counted as feeling, but the roles that reason and feeling each play in moral consideration differ as well. Nonetheless, as we can recognize in our daily moral experience, moral reason and feeling are also united. We cannot speak of one without the other.

All moral feelings that we experience in moral life are principled feelings. Conversely, moral reasons that we appeal to are always feeling-laden reasons. This is to say, like *yin-yang* forces in the cosmos, reason and feeling in moral consciousness are mutually penetrated by one another, conditioned by one another, defined by one another, complemented by one another, and enriched by one another. Equally important, what makes a person a moral agent is that the person has a human conscience consisting of both moral reason and feeling.

Moral feeling is principled and reason-laden. It is fundamentally normative. As Rawls correctly holds that the feeling of guilt, for example, is the feeling that one *ought to* have when one does something that is wrong according to the moral standards that are internalized in one's moral conscience. As he says, "[a person] feels guilt because he has acted contrary to his sense of right and justice" (Rawls 1971, 445). He points out, "it is a necessary feature of moral feelings, and part of what distinguishes them from the natural attitudes, that the person's explanation of his experience invokes a moral concept and its associated principles" (ibid. 481). Williams also suggests something similar when he says that morality "embraces a range of ethical outlooks.... It is the outlook, or incoherently part of the outlook, of almost all of us" (Williams 1985, 174). He argues that "the strength of feeling displayed about the matter is generally taken as one criterion of the man's having a strong or serious moral view about it" (Williams 1973, 219).

Indeed a person without moral beliefs has no moral feeling at all. For example, a person who does not believe in justice or righteousness would not have any feeling of shame, guilt or indignation in performing morally wrong actions. Moral feeling presupposes not only something to be felt about, but also *a standing point* from which a person feels about what is felt. In other words, to feel morally about an action or a state of affairs is not to feel from nowhere, but to feel from a specific standing point, which need not be an Archimedean point, but is nonetheless a point upon which a person stands. Therefore, we can say, whatever a moral feeling is, reason or principle is the light under which it is enlightened.

In addition, a moral feeling is not an inchoate passion, but a structured and cultivated sentiment. It is true that moral feeling is not as well delineated and defined as moral reason. Nonetheless it is part and parcel of it to have a pattern and be structured. And it is moral reason that provides feeling with structure. Thus, neo-Confucians call moral reason the principle. How a moral feeling is structured determines what it is. Not only different moral feelings are structured by different beliefs (for example, compassion is structured by the belief of humanity, the feeling of shame is structured by the belief of righteousness), but also feelings of the same category might be different precisely because they are structured differently in different cultural worlds (for example, a Chinese feeling of shame and dislike differs significantly from that of an American).

Here we should make a distinction between moral feeling and physical response. A moral feeling is a refined (sentimental) act of the conscience. A physical response is a crude act of the body. At times certain moral feelings are indeed accompanied by some physical sensations or disturbances; for example, a strong feeling of shame, guilt or indignation might make a person's face red (or pale), causing experience of a tightening of stomach or mental blank and so on. However, these physical sensations or disturbances do not contribute anything to make moral feelings as they are. Nor do they constitute the basis for the intensity of moral feeling. Physical responses, at their best, only express specific moral feelings as they are. What make moral feelings *as they are* is a set of moral principles and beliefs internalized in a moral agent. What moral feelings as they are is the moral agent's distinct concept of the self and the agent's distinct notion of what the agent can "live with" and what she or he cannot "live with."

We must also make a distinction between moral feeling and amoral feeling. Consider my hatred of injustice and my hatred of hot weather. My hatred of injustice involves and expresses my moral reflection of right and wrong, good and evil. It expresses my judgment that injustice is wrong and deplorable. It also expresses my understanding that I am right and totally justified in hating injustice (and unjustified if I do not hate injustice). However, my hatred of hot weather is different. It has nothing to do with the issues of right and wrong, good or evil and reasonableness. Thus, it would not make sense to ask if I am right (or wrong) to hate hot weather. Nor does it make sense to ask whether hot weather is good or evil. If I hate hot weather, I can still live with the fact that everyone else likes hot weather and my dislike of hot weather is unreasonable in the eyes of others. In other words, it is one thing to hate injustice, or to hate a friend's betrayal, dehumanizating institutions, and practice of disgrace, it is quite another to hate hot weather, greasy food, and a car that often breaks down. The former expresses a moral judgment of right and wrong as well as good and evil while the latter has nothing to do with such a judgement.

Now the reverse thing can be said of moral reason. Moral reason is always feeling-laden. Not only the moral concepts, values and norms that we employ as analytical tools are moral feeling-laden, but also the procedure of moral reasoning that we practice is moral feeling-laden. When we really think as a moral agent, we think as a human agent; when we think as a human agent, we think as concrete men and women who have strong feelings of what we can live with and what we cannot live with. Indeed, out moral reason is not only intrinsically intertwined with our moral feeling, but also enriched and empowered by feeling. Our moral sensibility is nurtured and enriched by our moral feeling as much as our resources of moral reasons are enriched by our moral feelings. Conversely, if moral feeling is absent, not only can our moral sensibility not be developed or sustained, but our store of reasons would become empty. Thus, when asked how a person should cultivate his or her filial piety toward parents, Confucius answered, "just remember when you were ill, how anxious your parents were" (*Analects*, 2:6). By this answer, Confucius suggested that one's piety is rooted in one's gratitude toward and feeling of love for one's parents; that is, when one recalls his or her parents' anxiety and care when he or she got ill, one thus keeps alive the warm love of the parents, which in turn becomes the source of the idea of piety. Mencius also held that one's compassion was the source of one's sensitivity to humanity; one's feeling of shame and dislike, the source of one's sensitivity to righteousness; one's feeling of respect and courtesy, the source of one's sensitivity to propriety; and one's feeling of right and wrong, the source of one's sensitivity to wisdom.

Two further observations follow. First, as suggested in the preceding discussions, under some circumstances, a moral feeling—for example, the feeling of outrage or shame or indignity—itself constitutes a ground or reason for an agent to act or abstain from action. In other words, under certain circumstance, moral feeling itself has a reason-giving force. For example, a person's feeling shameful of doing something is a good and sufficient reason for the person to abstain from doing it or to do something to correct the wrong done (*Mencius*, 6B:1).

Second, moral feeling internalizes moral beliefs within an individual (*Analects*, 2:3). Internalization is understood as the process to make specific moral beliefs and norms become personal ones. James J. Liszka points out,

> Internalization occurs when people feel that a set of beliefs, norms or codes are their own, so to speak; that is, at the point of internalization, they are willing to correct their own behavior without external prompts, and when they violate those norms, there is some anxious emotional response to it—that is, one of the more negative moral feelings and emotions become integrated with these beliefs or norms. (1999, 30)

Thus, if the moral reason that guides a moral agent are beliefs, norms, and standards, then these beliefs, norms, and standards are internalized through sentimental attachment and emotional integration. Of course, as a crude approximation, internalization of P as a principle of an agent does not vouch for the truth of P. Instead, it makes P operate as a reason of an agent when it makes P as a principle of the agent. It gives P the reason-giving force.

Here, we should also make a distinction between amoral reason and moral reason. For example, my reason not to walk on the streets of the Bronx in New York City between 9:00 P.M. and 6:00 A.M. is an amoral reason, while my concept of role obligation that guides me to carry out my professional duties as a professor is a moral reason. Amoral reason can be merely instrumental, calculating and, thus, feeling free. For example, if I decide that walking in the streets of the Bronx at midnight is not safe, then I can just avoid doing so without evoking any moral feelings, such as hatred, shame, indignation, and so on. It makes sense to ask if I am rational or wise not to walk on streets of the Bronx. It does not make sense to ask if I should be shameful of not walking on the streets of the Bronx. Moral reason is, however, different. The reason that informs me to fulfill my role obligation as a professor cannot help involving my distaste of failure to do my duty and feeling of shame if I fail to do my duty. It involves a personal feeling of commitment and bond to my role, which in turn evokes the feeling of honor and shame. Thus, if I fail to do my duty, it makes sense for someone to ask: should you not be shameful of such a failure?

In short, moral reason and feeling penetrate one another. Together they create an integrated moral horizon of a moral agent, a horizon in which sentimental approval or disapproval goes hand in hand with rational justification or rejection. To attempt to separate them is like trying to separate the *yin-yang* forces in the cosmos, which will not only be impossible but also fruitless. Of course, to emphasize the unity of moral reason and feeling is not to conflate their differences in nature, role, and feature, just as to emphasize the unity of *yin-yang* is not to suggest that these two are identical. Rather it is to insist that we should have a dialectical perspective of them and therefore properly appreciate their inseparability in morality, and appreciate that morality is featured not only by a set of thoughts, principles, norms, values, duties, and ideals, but also by a set of moral feelings that are part of us *as what we are* (cf. Williams 1985, 174).

Speaking of the unity of moral reason and feeling, I shall add that what makes us a moral agent is not only that we exercise rational constraint over our action and live what Socrates called an examined life, but also that we enrich our lives, beings, and experience with a set of moral feelings that are constitutive of humanity. In other words, what characterizes us as moral agents is not just that we appeal to reason—issued from beliefs and values that are bound with our moral selves—in making moral judgment, but also that we listen to our moral feelings that are expressions of our moral selves. What characterizes us as moral agents is not only that we are rational creatures, but also that we are reasonable human beings; we are neither super-computers nor other animals. Accordingly, morality is important not only because it makes us rational, but also because it enkindles us and makes us humans.

Now allow me to conclude this paper with these remarks. As moral agents, we always evoke both moral reason(s) and feeling(s) when we make a moral judgment of an action in a concrete practical context. Our judgment expresses our beliefs in specific moral principles and truth pertaining to the action and our feeling about the action. Accordingly, moral praise-worthiness or blame-worthiness is essentially a conclusion of both moral reason and feeling, not either one alone. Of greater importance, moral reason and feeling are inseparable in a moral agent. An agent's moral sensitivity to what the agent owes to others and to society, justice as fairness, obligation, happiness, good, and so on is enhanced and enriched by the agent's moral feelings. Conversely an agent's moral feelings of shame, guilt, indignation, and so on are deeply cultivated and refined by deeply seeded moral beliefs. Our capacity to think reasonably is complemented, enkindled and enriched by our capacity to feel morally. Conversely, our capacity to feel morally is enhanced, empowered and refined by our capacity to think reasonably. Therefore, both moral formalism and emotivism are one-sided. Accordingly, an adequate understanding of morality must go beyond both of them.

REFERENCES:

Cheng, Chung-ying. 1991. *New Dimensions of Confucian and Neo-Confucian Philosophy*. Albany: State University of New York Press.

Confucius. 1974. *Analects*. Edited by the Department of Philosophy, Beijing University. Beijing: Beijing University Press.

Habermas, Jürgen. 1996. "Morality and Ethical Life: Does Hegel's Critique of Kant Apply To Discourse Ethics?" In *Twentieth Century Continental Philosophy*, edited by Todd May. Upper Saddle River: Prentice Hall.

Hume, David. 1888/1987. *A Treatise of Human Nature*, Oxford: Oxford University Press.

Kant, Immanuel. 1989. *Foundations of The Metaphysics of Morals*. New York: Macmillan.

Lau, D. C. (trans). *Mencius*. 1970. New York: Penguin Books.

Liszka, James J. 1999. *Moral Competence*. Upper Saddle River: Prentice Hall.

MacIntyre, Alasdair. 1984. *After Virtue*. Notre Dame: University of Notre Dame Press.

Mencius. 1998. *Mencius*. In *The Four Books and The Five Classics*, edited by Yang Xiaomei.

Nozick, Robert.1974. *Anarchy, State and Utopia*. New York: Basic Books.

Parfit, Derek. 1984. *Reasons and Persons*. Oxford: Clarendon Press.

Rawls, John. 1971. *A Theory of Justice*. Cambridge: Harvard University Press.

———. 1993. *Political Liberalism*. New York: Columbia University Press.

Scanlon, Thomas. 1998. *What We Owe To Each Other*. Cambridge: The Belknap of Harvard University Press.

———. 1982. "Contractualism and Utilitarianism." In *Utilitarianism and Beyond*, ed. Martya Sen and Bernard Williams. Cambridge: Cambridge University Press, 103-128.

Shun, Kwong-loi. 1997. *Mencius and Early Chinese Thought*. Stanford: Stanford University Press.

Williams, Bernard. 1985. *Ethics and the Limits of Philosophy.* Cambridge: Harvard University Press.

————. 1973. *Problem of Self.* Cambridge: Cambridge University Press.

Yang, Xiaomei (ed.). 1998. *The Four Books and The Five Classics.* Chengdu: Ba Chu Publishing House.

————. 1998. *The Doctrine of Mean,* in *The Four Books and The Five Classics,* edited by Yang Xiaomei.

5

The Confucian Account of Freedom[*]

Peimin Ni

Since the early twentieth century, Confucianism has often been criticized harshly for being fundamentally authoritarian, and for imposing
rules of propriety (*li*) to limit individual freedom. The Western ideas
of "choice" and "freedom" seemed to have no place in the works of
Confucius or his successors. To the contrary, Confucians advocated
abundant traditional ritual codes of behavior and required every individual member of the society to observe these rituals. Not only out-
ward behavior patterns were regulated, even a person's thoughts were
supposed to follow what is ritually appropriate. From social and political realms to family relationships, Confucianism was taken to be
the foundation of a hierarchic order. Emperor Xian Zong of the
Ming Dynasty (明憲宗) wrote,

> Under Heaven, not one day can pass without the Way of Confu-
> cius. Why is this so? Because when the Way of Confucius is

[*] Earlier versions of the paper were delivered at the symposium: "Race, Liberty and
Chinese Moral and Political Philosophy," a special session in the Seventieth Annual
Meeting of the American Philosophical Association Pacific Division. Seattle, WA.
April 6, 1996, and the fifth conference of the International Society for Philosophy
and Psychotherapy, on "Liberation: Secular and Spiritual," held at Hsi Lai
University, Rosemead, California, Aug. 12-15, 1996. The main ideas of the paper
were also included, in a much abbreviated form, in the section "Freedom" of my
book *On Confucius* (Belmont, CA: Wadsworth, 2002). I would like to thank
Chenyang Li and an anonymous reviewer of the paper for giving me helpful
comments and suggestions.

there, the social order is straight and the ethical principles are manifested; everything under Heaven is placed appropriately in their positions. ...Confucianism is where the weal and woe of the people are dependent upon, and the peace and chaos of the state are contingent on. Those who rule the land under Heaven really cannot spare Confucianism even for just a single day.[1]

Within this social order, those who were in subordinate positions had to follow the superordinate, though the superordinate were supposed to take the responsibility of guiding and protecting the subordinate in return. Not only social and political suppression was legitimized under the banner of Confucianism, family tragedies often resulted in part from the enforcement of Confucian rules of propriety. As Wm. Theodore de Bary says, during the revolution in the early twentieth century in China, especially in the May Fourth Movement of 1919, which was a breaking point between old and new, Confucianism was made to stand for all that was backward and benighted in China, including political corruption and repression, the suppression of women, concubinage, female infanticide, illiteracy, etc. Even today, says de Bary, Confucianism is still employed to justify the rulership by a political elite and by a party dictatorship allegedly for the people. The "dramatic appearance of the 'Goddess of Democracy' at T'ian-an-men," which is either "inspired by the Statue of Liberty (a French creation) or by the classic female impersonation of 'Liberté, Egalité et Fraternité'" would "least of all be identified with anything Chinese or with Confucian tradition" (see de Bary 1991, 103-8). Christina Whitman points out that "the Confucians rejected the Legalist position precisely because it left some areas free. Persuasion was preferred to compulsion as a means of regulating behavior—not because it would leave more room for deviance from social norms, but because it would result in more consistent conformity" (Whitman 1985, 93).

These assessments of Confucianism contain a great deal of truth. Without the slightest intention to defend any oppressive or re-

---

[1] Quoted from a stone tablet erected in 1468 in the Confucius Temple at Qu Fu. The tablet is known as "Da Cheng Bei"—the Tablet of Great Completion.

pressive form of government or tradition, I will argue, however, that Confucianism entails a positive account of freedom. I will try to show that Confucius, and his main successor Mencius, upheld values that are expressed in Western philosophy by the term "freedom," though their views about necessary conditions for freedom and how to achieve freedom are different from the predominant views on the same subject in the West. I will also try to explain that their views on freedom are no less plausible than their popular Western rivals, and that they are highly relevant and significant to the contemporary world.

Since "freedom" is itself a complicated and controversial notion, for the convenience of our discussion, I would like to provide a rather simplified working map of differing concepts of "freedom," and argue from there that the Confucian account of freedom makes good sense in all areas of the map. We may first follow the convention of differentiating a "negative sense of freedom" from a "positive sense of freedom." "Negative" refers to the absence of constraints and coercion, and is thus known as the *"freedom from."* "Positive" refers to the ability to choose and initiate one's own action, and is thus also known as the *"freedom to."* According to this distinction, a prisoner in a cell may be free in the positive sense but not in the negative sense. We may further divide both the "negative freedom" and the "positive freedom" into two senses. The two senses of the "negative freedom" are (N1) the lack of internal constraints and coercion, including, but not limited to the lack of necessary knowledge to perform certain action, and (N2) the lack of external constraints and coercion, including, but not limited to the availability of alternatives and information. According to this distinction, a new chess player may be free to make her moves in the second sense but not in the first, and a prisoner may be free to escape in the first sense but not in the second. The two senses of the "positive freedom" are (P1) the freedom of the will or the possibility of choice, and (P2) self-determination or the exercise of initiative. According to this distinction, a person who is brainwashed to act in no way but that which his master wishes him to would be free in the sense of self-determination but not in the sense of having free will, and the Buridan's ass, which I will discuss later, would be free in the sense of having free will, but lacks freedom in the sense of self-determination.

I

In his famous short autobiography, Confucius says "At the age of seventy, I was able to follow my heart-mind (*xin*)'s desires-wills (*yu*) without overstepping the lines 七十而從心所欲, 不逾矩."[2] This short statement entails rich layers of meaning that are directly and profoundly relevant to the topic of freedom.

First of all, the phrase "to follow the heart-mind's desires-wills without overstepping the lines" indicates a state of *freedom to* do what he wants (positive freedom). Though the word *xin* 心 in Chinese means both heart and mind, and the word *yu* 欲 means both desire and will, the statement entails that the "heart" part and the "mind" part of the *xin* (and thus desires and will) were not in perfect union before Confucius reached the age of seventy. Here we see a power of the mind that is not simply identical with the heart's desires. When the mind informed him where the "lines" were, before the age of seventy, his heart still wanted to do otherwise. For this reason he (the mind) was not able to let his heart take the lead to do whatever it desired. He had to exercise his free will to choose the right path, and regulate his heart's desires so they would not go out of the lines. At the age of seventy Confucius felt he could finally trust his heart's desires. The trust was an authorization from the mind that supervised the heart's desires, based on the fact that the heart was cultivated well enough that it had no more desires to overstep the lines. This interpretation does not necessarily require us to split the Confucian heart-mind into two separate entities. It only requires us to see the sophisti-

---

[2] Confucius, The *Analects*, 2:4. Further references to the book will be marked by the relevant chapter and passage numbers in parentheses. The translation is mainly based on D. C. Lau's (New York: Penguin Books, 1979) and Ames/Rosemont's (New York, Ballantine Books, 1998). Occasionally I take the liberty of altering a few words to make the translation more accurate in the given context.

cation of the Confucian heart-mind, to see that it performs multiple functions of thinking, feeling, willing, desiring, and decision-making.

Also entailed in the passage is an idea about the *freedom from* constraints, restrictions, and coercion. Even though the statement looks exactly like the opposite, as it clearly says that there were lines that Confucius was not supposed to overstep, the real message, however, is that the lines, which were restrictions to him, no longer existed to him as restrictions. After his life-long cultivation, his heart had no more improper desires or ill wills that had to be regulated and restricted. When a person has no intention to shoplift, the surveillance cameras in the shop means no restriction to the person. Similarly, when a person has cultivated herself so well that there is no more desire to do anything inappropriate, the person is free from moral restrictions in the same sense. It does not mean that there are no more moral codes and other norms; it means that those codes and norms are no longer restrictions to the person. They are restrictions only when the agent feels uncomfortable with them and has a desire to go against them.

Having said that, the statement entails both the "freedom to" and the "freedom from," it must be noted that the freedom is not a state of indifference to dispositions. It is rather a state of no-hindrance resulting from cultivated spontaneity, a state of having dispositions to do what the moral norms require effortlessly. The dispositions include developed benevolent tendencies (what Mencius calls "the Four Incipient Tendencies," namely, the Heart of Compassion, the Heart of Shame, The Heart of Courtesy and Modesty, and the Heart of Right and Wrong), and ritual habits guided by the rich knowledge and wisdom of how to apply them. They are so deeply embodied that they become the person's second nature, and the person is therefore able to act in accordance with them spontaneously and effortlessly. This state is essentially no different from the Daoist idea of *wuwei* 無爲, the action of non-action, wonderfully illustrated by Zhuangzi's famous story of Cook Ding. While Cook Ding is able to cut up an ox so skilfully that he lets his spirit move his arms and legs freely, like watching an event taking place by itself, and he enjoys his own action in an aesthetic spirit of "*you* 遊" (free wandering), the well-cultivated Confucian is also able to "set the sights on the Way, sustain with virtue, lean upon human-heartedness, and wander (*you*) in artistic creativity" (7:6).

People usually conceive freedom of the will as a state of autonomy. A free agent in this sense is one who makes autonomous decisions, and not being impelled by any inclinations or dispositions. If one decides to follow certain norms freely, the norms are chosen as right and good by the agent as one of the options that one is not impelled to take, not even by one's own psychological inclinations. In the autobiographic statement of Confucius, however, the norms are followed exactly as his psychological inclinations lean toward. This is the reason why Confucian ethics becomes "descriptive psychology," as Chad Hansen puts it. It describes what the sages incline. For this reason, Hansen concludes that "Confucianism has no doctrine of freedom" (Hansen 1972, 170). Under this concept of freedom, i.e. as a state of being indifferent to inclinations, not only Confucianism, but even the whole Chinese philosophical tradition lacks this dimension. When A. C. Graham said that it would be naive to look for the exact word for the Western idea of liberty or freedom in Chinese culture,[3] he also had this idea of freedom in mind. Graham was quite right in identifying the Chinese concept of *ziran* 自然—"being so of itself'—as the counterpart. In the state of being so of itself, there is no exercise of the will to limit and regulate actions done in accordance with one's dispositions. Graham also uses "spontaneity" to translate the concept of *ziran*, and says, "For Chinese moral philosophizing, the good is what the wisest spontaneously prefer" (Graham 1995, 302).

It might be puzzling that Chinese philosophers, Confucius and Mencius included, had never clearly raised the issue of freedom of the will. But this fact may be conceived as something fortunate, if not insightful, in Chinese philosophy. Upon close examination, we may notice a connection between P1 and N1, namely the freedom of the will and the freedom from internal constraints. If we take P1 to mean

---

[3] Graham uses the word "liberty." But his use of the word seems to be synonymous to the word "freedom."

total indifference to any inclinations, it would require the total freedom in the sense of N1. Yet the total freedom in the sense of N1 would be self-defeating, since it would mean that, on the one hand, the person is not constrained by the lack of knowledge, character, and other dispositions to perform the intended act, and on the other hand, the person is not even led in any direction by the presence of knowledge, character, and other dispositions necessary for a successful performance of the act. It would also make P2 (self-determination) impossible. Confucius and other major traditional Chinese philosophers never took an individual person as an indifferent choice-maker who can disconnect from his or her characters and dispositions. Not only is it impossible for anyone to be free from dispositions, but even if we assume that one could be totally indifferent to dispositions, the person would be like the Buridan's ass, which starved to death between two equally good piles of hay, because it could not find a reason to go to one pile and not the other. Some may take Buridan's ass as an exceptional case, as rarely a person would confront alternatives that are exactly equal in goodness. But in every rational deliberation, if one does not have any inclination, how can one even find reason to go to one alternative and not another? Furthermore, if freedom is indifference, the person should be indifferent to the choice he makes and be able to choose between making the choice and not making the choice. The person has to choose the choice, and for the same reason, he has to choose the choice to choose the choice. This regress will go backward infinitely. The result is obvious—the person will not be able to make any choice, unless, at some point she lets it go and simply chooses! Once when Confucius was asked whether a person should think three times before taking an action, Confucius said "twice is enough" (*Analetcs*, 5:20). Clearly Confucius was aware of the fact that too much deliberation is restrictive, and having to deliberate too much is a sign of lacking freedom. To be free in the positive sense, one has to avoid two extremes. One extreme is to be impelled by blind impulses, and the other extreme is to have no impulses that lead in any direction. Neither of the extremes is a state of freedom. The freedom has to be somewhere in between. The Confucian cultivated spontaneity is such a golden mean. A good example is playing chess. A chess master obviously enjoys more freedom than an uncultivated newcomer who knows nothing about chess. The newcomer either follows blind impulses or holds a chess piece without even knowing how to deliberate. The freedom that the master enjoys is the result of the master's rich experience, knowledge, talent, and the ability of maintaining an optimal psychological and physiological condition.

Many Western philosophers had more or less awareness of the problems entailed in the notion of freedom as indifference, and expressed reservations toward the notion. For example, Descartes takes it to be the "lowest grade" of freedom. He writes,

> [T]he indifference that I observe when no reason moves me more in one direction than in another is the lowest level of freedom; it evinces no perfection in it, but rather a defect in my knowledge, or a certain negation. Were I always to see clearly what is true and good, I would never deliberate about is to be judged or chosen. Thus, although I may be entirely free, I could never for that reason be indifferent. (Descartes 1980, 81)

The kind of freedom that Descartes upholds is called by David Hall and Roger Ames the "formalist" notion, a notion shared by Pythagoras, Plato, Spinoza and Hegel. According to the formalist position, freedom is the knowledge of the eternity or the necessity (see Hall & Ames 1995, 167 and 97-98). A. C. Graham interpreted Confucianism exactly in terms of formalism. For Graham, the Confucian sages are those who are wise; and the wisest, he says, are those who know all the relevant facts (Graham 1995, 302). But this interpretation renders Confucianism far too intellectual than it could permit. For Confucianism, being wise in the sense of knowing relevant facts or truth is not the only qualification, and not even the most important qualification, of a sage or even a *junzi* (君子 exemplary person). To know what is good by the intellect alone is not only impossible (one has to embody the good to know its goodness), but even if it were possible, it would not be enough for a person to be free in the Confucian sense of cultivated spontaneity. One must fully embody the knowledge and make it her own disposition. A person who has to fight against dispositions and desires to stay good is not as free as one who does not have to fight against these forces. Confucius advises a person to be cultivated in music, in literature, in rituals, in one's habits and temperament, etc., and become a well-rounded human being. "Those who know are not perplexed," Confucius says; but there is more. He also says that one must be *Ren* (仁 benevolent) to be not worrisome, and courageous to be not afraid (9:29). From a Confucian perspective these qualities are no less important than knowledge is with regards to freedom.

For the same reason, the Confucian cultivated spontaneity is also different from the Kantian absolute spontaneity (see Kant 1960, 45n). The Kantian absolute spontaneity is the spontaneity of pure reason, which is separated from inclinations such as desires and aversions. For Kant, our desires and aversions reflect the natural aspect of us. They are governed by causation, and cannot govern themselves. Only pure reason, in John Rawls's words, can be the "court of appeal concerning its own constitution and its principles and guidelines for directing its own activities" (Rawls 2000, 280). The Confucian would say, however, that absolute spontaneity is still spontaneity—it is impossible for reason to appeal endlessly of its own decisions. Secondly, if it makes sense to call the absolute spontaneity a state of freedom, it makes more sense to speak of the cultivated spontaneity as a state of freedom. In the Kantian absolute spontaneity, pure reason is not yet in harmony with inclinations, and is therefore endangered by the predeterminism from the natural forces of desires and aversions. In the Confucian cultivated spontaneity, the desires and aversions are attuned and are therefore no longer purely "natural" forces. They have been modified and purified by the subject and are therefore in harmony with the moral reason. They become the embodiment or the materialization of moral reason. This harmony allows the individual's moral actions to be more fully his or her own than the Kantian absolute spontaneity, in which the moral actions are still partially against the agent him/herself.

II

I have more than once indicated, in the previous section, that the autobiographic statement of Confucius entails that for Confucius, freedom is a state achieved after, or gained through, long time culti-vation. In Confucius' own case, he set his mind at learning since the age of fifteen, and he was not free in the sense of being able to follow his heart's will (P1) without overstepping the lines (N2) until the age of seventy. This point is not only important to the Confucian account of the positive freedom, including his approach to the freedom of the will, it is also important to the Confucian account of the negative freedom, the freedom from constraints and coercion. It is natural to infer from the statement that freedom of action in general, and politi-cal freedom as a particular part of it, is not simply a matter of some natural rights that a person is born into and enjoys without having to do anything to earn them. Though Confucius' failure to advocate ba-sic human rights is a drawback of his theory, the recognition of the importance of cultivation is his contribution. An individual's personal cultivation is certainly relevant to his or her freedom, political or non-political, both in the sense of how much one is able to exercise or gain one's rights, and in the sense of not "overstepping the lines" and consequently losing the rights one already possesses. In this section, I want to draw some further implications from the Confucian cultiva-tion with regard to the concept of negative freedom, or more specifi-cally, the relationship between N1 and N2.

Confucius' autobiographic statement informs us that the Con-fucian cultivation, as a way of achieving freedom, is primarily a culti-vation of oneself, not fighting against others or removing external constraints. The *Analects* of Confucius contains quite a number of passages that advise people to cultivate themselves rather than to put restrictions on others. For instance, "If one sets strict standards for oneself and makes allowances for others when making demands on them, one will stay clear of ill will" (15:15). "When you meet some-one better than yourself, turn your thoughts to becoming his equal. When you meet someone not good, look within and examine your own self" (4:17). "It is not the failure of others to appreciate your abilities that should trouble you, but rather your failure to appreciate theirs" (1:16). When things go wrong in a country, the Confucian ideal ruler blames himself (20:1). "What the gentleman seeks, he seeks within himself; what the small man seeks, he seeks in others" (15:21). Confucius even describes *ren*, the central quality of an exemplary person, in part as "overcoming the self" (12:1). Through self-cultivation a person should become morally sensitive, compassionate, courageous, and wise. With these qualities, one's heart-mind is able to remain undisturbed (*budongxin* 不動心) confronting seductions and threats. The *Daxue* (大學 *Great Learning*) shows clearly how this self-cultivation will bring one freedom to make great achievements, such as regulating a family, governing well a state, and bringing peace to the world.

Indeed, all major Eastern philosophical traditions stress self-cultivation as a way of achieving freedom. The fundamental teaching of Hinduism is that "Atman [the true self] is [identical with] Brahman [the 'self' of the universe]." For the Hinduist, to achieve freedom is to eliminate the illusory self, which people normally conceive to be an entity separated from, and in opposition to, the world. Buddhism denies the existence of any substantial self, whether Atman or Brahman. Buddhists believe that the craving for getting a hold of the self is the very source of suffering. To achieve freedom (mainly from suffering) is for the Buddhist essentially getting rid of the illusion and living accordingly. Daoism advocates harmony with nature, and for that purpose it teaches the virtue of non-striving. By "daily drop" (of conventional knowledge and moral codes, of desires and expectations), and "sitting forgetfully," one achieves the freedom of being in harmony with the universe. In an overall comparison to these other Eastern traditions, Confucianism stands out as the most positive and constructive one. The other three major Eastern traditions are all predominantly oriented toward some kind of "negation,"—as their emphasis on "elimination," "detachment," "drop" and "non-striving" indicates. Confucianism aims more at constructing and establishing the moral subjectivity. If we say that all the four major Eastern traditions aim at the unity between "Heaven and human," and they all try to achieve the unity through self-cultivation, we may say that the other three tend to get the unity by negating the self so that there will be nothing to be constrained, but the Confucian tradition tries to construct a self and let Heaven be displayed through human moral subjectivity. No other tradition had the aspiration to say "to establish the heart for Heaven and Earth 爲天地立心" like the Confucians. The sense of mission makes the secular sacred, and it turns external constraints into conditions through which the moral subjectivity (and thus autonomy) is able to display itself and realize its value. Mencius discovered through his own experience that this is not a mere devotion of faith, for he was able to actually feel his vital energy, *qi* 氣, filling the space between Heaven and Earth.[4] Mencius says: "An exemplary person steeps himself in the Way because he wishes to find it in himself. When he finds it in himself, he will be at ease in it; when he is at ease in it, he can draw deeply upon it; when he can draw deeply upon it, he finds sources of help wherever he turns" (4B:14). The cultivated person can have such a powerful presence in front of others that he or she can affect others without using physical power. The force is much more effective than physical power—while physical power enforces from without, moral power affects others from within. Physical power can only result in uniformity; internal affection results in harmony. Mencius even claims that "the myriad things are all here at my disposal" (7A:4).[5] This level of "freedom to" do whatever one likes to do does sound quite mystical, but the philosophical point relevant to our current topic is that the passages in Mencius show how the Confucian cultivation is a positive construction of the greater self, in which the autonomy becomes more than the autonomy of an individual person, but an extended autonomy of the unity between the individual and Heaven.

One may raise the objection that two things normally considered vital to the freedom of action are not stressed by Confucius. One is the availability of alternatives to choose from, and the other is the availability of information about options or alternatives. One may also argue that Confucius' self-cultivation is in fact a way of internalization or indoctrination of social norms that restricts freedom. However, it is not difficult to understand the reason behind this. What is more vital to freedom, the availability of many alternatives to choose

---

[4] *Mencius*, Book 2, Part A, Section 2. Further references to the book will be marked by relevant book numbers, parts and section numbers in parentheses. The translation is mainly D. C. Lau's (New York: Penguin Books, 1970).

[5] Here I use A. C. Graham's translation in his *Disputers of the Tao*, which I think to be closer to the original Chinese text than the translation "all the ten thousand things are here in me," by D. C. Lau.

from or the ability to choose what is good for oneself? Which of the two gives me more freedom, the availability of drugs that destroy myself or the knowledge and disposition to stay away from them? When the latter is absent, the availability of the former is actually a threat to my freedom. Before one can reach the stage of cultivated spontaneity, one still needs to be constrained by "the lines," and the lines are necessary guides for one to reach the stage. Confucius' saying that "the common people can be made to follow a path, but not to know" (8:9)[6] is often criticized, for nothing seems more evident than from this saying that Confucianism is authoritarian, and is oppressive of human freedom. But it does not take much investigation before one realizes that by this saying Confucius could not have meant that it would be better to keep the common people ignorant and powerless unconditionally. The entire spirit of Confucianism is to establish humanity and not to just establish an elite class. One obvious indication is that his school was open to anyone who sincerely wanted to learn (7:7, 15:39). What he meant must be that, before a person reaches a certain level of maturity in cultivation, the person is unable to understand the reason for following the lines. Therefore, pedagogically, the rulers (as common people's guardians) should first work on letting people follow the correct path rather than trying to let them understand it and have the power to go astray. His intention must be like the intention behind today's movie ratings and drug regulations—it is for their own good that we keep our children away from seeing or having something. Because the availability of these things tends to deprive the availability of what is genuinely good for them. In this sense, too much freedom in the sense of N2 is deprivation of the possibility of the freedom in the sense of N1, that is obtainable only through self-cultivation.

---

[6] There can be (at least) two mutually compatible interpretations of the saying, —I mean they can both be right—one descriptive and the other normative: Under one interpretation it is saying that it is a fact that the common people are difficult to be made to understand, and under the other it is saying that the rulers should just let the common people follow and not let them know. As the two are not incompatible, I take it both ways.

III

There is yet another important dimension of the Confucian account of freedom—relatedness. Though the dimension is not as clearly entailed in the autobiographic statement as those discussed in the previous two sections, it can be readily seen from the overall spirit of Confucianism. The "lines" that Confucius was able to follow effortlessly at the age of seventy are not absolute commandments issued from God or from some lawmakers, nor are they totally subjective choices of autonomous individuals. They are insights about what is most appropriate in one's encounters with others, mostly formalized as ritual proprieties and passed down from generation to generation as traditional social customs. One metaphysical background of the "lines" is the Confucian notion of a human being as essentially a social existence, not an abstract autonomous choice maker. Every person is an axis of social relationships, and is defined by the relationships. It implies that, for any one to be free, he or she has to achieve the freedom within the relationships, and not in isolation from them. David Hall and Roger Ames made this point very clear in their classical work *Thinking through Confucius*:

> Western social theories are weighted in favor of the notion of individual absoluteness which suggests that they have difficulty making an appropriate case for social interdependence without challenging the viability of the notion of freedom and autonomy. The case is the opposite for the classical Confucian view. There the preference for individual relativity is quite evident. Any attempt to shift that view in the direction of individual absoluteness threatens the very structure of the Confucian social vision. (Hall & Ames 1987, 152.)

According to Confucianism, not only is an individual unable to be isolated from others, whether it is one's family, friends, neighbors, colleagues, rulers, the society, or *tian* 天—Heaven; one's relatedness to others is in fact a necessary condition for one to be free. The point can be illustrated nicely by comparing two stories. One is Sartre's story about a student who came to him for advice on whether he should leave France to join the forces against Nazi Germany, or stay with his mother and help her to carry on. The young man was torn between two moral duties that apparently couldn't both be fulfilled at the same time. On the one hand was his duty to take care of his mother, who was suffering tremendously from the half-treason of her husband and the death of her older son, and on the other hand was his duty to his country.

Sartre tells us that nothing could help the student to make his decision. Ethical theories could not help because he had to choose which theory to follow and how to interpret a theory in the given situation. Instincts or feelings could not help because it was his decision and his final action that would give a feeling value, not the other way around. Other people could not help because before others could offer him advice, he had to choose whom he should go to for advice; in that case, he already knew, more or less, what advice he was going to get. Sartre's answer to the student was: "You are free, choose, that is, invent" (see Sartre 1993, 24-28). By using this example, Sartre wants to show the "forlornness" of a free individual, and show that the forlornness will inevitably be accompanied by the feelings of anguish and despair.

Interestingly, there is a well-known Chinese story that parallels the Sartrean story cited above, yet the Chinese story leads to an opposite conclusion. Song dynasty Chinese general Yue Fei 岳飛 (1103-1142) had a dilemma similar to Sartre's student—He had to choose between either to defend his country against invaders, or to stay at home to take care of his aged mother. The solution, however, did not come from his own "invention," it came to him from his mother— she urged him to go to defend his country so strongly that she even tattooed four Chinese characters, "*jinzhong baoguo* [盡忠報國, to exert absolute loyalty and repay your country]" on his back. Her action dismissed Yue Fei's dilemma; because given her action, he would be going against her will if he would still chose to stay with her, and that would not be a way of caring for her.

The difference between the two stories is not that Yue Fei was simply lucky and the young man in Sartre's story unlucky, or that the Chinese society and the French society were different. The Confucian would say that a person is not a "nothingness" who in loneliness faces all the choices. A person lives in a particular society and is in particular relations with the people around him or her. As Henry Rosemont puts it,

> For the early Confucians there can be no me in isolation, to be considered abstractly: I am the totality of roles I live in relation to specific others. Moreover, these roles are interconnected in that the relations in which I stand to some people affect directly the relations in which I stand with others, to the extent that it would be misleading to say that I 'play' or 'perform' these roles; on the contrary, for Confucius I am my roles. (Rosemont 1991, 72)

In other words, the Sartrean idea of a human being as an absolute autonomous, self-determining individual, detached from all the relations and lonely makes decisions, would be considered by the Confucians to be fundamentally flawed. Neither Yue Fei nor Sartre's student was an isolated individual. The fact that Yue Fei became a model of both a good son and a patriot was not simply the result of his own choice. His mother made it possible for him to become both. She did not stand outside as a passive observer, waiting for her son to make a decision. The original dilemma was one of human relationship, and it was resolved through the human relationship. The deciding factor in the solution was not Yue Fei's decision of accepting his mother's help; it was his mother's help that made his consequential decision part of a good solution. Certainly it was possible for Yue Fei's mother to offer no help. But even if that were the case it would still not change the fact that Yue Fei and his mother were related in a specific way and they were both responsible for the outcome of the situation. Yue Fei would still not be alone, and the result would still be the consequence of the actions of all the parties involved.

In Sartre's student's case, Confucius would say that whether the student came to Sartre or not, he and Sartre were in a student-teacher relationship. This relationship was not the student's choice. It was a fact that both the student and Sartre had a moral obligation to acknowledge. As a teacher, Sartre could have given his student some more practical suggestions or help, such as making some arrangements for taking care of his mother, suggesting that there may be ways of joining the resistance against Nazi without leaving France, so that he can take care of his mother at the same time, etc. Even if after all these efforts, the problem still remained, it would still be different from what he actually did—a cold rejection of offering any help. What Sartre did to the student was not simply telling the student a factual situation about the student; it was a demonstration of his attitude toward the student. Furthermore, Sartre's words were not simply descriptive; they were also performative. His advice was an action that had effects on the student—it deepened the student's feeling of loneliness, anguish and despair. The difference between the two stories, according to the Confucian, is that in one story, the related individuals' joint action led to a solution of a dilemma whereas in the other, the related individuals' actions deepened a dilemma. In both cases, the dilemmas did not belong to one individual. They were both dilemmas confronting all the relevant parties.

Just like water is a necessary condition for swimming, and adjusting bodily movement according to the nature of water increases a person's freedom in the water, one's relationship with a specific environment is a necessary condition for an individual to be free within the given environment, and adjusting the relationship accordingly increases the person's freedom in it. Separated from social relations, one cannot even talk about being free in the society. In order to be free in a given society, a person has to deal with the people that he or she is in a specific relationship with. To be free in a given society requires a clear sense of one's own social position and relationship with others, and adjustment of the relationships to the best possible state. To "let the ruler be a ruler, the subject a subject, the father a father, the son a son" (12:11), looking from this perspective, is also advice for getting freedom. Of course, one should not misinterpret the Confucian point of having a harmonious relation with the "other" as having no conflict with the "other" at any cost. The state of "harmony" is different from the state of a peaceful co-existence. People can have a peaceful co-existence with a tyrant in a totalitarian state, as long as they submit to the force of the tyrant. Harmony means a peaceful, pleasant, and mutually benefiting and constructive state of co-existence. It is a state in which one is both autonomous and essentially dependent on others. The dependency on others is such that one is unable to be free without the others, and the autonomy is such that one is able to express one's own humanity and individuality within the relationships, as one engages oneself in dynamic interactions with others, including transforming and being transformed by others. Self-cultivation and interaction with others are not two separate stages, as we can see that Confucius himself did not wait until the age of seventy to teach his students.

It is said that by stressing the importance of self-cultivation, of relationships and social responsibilities of the traditional feudalistic Chinese society, Confucius should be held responsible for China's lack of the concept of human rights, which in turn implies the lack of freedom. Individuals should be respected as such, and have the right to make their own choices, not merely act as a part of a social structure. From the Confucian point of view, however, the idea of human rights is justifiable only if the people will be better off with the rights than without the rights, and that is not always the case. It would be silly to grant young children the right to play with fire. When common people have not cultivated themselves to a certain level, some amount of paternalism is always needed. On the other hand, for those who have well cultivated themselves, and harmoniously interact with each other, the emphasis of rights is not only redundant; it impairs the very harmony itself. [7] It would be silly and hurtful for Yue Fei to claim to his mother that it was his choice, and she had no right to give him an order. The idea of human rights entails a contractual relation to bind the government and the people externally, not a reciprocal correlative relation that connects people internally in harmony.

We must not gloss over the fact that partly because Confucianism lacked some features of the right-oriented idea of freedom that is prevalent in the West, the Chinese suffered greatly from totalitarianism, from exploitation and manipulation by their corrupted rulers. It seems to me that the Confucian view of freedom can be applied mainly in two stages of human/social development. One is an early stage of human civilization when common people needed more guid-

---

[7] Chenyang Li also made this point in his book, *The Tao Encounters the West* (see Li 1999, 175).

ance than the exercise of autonomy, and sage rulers were in power, and the other is a stage when common people on average and the society as a whole are civilized enough to live harmoniously in a reciprocal and correlative way. Between these two stages, the right-oriented idea of freedom ought to be on duty to a great extent, since Confucianism provides ordinary individuals no powerful protection against tyrants, nor does it put legal restrictions on rulers. However, it does not mean that Confucianism has no value today. In today's world, the spirit of self-cultivation needs to be revitalized. Under the strong influence of modern Western individualism, self is assumed and even worshipped as simply an entity that deserves respect, understanding, and satisfaction, not something that also needs to be cultivated, rectified, and transformed in its relationship with others. Lacking proper cultivation within human relationships, many young people are now slaves of the "wants" created by the public media. To cultivate oneself and regulate wants/desires is an important way of achieving freedom. Education must help a person to get freedom by transforming a person, rather than just letting the person know relevant information on how to remove external constraints. More humane personal relationships must be built in our more and more right-oriented individualistic societies for people to re-acquaint with others as conditions of, rather than limitations to our freedom.

IV

To summarize the discussion, with the conceptual "map" provided at the beginning of this paper in mind, we find that for Confucians, "positive freedom" or freedom to do what one wants should be defined as a cultivated spontaneity, and not a fictitious state of indifference. The Confucian autonomy is a state of embodied moral subjectivity, and not merely the possession of knowledge about what is good and right, nor the dictatorship of the pure practical reason. We also find that, with regard to "negative freedom" or freedom from constraints, Confucians placed self-cultivation over the removal of external constraints. Their cultivated spontaneity requires positive establishment of moral subjectivity, and not merely negative removal of constraints, whether internal or external. The presence of some constraints can be constructive to the development of freedom. Furthermore, we find that for Confucians, inter-relatedness between individuals is not only inescapable, it is a necessary condition for an individual to be free in her social environment. The notion of an autonomous decision-maker separated from social relations is conceptually flawed and practically prohibitive to the emergence of genuinely free members of a free society. In comparison to this account of freedom, the conceptual map of the "negative" and the "positive" senses of freedom looks pale, mechanical, and disintegrated, even though it served the purpose of guiding us to see the fully embodied, integrated parts of the Confucian account.

REFERENCES

Ames, Roger T. and Rosemont, Jr. Henry (trans). 1998. *The Analects of Confucius: A Philosophical Translation*. New York: Ballantine Books.

de Bary, Wm. Theodore. 1991. *The Trouble with Confucianism*. Cambridge, MA: Harvard University Press.

Descartes, René. 1980. *Discourse on Method and Meditations on First Philosophy*. Trans. by Donald A. Cress. Indianapolis: Hackett Publishing Company.

Graham, A. C. 1989. *Disputers of the Tao*. La Salle, Ill.: Open Court.

Hall, David and Roger Ames. 1987. *Thinking Through Confucius*. Albany: State University of New York Press.

———. 1995. *Anticipating China*. Albany: State University of New York Press.

Hansen, Chad. 1972. "Freedom and Moral Responsibility in Confucian Ethics," *Philosophy East and West* 2:169-186.

Kant, Immanuel. 1960. *Religion within the Limits of Reason Alone*. Trans. by T. M. Greene and H. H. Hudson, New York: Harper and Row.

Li, Chenyang. 1999. *The Tao Encounters the West*. Albany: State University of New York Press.

Rawls, John. 2000. *Lectures on The History of Moral Philosophy*. Edied by Barbara Herman, Cambridge: Harvard Univ. Press.

Rosemont, Jr. Henry. 1991. *A Chinese Mirror, Moral Reflections on Political Economy and Society.* La Salle, Ill.: Open Court.

Sartre, Jean-Paul. 1993. *Existentialism and Human Emotions.* New York: Citadel Press.

Whitman, Christina. 1985. "Privacy in Confucian and Taoist Thought." In *Individualism and Holism: Studies in Confucian and Taoist Values*, edited by Donald J. Munro. Ann Arbor: Center for Chinese Studies, the University of Michigan.

6

Mencius on Moral Responsibility

Xinyan Jiang

Is there a theory of moral responsibility in Confucian ethics? The answer seems to depend on how "moral responsibility" is understood. It has been argued that not only is there no account of moral responsibility in Confucian ethics, but also there is no appropriate context for such an account. The argument is made on the following grounds: whereas a theory of moral responsibility is associated with an action-based ethical theory, which seeks to establish moral rules or formulas, Confucian ethics is not an action-based ethical theory but a virtue-based one that rejects the formulation of abstract rules. Therefore, there is not a theory of moral responsibility in Confucian ethics. The reason why the account of moral responsibility relies on an action-based ethics is this: if to be moral is to follow moral rules, moral failure means failing to perform acts according to moral rules. Since there always will be some exceptions to rules, there is a need to define those conditions under which one ought not to be morally blamed for failing to act according to moral rules. If we call those conditions "excusing conditions," then, theories of moral responsibility are philosophical attempts to systematize and justify excusing conditions. If an ethical theory does not emphasize the application of moral rules, it will have no need to define excusing conditions and therefore no need to account for moral responsibility (see Hansen 1972, 169-186). However, such an argument is problematic. Even if we take it for granted that Confucian ethics is totally virtue-based and has no account for moral action, we still cannot conclude that there is no Confucian theory of moral responsibility. If "moral responsibility" is defined in a much broader sense and connected with character development and moral duty as well, undoubtedly, Confucian ethics provides a rich account of moral responsibility.

In a virtue ethics, we might not define the exceptional conditions to the rules in order to excuse an agent's action, but we do need to ask about the conditions under which one fails to form a virtuous character. If in an action-based theory moral failure is related to the failure to observe rules, in a virtue-based theory moral failure is related to the failure to cultivate virtue. Hence, if a theory of moral responsibility is to define excusing conditions under which one ought not to be morally blamed for his/her moral failure, virtue ethics also needs an account of moral responsibility. The difference of a virtue-based theory from an action-based theory might suggest that it requires a different theory of moral responsibility, but this is no reason to deny it such a theory. Confucian ethics, especially Mencius' ethics, does address those excusing conditions for moral failure in character. Furthermore, Confucian theory of moral responsibility goes beyond the problem of moral failure. It also addresses moral responsibility in terms of moral obligation in social context. This paper is a tentative explanation of Mencius' view on moral responsibility.

Mencius proposes that for the formation of moral character, there are two indispensable conditions: certain environmental conditions and self-cultivation. On the one hand, a minimally good environment is necessary for one to obtain sound moral beliefs and good character. Such a necessary condition for moral development is external to individuals. Therefore, when it is not met, the agent cannot be held responsible for what he/she is. On the other, self-effort is crucial in moral development, and no one can be virtuous without self-cultivation. Given a minimally good environment, it is up to individuals to cultivate their character. One is responsible for his/her moral failure due to the lack of self-effort. Furthermore, once one's morality and character are established, one not only can overcome adverse environmental influences but also can transform the environment. Based on these beliefs, Mencius holds that those who lack a necessary environment for moral development can be morally excused for their moral failure, and that those who are in the position to make social changes and provide the environment necessary for moral development are not only responsible for their own character but are also at least partially responsible for the character formation of others. They have a heavy moral responsibility for building up a good society and producing more responsible agents. That is why Mencius urges the ruling class to practice benevolent government (*ren zheng* 仁政) and teaches intellectuals to take the responsibility for the world.

I

To understand Mencius' position on moral responsibility, we first need to discuss his well-known theory that human nature is originally good. For it is this belief in the goodness of human nature that provides the foundation for Mencius' theory of moral responsibility.

At Mencius' times, the term "nature" (*xing* 性) was often used to refer to a thing's tendency and inclination. The *xing* of an animate thing meant the course on which life completes its development if not injured and adequately nourished (Graham 1967, 232; 1989, 124). *Xing* was both a descriptive and prescriptive concept. On the one hand, the *xing* of a thing referred to the course of life proper to the thing; on the other, it referred to the way the thing will develop when free from interference (Graham 1989, 125). Given this understanding of *xing*, we can see that, by "human nature," Mencius refers to the natural and proper tendency of human beings.

According to Mencius, human beings are disposed to be virtuous just as water is disposed to flow downward (*Mencius*, 6A:2). All human beings have the four beginnings or innate seeds of virtues: the heart (*xin* 心) of commiseration, the heart of shame and dislike, the heart of deference and compliance, and the heart of right and wrong. The heart of commiseration is the beginning of benevolence. The heart of shame and dislike is the beginning of righteousness. The heart of deference and compliance is the beginning of propriety. And the heart of right and wrong is the beginning of wisdom (*Mencius*,

2A:6). These four beginnings are four kinds of senses or feelings.[1] They consist of human nature and distinguish human beings from other species. If they are properly developed, the person will become virtuous, just as a seed of a tree will become a tree if it is properly nurtured.

Clearly, by "human nature is good," Mencius does not mean that the human being is born with perfect virtues—like a sage. Instead, he means that every human being has some seeds of virtues and has a natural basis for moral perfection. Speaking of human moral potential, every person can be Yao and Shun[2] (*Mencius* 6B:2). "The sage and I are of the same kind"(*Mencius* 6A:7). However, to be capable of attaining sagehood is not the same as to actually become a sage. The fact that every one has some seeds of virtues does not mean that these seeds can be actually developed. The goodness of human nature does not entail that each human being will naturally or spontaneously become a virtuous person. For Mencius, moral development is a long and dynamical process. Good seeds need to grow up. To become a virtuous agent, one must have his/her seeds of virtues, i.e., his/her four beginnings or four feelings, properly nurtured.[3]

It is within this context that the issue of moral responsibility arises in Mencius. If for moral development it is essential to make the seeds of virtues grow, what, then, is responsible for their growth?

For Mencius, whether one's good nature can be properly nurtured is dependent on both internal and external conditions: the agent's self-attention and self-effort, and outside economic, political and social environments. In other words, the lack of self-attention or cultivation and the lack of a suitable environment are two factors responsible for the failure of the innate good nature of human beings to develop. Although the former is up to the individual's effort, the

---

[1] The idea of innate sympathy is also put forward by some Western philosophers such as Rousseau and Hume, but no Western philosopher has proposed the other three moral senses discussed by Mencius.

[2] Yao and Shun were both legendary sage-rulers of the 3rd millennium B.C.

[3] See Jiang 1997 for a more detailed discussion on human nature and moral cultivation.

latter is not. When one's failure in moral development is due to an external reason that is beyond one's control, one could not be responsible for it. Therefore, necessary external conditions for moral development are also preconditions for moral responsibility. In the next section such external conditions will be discussed in some detail.

II

Since whether those external conditions for moral development can be met is not determined by the individual, whether one can be responsible for his/her morality is not totally up to oneself. In this aspect, Mencius would agree with those contemporary Western philosophers such as Bernard Williams and Thomas Nagel who believe that morality is subject to luck, and moral life is not free from external contingency.[4]

For Mencius, the most important external condition for one's being virtuous is the environment in which one grows up and lives. Although human nature is disposed to morality, a person can be made bad by an external force, just as water can be forced to go uphill (*Mencius*, 6A:2). Although human nature is the same in everyone, people may behave differently under different environmental circumstances. He says in 6A:7 that in good years most young people behave well, while in bad years they abandon themselves to evil. Such a difference in behavior is clearly not caused by the difference in human nature but by differences in the environment. In 6A:8, the same point is illustrated by the metaphor of Niu Mountain.

> The trees of Niu Mountain were once beautiful. But can the mountain be regarded any longer as beautiful since, being on the border of a big state, the trees have been hewed down with axes and hatchets? Still, with the rest given them by the days and nights, and nourishment provided them by the rains and the dew, they were not without buds and sprouts springing forth. But then the cattle and the sheep pastured upon them once and again. That is why the mountain looks so bald. When people see that it is so bald, they think that there was never any timber on

---

[4] See Bernard Williams 1981, 20-40, and Thomas Nagel 1979, 24-38.

the mountain. Is this the true nature of the mountain? Is there
not [also] a heart of humanity and righteousness originally existing in man? The way in which he loses his originally good mind
is like the way in which trees are hewed down with axes and
hatchets. (Chan's trans., 56)

This metaphor of Niu Mountain first shows that people's bad behavior does not indicate that they are not originally good, just as the
mountain's being bald now does not prove that it is not the nature of
the mountain to grow buds and sprouts. Furthermore, the metaphor
suggests that despite their original good nature, people might become
bad and remain bad due to external forces, just as the mountain became bald as the result of overwhelming external destruction and
cannot restore its original beauty unless its environment is changed.
This shows that, as certain external conditions are necessary for the
mountain to maintain its original natural beauty, the economic, social
and political environment is extremely important for preserving and
developing good human nature. "Therefore with proper nourishment
and care, everything grows, whereas without proper nourishment and
care, everything decays"(ibid. 57).

What, then, are the minimal environmental conditions for being
morally good? When may we judge that one's being bad is due to environmental reasons? For Mencius, the first indispensable environmental condition is that people have the necessities of life without
which their survival is impossible. Extreme poverty will force people
to do whatever helps them survive. That is why Mencius strongly believes that those who become criminals, because of extreme poverty
caused by corrupt rulers and unfair distribution in society, should not
be blamed. Instead, those rulers who put their people in such terrible
living conditions are largely responsible. Such a point is clearly made
in passage 1A:7.

When they are thus involved in crime, to follow them up and punish them—this is to entrap the people. Therefore, a wise ruler will
ensure the livelihood of the people, so that, above, they have
wherewithal to serve their parents and, below, sufficient wherewithal to support their wives and children; in good years they shall
always be abundantly satisfied, and in bad years they shall escape

death by starvation. Only then does he drive them toward goodness; in this way the people find it easy to follow him. (Yang's edition, 17)[5]

This passage suggests that, though Mencius and contemporary philosophers do not have the same terminology of "moral responsibility," they are concerned with the same issue. Mencius might not say
that those who have committed crimes for the sake of survival are
completely free from responsibility for their wrong doing and character, but he is clearly saying that the ruler's failure to provide for their
people's necessities of life is mainly responsible for those people's
wrong doing. Obviously, Mencius believes that such unfortunate
people are morally excused for their crimes, and the punishment imposed on them is unfair.

With the belief in the goodness of human nature, Mencius holds that
people will not do evil if they are properly educated and are not
driven to evil by external forces, just as Niu Mountain will grow trees
if it is free from external destruction. Therefore, for Mencius, the efficient way to make people moral is to remove those conditions that
force people to do evil. More specifically, the main means to bringing
about morally responsible agents is not imposing legal punishment
but providing good economic, social, and political environments and
proper moral education. In practice, Mencius does not advocate abol-
ishing legal punishment. He might not deny the expressive function
of punishment, that is, to announce in the strongest terms the society's disapproval of certain behaviors.[6] But he seems not to believe
that punishment is the most efficient means to stop crimes and develop moral persons. First, for those criminals who commit crimes
due to their lack of the necessities of life, punishment will not stop
their crimes. As long as their necessities are not met, they will continue to commit crime. Second, for those who commit crimes due to
flaws in their character, punishment cannot make them morally good

---

[5] This is my translation from Yang's edition, but I have referred to some other
translations.
[6] Lawry Finsen brought to my attention some contemporary discussions on the
expressive function of punishment.

but encourages sophisticated selfishness. They will not commit a crime when they believe that they can be caught, but they will whenever they think they can get away with it. This is in line with Confucius' following remarks:

> Lead the people with governmental measures and regulate them by law and punishment, and they will avoid wrongdoing but will have no sense of honor and shame. (*Analects*, 2:3. Chan's trans., 22)

The Confucian attitude to punishments has been summarized by Chad Hansen as follows: according to the Confucians, governing by laws will produce endless litigation and nurture the selfish instinct for avoiding punishments. The essentially immoral population will only consider ways to enrich themselves through loopholes in laws. Under such circumstances, it is almost impossible to develop a morally good person (Hansen 174). Such a Confucian belief explains why Mencius did his best to urge rulers to practice the kingly way to rule and establish the benevolent government. Due to the influence of such Confucian philosophers as Mencius, in traditional Chinese culture law is regarded as the last resort to appeal, and rulers are expected to be moral examples and love their people as parents love their children. Although very few rulers actually lived up to such a Confucian ideal, most rulers labeled themselves as practitioners of such a Confucian benevolent government and take this as the moral basis of their rule.

For Mencius, those who have to work all the time in order to survive and live in extreme poverty have the same human nature as others and have the potential to be moral sages, but their moral potential cannot be developed because of their terrible living conditions. Therefore, they are objects of love and pity but not of blame. In the *Mencius*, there are many passages which show Mencius' deep sympathy for the working poor, as well as great anger at corrupt rulers. [7]

---

[7] What Mencius has said about working people who constantly struggle to obtain the necessities of life is also compatible with some contemporary analyses of conditions of responsibility. Contemporary philosophers, such as Herry Frankfurt, Gary Waston, and Richard Taylor, all agree that in order for an agent to be responsible,

However, for Mencius, extreme poverty is not the only external force which can make a person lose his or her good nature and therefore become a morally bad being. Mencius clearly recognizes the moral relevance of socialization. Sometimes, socially corrupting forces can impede one's moral development to such an extent that one becomes morally blind or unavoidably embraces mistaken values. For example, if a person is surrounded by evil people all the time and has never had a chance to understand what a morally good person is, it will be impossible for him or her to know what is right and what is wrong. Just as in order to learn a language one needs to have a proper language environment, so also in order to be morally good, one needs to have a proper social environment. The following passage from the *Mencius* shows this point.

> Mencius said to Dai Busheng, "Do you wish your king to be good? I shall speak to you plainly. Suppose a Counselor of Chu wishes his son to speak the language of Qi. Would he have a man from Qi to tutor his son? Or would he have a man from Chu?"

> "He would have a man from Qi to tutor his son."

---

the agent must have freedom of will in the sense that he or she not only can act according to his or her desires but also can act according to those desires endorsed by his or her true self (see Frankfurt, 1971, 5-20, Watson, 1975, 205-20, and Taylor, 1976, 281-99). For all of them, human beings have the ability to evaluate, reflect on, and correct selves and therefore are able to choose their first order desires. Because children, insane people and animals do not have this ability, they are not responsible for themselves. Because victims of mental manipulation are not acting upon the values they choose, they are not responsible either. Susan Wolf labels the Frankfurt-Watson-Taylor type of theory as "the deep-self view" since it holds that one is responsible only if one's will is governed by one's deep self (see Wolf: 1987, 50-51). If we apply such a theory to those who have been constantly struggling for the necessities of life such as food and clothing and have never had time and opportunity to speculate about anything, it is not hard to see that such people cannot have deep selves as long as their living conditions are not changed for the better. Although as human beings they have the ability to form deep selves, they do not have the opportunity to use this ability and fulfill their full humanity. If "the deep self" is a necessary condition for responsibility and these people are not able to form deep selves due to extreme poverty, they cannot be responsible for themselves.

"With one man from Qi's tutoring the boy and a host of Chu men chattering around him, even if you caned him every day to make him speak Qi, you would not succeed. Take him away to some district like Zhuang and Yue (names of streets in Qi) for a few years, then even if you caned him every day to make him speak Chu, you would not succeed. You have placed Xue Juzhou near the King because you think him a good man. If everyone around the King, old or young, high or low, is a Xue Juzhou , then who will help the King to do evil? But if no one around the King is a Xue Juzhou, then who will help the King to do good? What difference can one Xue Juzhou make to the King of Song?" (*Mencius*, 3B:6. Lau's trans., 111-12)

If a child is placed among evil people all the time, there is no way for him or her to distinguish what is right from what is wrong and become a morally good person. In Susan Wolf's words, in such a situation, the child cannot have "a sane deep self."[8] By "a sane deep self" she refers to a self which contains the ability to know right from wrong and therefore enables the agent to correct and improve himself or herself. Whether one can have a sane deep self is not up to oneself, but as long as one has a sane deep self, one is a responsible agent. Therefore, Wolf believes that we who have sane deep selves may not be metaphysically responsible for ourselves in the sense that we did not create ourselves from nothing, but we are morally responsible for ourselves, because we are able to understand and appreciate

---

[8] Wolf uses the following example to make the same point Mencius shows above. Let us call Wolf's example "the example of JoJo." JoJo is the favorite son of Jo the First, an evil and sadistic dictator of a small, undeveloped country. JoJo is allowed to accompany his father and observe his daily routine. Since little JoJo takes his father as a role model, he develops values very much like his father's. When he becomes an adult, he does many of the same sorts of things his father did, including sending people to prison or to death or to torture chambers on a whim. It seems that it is not very plausible to say that JoJo is really responsible for what he has become. JoJo acts according to his desires and values, therefore he has a deep self that controls his desires and actions (see Wolf 53-54). But, unfortunately, his deep self does not have the ability to know right from wrong and therefore lacks the resources and reasons that might have served as a basis for self-correction. Wolf calls the JoJo type deep self "insane deep self" and deep selves of people who live in a normal environment "sane deep self" (see Wolf 56-59).

right and wrong, and to change our characters and our actions accordingly (Wolf 1988, 59). A sane deep self is a necessary condition for being morally responsible, and those who have insane selves are not responsible for themselves. Such a theory is in total agreement with Mencius' view that some human beings are not responsible for their moral failure since adverse external forces such as extreme poverty and bad upbringing are so overwhelming that they are not able to be morally good.

It is because of Mencius' sensitivity to the influence of the environment on one's moral development that he cares so much about social and political affairs. He advocates social changes from top down due to his belief that the best strategy for inculcating morality in society is to win over a ruler who will provide the environment necessary for moral growth.

Certainly, Mencius's view on the significance of the minimally good environment for moral growth does not accord with our intuitive and widely shared understanding of moral responsibility. According to the latter, one is morally responsible as long as one's actions and character do not directly result from coercion and involuntary movement. If such a concept of moral responsibility is correct, extreme poverty and bad upbringing cannot exempt one from being morally responsible, even though they make the formation of one's sane deep self impossible. But, this concept of moral responsibility, as Nagel points out, is deeply paradoxical. The paradox lies in this:

> A person can be morally responsible for what he does; but what he does results from a great deal that he does not do; therefore he is not morally responsible for what he is and is not responsible for. (Nagel 1979, 34)

The concept of responsibility that is so deeply paradoxical cannot provide the justification for moral blame and praise. So, to hold those who are not able to obtain a sane deep self responsible for what they are and what they do in this sense does not make them deserve blame and punishment. If the concept of responsibility ought to justify moral blame and praise, those who are not able to form a sane deep self due to external reasons are not responsible for their moral failure.

III

The discussion above shows that, in Mencius' ethics, the excusing condition for moral failure is the lack of a minimally good economic environment or the lack of a minimally good social environment for moral development. Basically, when people do not have such a minimal economic or social environment for their moral development, they are not responsible for their moral failure. Then, who is responsible, or at least mainly responsible for it? Logically, those who are in the position to create or change people's economic or social environments are responsible. To release moral responsibility from those who lack the external conditions necessary for moral development and to put heavy moral responsibility on the elite are two indispensable sides of Mencius' theory of moral responsibility. In this section, I will focus on the latter and show why members of the elite, such as rulers and intellectuals, are more responsible than are others for the wellbeing of society and people's moral development.

Chinese culture has been a culture of responsibility in the sense that it emphasizes that every person has certain responsibilities to others, to the state, and to the whole world, given his/her social role. On the one hand, to a certain degree each person is responsible for building up a good society. This idea is expressed in the old Chinese saying "Everyone has a share of the responsibility for the fate of his/her country." On the other hand, not all people are equally responsible for it. Given their special positions in society, members of the ruling class and intellectuals have heavier responsibility than other members of society have. Confucian ethics definitely represents such a way of thinking on responsibility. "Intellectuals' responsibility is heavy and their road is long" is a well-known saying from Confucius' *Analects*.[9] Both Confucius and Mencius were good examples of responsible intellectuals. They did their best to bring about desirable social changes. Although they did not have much success in it, they never gave up trying. They regard that as what they ought to do no matter whether they could attain desirable consequences.

---

[9] Confucius' *Analects*, 8:7.

One's moral responsibility needs to be understood in a social context. There is a close relation between one's responsibility and one's social role. As far as such a relation is concerned, one's responsibility might be either an activated one or a deactivated one, as Robert Neville has classified (Neville 1995, 151). A person's activated responsibilities remain with the person because they belong with the person's social role and because no one else has taken them over. A person's deactivated responsibilities are set in abeyance because other people have roles to fulfill them (ibid.).

> A primary element of social bonding is that each person serves as a token to fulfill some of the responsibilities of others; ... together the society can address the array of its obligations with some hope of success. (Neville 1995, 151)

In an ideal situation, as long as individuals take their responsibilities according to their social roles, the full range of obligations in society will be addressed. But, if the social organization fails to effectively address certain obligations, everyone's responsibilities to those obligations are activated and therefore individuals' ranges of activated responsibilities increase (ibid.). Nevertheless, one will always have those activated responsibilities derived from his/her social roles. Given the social roles of rulers, according to Confucianism, to provide people with the necessities of life and to teach people virtue are among rulers' activated responsibilities. As parents are largely responsible for their children's moral development and wellbeing, rulers are greatly responsible for the moral development and wellbeing of their people. If rulers fail to take such responsibilities, they should be morally blamed. As far as intellectuals' social roles are concerned, their activated responsibilities at least include educating the ruling class and common people to be virtuous, setting up good examples of virtue, and directly or indirectly contributing to a good government. If they fail in such responsibilities, they are morally blameworthy too. Those responsibilities of rulers and intellectuals are not just for the past and present, but more about the future. Therefore, they are prospective rather than retrospective.[10] Rulers and intellectuals have a heavy responsibility for bringing about a better society in the future. What Confucianism emphasizes is such a kind of forward-looking responsibility.

In Confucian ethics, there is no dichotomy between private and public morality. On the contrary, for Confucians, one's taking responsibilities for others and society presupposes one's being a virtuous agent. Self-cultivation is the foundation of the fulfillment of moral responsibility for society. In China, "to cultivate one's character, to regulate one's family, to govern the state well, and to make the world tranquil and happy" is a well-accepted idea from Confucianism.[11] In order to fulfill their responsibility for society, rulers and intellectuals need to take responsibility for their own moral development first. As discussed earlier, the formation of good character requires a minimally good environment and self-cultivation. Rulers and intellectuals in general do not have a problem in attaining a minimally good environment (economically and socially). Then, self-cultivation is the main issue for their moral development.

An important characteristic of Mencius' ethics is the emphasis on self-cultivation. Given a minimally good environment, it is one's responsibility to preserve and develop one's good nature and to form moral character. The growth of the goodness in one's nature requires one's constant self-effort. But, why does moral development require so much self-effort if one's nature is disposed to virtue and if one has a minimally good environment? Because there is also a part in one that may drive one to immorality. For those who have minimal environmental conditions for the satisfaction of moral development, the key to being morally well-developed is to cultivate the noble part inside (the four moral seeds) so much that the lower part becomes minimal. Although for Mencius human nature is good in the sense

---

[10] I borrow this distinction from Michael S. Moore. Moore classifies responsibility for some event in the past as "retrospective responsibility," and responsibility for the future as defined by individuals' social roles as "prospective responsibility" (see Moore, 1984, 50). It was Robert Shope who brought my attention to Moore's distinction.

[11] This idea is from the *Great Learning*. See its chapters 4-5.

that unique human qualities incline us to be moral, there is part of the innate nature of human beings that is shared with animals and that may lead to evil. What we share with animals is the lower part inside human beings. It consists of those natural desires and instincts for material and physical needs. These desires and instincts are not evil in themselves, but the pursuit of the satisfaction of them without regulation will make people part from morality. Therefore, to be virtuous, one needs to build up the nobler part of his nature and overcome the lower part. Given similar environments, the reason why some people become moral but some do not is that they do not cultivate their inner selves to the same degree. So Mencius believes:

> Those who follow the greater qualities in their nature become great men and those who follow the smaller qualities in their nature become small men. ... If we first build up the nobler part of our nature, then the inferior part cannot overcome it. It is simply this that makes a man great. (*Mencius*, 6A:15. Chan's trans, 59)

In the course of the process of growth of the innate goodness, one gains greater and greater moral strength. When one achieves a high level of moral perfection, one will obtain what Mencius called *hao ran zhi qi* (浩然之氣 flood-like *qi* or energy). Although *qi* (氣 vital energy or force) was widely used in Chinese philosophy before Mencius, *hao ran zhi qi* is a term invented by Mencius (Fung 1948, 78). According to Mencius, the flood-like *qi* is not a kind of ordinary vital force. It unites the moral ideal with physical force. It is, to the highest degree, vast and unyielding. It is accompanied by righteousness and the Way. It is produced by the accumulation of righteous deeds but not by incidental acts of righteousness (2A:2). As one's moral strength grows, one is able to perform more and more difficult moral actions. The person who has obtained flood-like *qi* will display great moral courage and be able to face great dangers for the sake of righteousness with an unmovable mind.[12] Eventually, one will be an ideally moral person like this:

---

[12] I have discussed Mencius' view on courage in detail elsewhere. See Jiang, 1997.

> When he achieves his ambition he shares these with the people; when he fails to do so he practices the Way alone. He cannot be led into excesses when wealthy, and honoured or deflected from his purpose when poor and obscure, nor can he be made to bow before superior force. This is what I would call a great man. (*Mencius*, 3B:2. Lau's trans., 107)

The morally ideal person portrayed above has been the moral inspiration of Chinese intellectuals for more than two thousand years. It still inspires and will continue to inspire the Chinese—especially Chinese intellectuals— to take moral responsibility and keep integrity under any circumstance.

Although, for Mencius, adverse external forces can make a person whose virtues have not been developed morally bad, they cannot make a truly virtuous person non-virtuous. Proper environment and education are indispensable for developing the goodness of human nature and forming good character. But once the goodness in one's nature has been well developed, and one's character has formed, one will be able to transcend the environment. The stronger the nobler part of one's nature is, the less the environmental influence. When one has achieved a high degree of moral perfection, no environment can negatively affect one's morality. That is why Mencius says "Only men of education can have a constant heart without a certain livelihood" (*Mencius*, 1A:7).[13] Furthermore, a virtuous agent may become morally stronger by overcoming and transforming adverse environments. So Mencius said:

> When Heaven is about to confer a great responsibility on any man, it will exercise his mind with suffering, subject his sinews and bones to hard work, expose his body to hunger, put him to poverty, place obstacles in the paths of his deeds, so as to stimulate his mind, harden his nature, and improve wherever he is incompetent. (*Mencius*, 6B:15. Chan's trans., 78)

Clearly, according to Mencius, a truly virtuous person will regard extreme hardship and adverse environments as a means to test and

---

[13] This is my translation from Yang's edition, but I have referred to some other translations.

strengthen his character. Therefore, as Tu puts it, "a difficult personal ordeal may turn out to be a blessing in disguise" (Tu 1976, 62). Mencius does not deny that, in general, adverse environments impede moral development. Nevertheless, negative influences of adverse environments on virtuous agents are much smaller than on other people. Furthermore, virtuous agents may turn the negative environmental forces into positive factors for moral cultivation.

When one cultivates his person so well, he is ready to take great responsibility for the world. That is why Mencius says that the virtuous person starts with self-cultivation and aims at bringing order to the world (7B:32). Deeply influenced by Confucianism, typical Chinese intellectuals from ancient times to the present always have had a strong sense of mission and responsibility. That is why most Chinese intellectuals regard bringing happiness to the people as their duty.

In general, in Mencius' ethics, sensitivity to the influence of the environment on moral development, and the emphasis on responsibility coexist without any contradiction. Meanwhile, given Mencius' belief both that all human beings have the same moral potential and that certain minimal environmental conditions are indispensable for moral development, there is no inconsistency for Mencius to hold both that all people are morally equal and that, realistically, not all people have the same degree of moral responsibility for their moral development. To minimize the inequality of this responsibility among people, improvements in economic, political, and social conditions must be made. Furthermore, those who are in the position to bring about such changes in society not only have responsibility for their own self-cultivation but also have a heavy responsibility for the world.[14]

REFERENCES

---

[14] I would like to thank Jiyuan Yu, Lawry Finsen, Robert Shope, Peimin Ni, and other readers for their valuable comments and suggestions. I am also grateful to Grand Valley State University for awarding me a faculty research grant in the late 1999 for working on this and another essay.

Chan, Wing-Tsit (trans. and complied). 1963. *A Source Book in Chinese Philosophy*, Princeton: Princeton University Press.

Fung, Yu-lan. 1948. *A Short History of Chinese Philosophy*. New York: Macmillan.

Frankfurt, Harry. 1971. "Freedom of the Will and the Concept of a Person," *Journal of Philosophy* LXVIII, 5-20.

Graham, A. C. 1967. "The Background of the Mencian Theory of Human Nature," *Qinghua Xuebao* (Qinghua Journal of Chinese Studies) 6: 215-71. Reprinted in his *Studies in Chinese Philosophy and Philosophical Literature*. Albany: State University of New York Press, 1990.

———. 1989. *Disputers of the Tao*. La Salle: Open Court.

Hansen, Chad. 1972. "Freedom and Moral Responsibility in Confucian Ethics," *Philosophy East and West* 2: 169-186.

Jiang, Xinyan. 1997. "Mencius on Human Nature and Courage," *Journal of Chinese Philosophy* 24: 265-289.

Lau, D. C. (trans.) 1970. *Mencius*. London, Penguin.

Moore, Michael S. 1984. *Law and Psychiatry*. Cambridge: Cambridge University Press.

Nagel, Thomas. 1979. "Moral Luck," In his *Mortal Questions*. Cambridge: Cambridge University Press.

Neville, Robert Cummings. 1995. *Normative Cultures*. Albany: State University of New York Press.

Taylor, Charles. 1976. "Responsibility for Self," in A. E. Rorty ed. *The Identity of Persons*. Berkeley: University of California Press.

Tu, Wei-ming. 1976. *Humanities and Self-Cultivation: Essays on Confucian Thought*. Berkeley: Asian Humanities Press.

Watson, Gary. 1975. "Free Agency," *Journal of Philosophy* LXVII, 205-20.

Williams, Bernard. 1980. "Moral Luck." In his *Moral Luck*. Cambridge University Press.

Wolf, Susan. 1987. "Sanity and the Metaphysics of Responsibility." In *Responsibility, Character, and the Emotions: New Essays in Moral Psychology*, edited by Ferdinand David Schoeman. New York: Cambridge University Press.

Yang, Po-Chun (ed. and complied). 1984. *Meng Tzu Yi Zhu*. Hong Kong: Zhong Hua Shu Ju, Hong Kong Ltd.

Zhu, Xi (edited and annotated). 1985. *Great Learning.* In Zhu Xi (edited and annotated). *Collected Commentaries on the Four Books.* Rerprint. Changsha, China: Yuelü Press.

7

Can *Shu* Be the One Word that Serves as the Guiding Principle of Caring Actions?

Sin Yee Chan

In this paper, I aim to explicate the meaning of the Confucian concept of *shu* (reciprocity 恕) and show how it can be applied in the ethics of care, as described by some feminist theorists (Gilligan 1982). *Shu* is explained as "what one does not want, do not do to others" (*Analects* 15:23).[1] Confucius refers to it as the one word that can serve as the guiding principle of conduct throughout life (*Analects* 15:23). And Confucius' disciple Zhengzi describes *shu*, together with the virtue loyalty (*zhong*), as the one thread that runs through Confucius' doctrine(*Analects* 4:15).[2]

I believe that *shu* also sheds interesting light on one significant issue in the ethics of care: When caring for another person, should we go by her perspective or ours in deciding what to do on her

---

[1] Thus *shu* is often compared to the Christian Golden rule. The comparison however is complicated by the fact that the Golden Rule itself is subject to numerous interpretations. For example, it has been variously seen as expressing the Universalization Principle (Sidgwick 1962, 379-380); as only about the general principles the agent accepts, and not about her particular wishes or desires (Singer 1963, 293-314); and as about proscriptions of our actions towards strangers and generalizations about human needs and desires (Thomas 1996, 271-294). For a comparison between *shu* and the Golden Rule, see Allison 1992.

[2] Bruce and Taeko Brooks challenge the authorship of the *Analects* (Brooks 1998). In this paper, I do not intend to address this intriguing question and shall just assume that the *Analects* largely reflects the thoughts of Confucius rather than those of his successors.

behalf?[3] The question poses a dilemma. On the one hand, if we follow our own perspective, we may be acting paternalistically without giving due regard to the autonomy of the cared-for. On the other hand, if we follow the perspective of the cared-for blindly, we may not be really benefiting the cared-for. Furthermore, it could be argued, we would sacrifice our autonomy and be reduced to mere tools, as we would no longer be guided by our best judgment of what should be done.

Shu can help us on this question. For *shu*, as I shall show, implies the affirmation of both the perspective of the caring agent and that of the cared-for, but assigns a priority to the former.

This paper has two goals. The first and main goal is to provide a philosophical analysis of the meaning of *shu*. Specifically, I aim to defend and further develop Herbert Fingarette's insightful interpretation of *shu* as *identifying with another person while remaining her critic* (Fingarette 1980, 373-405). I shall base my analysis on the text of the *Analects*. The second goal of the paper is to show how *shu* can offer a viable solution to the question mentioned above. However, my work in this regard is programmatic and meant primarily to point to a promising direction for further exploration.

I. The Meaning of "Shu"

1. *Shu*: Positive and Negative Analogical Thinking

The concept of *shu* in the *Analects* refers to a method of moral thinking. More specifically, *shu* is a kind of *analogical thinking*: taking oneself as a measure when one decides how one should treat others. However, it is not very clear whether *shu* refers only to negative analogical thinking, i.e. thinking about what one should *not* do to others when one takes oneself as a measure for them, or whether it also includes positive analogical thinking, i.e. thinking about what one

---

[3] Following Nel Noddings, I shall call the person whom we care for the cared-for. (Noddings 1984).

should do to others when one takes oneself as a measure for them.[4] What is obvious, nevertheless, is that Confucius assigns equivalent roles to negative and positive analogical thinking. Both are used to explicate the Confucian ideal virtue of *ren* (benevolence):

> #1. Confucius said, ".... A man of *ren* (benevolence), wishing to establish himself, also establishes others, and wishing to be prominent himself, also helps others to be prominent. To be able to draw upon what is close as an analogy is called the method of *ren* (benevolence)." (*Analects* 6:28)

> #2. Zhonggong asked about *ren* (benevolence). Confucius said, "When you go abroad, behave to everyone as if you were receiving a big guest.... What you do not want, do not do to others." (*Analects* 12:2)

Since the discussions I make in this paper hinge only on Confucian analogical thinking, but not on whether it is positively or negatively formulated; and given that positive and negative analogical thinking, philosophically speaking, express the same basic ideas; for the sake of simplicity, I will use the term *shu* to cover both types of analogical thinking.

2. *Shu*: Reversibility or Projection of One's Preference onto Others?

Shu is also concerned with reversibility: one will do to others only what one oneself would be willing to accept if the positions were reversed. The following passage highlights the recipient's position:

> #3. Zhilu said, "What I do not want others to inflict upon me, I do not want to inflict upon others." (*Analects* 5:11)

---

[4] Both Feng Youlan and Robert Allison believe that *shu* is only about negative analogical thinking. See Feng 1953 and Allison 1982.

Yet one may argue that a literal reading of passages #2 and #3 together seems to suggest an alternative interpretation of *shu*: only ne*gative* analogical thinking involves *reversibility*. *Positive* analogical thinking means *projecting* one's own *selected* preferences (e.g. the desire to establish oneself and the desire to be prominent) onto others, *without imagining oneself in the recipient's position*. This interpretation makes sense, one may argue, because in case of proscriptions (negative analogical thinking), if one errs and one's dislikes do not match those of the other person, the worst is that one abstains from beneficial actions. But when a mismatch occurs in case of prescriptions (positive analogical thinking), one may actually inflict harm on the other person.[5] Since inflicting harm is, in general, much worse than withholding benefit, caution advises more restrictions on positive analogical thinking. Hence one should only project *selected* preferences onto others. Negative analogical thinking, on the other hand, need only be conditioned by the hypothetical position of the receiving end.

However, even if we assume that proscriptions and prescriptions have different implications, a stronger emphasis on the use of negative analogical thinking, as compared to positive analogical thinking, should be cautious enough. It is not necessary to assign to positive analogical thinking a radically different meaning from negative analogical thinking. And we do see a predilection in favor of negative analogical thinking in the *Analects*. In contrast to three passages on negative analogical thinking (*Analects* 15:23, 12:2, 5:11), there is only one passage (#1) on positive analogical thinking.

Moreover, if positive analogical thinking meant projecting one's *selected* preferences onto others, then presumably, Confucius would have given us a list of projectible desires. But he did not. More basically, if there were such a list, analogical thinking would be made redundant. For we would know what to do by following the desires on the list. But Confucius does allude to analogical thinking

---

[5] This is also the reason Allison gives for saying that *shu* only involves negative analogical thinking. See Allison 1982.

immediately after he exhorts us to help others to become prominent if we want to be prominent ourselves (passage #1).

Since there is only one passage about positive analogical thinking, perhaps we should not read the passage too literally. For the sake of theoretical consistency and simplicity, and with no strong evidence to suggest otherwise, we should perhaps take *shu* as meaning the same thing for both positive and negative analogical thinking: it involves reversibility.

3. *Shu*: Reversibility—With or Without Imagining Oneself in The Other Person's Position

What exactly does it mean to say that we imagine ourselves at the receiving end? Does it mean something like "I imagine myself *as I am now* at the receiving end?" Or does it mean "I imagine myself *in the position of Ann*, the actual recipient of the proposed action?" In brief, the question is whether *shu* involves imagining oneself in *the other person's* position or not.[6] And does this matter?

Certainly it does. When one contemplates an action, one considers its morally relevant features such as consequences, practicability, social meanings, etc. But what is counted as relevant depends upon the specifics of one's own position, i.e., on factors such as one's circumstances, aptitudes, past experiences, values, etc.[7] For example, the sugar content of a meal is an extremely significant feature to a diabetic, but not to me. Now the point of assuming the reversed position is to see if one would be willing to accept the action, with its full implications, if one were at the receiving end. And since the implications of the action are mediated through one's position, one cannot judge them correctly without imagining oneself

---

[6] I am indebted to David Christensen for drawing my attention to this distinction between imagining oneself at the receiving end and imagining oneself in the position of the person who is the recipient of the action.

[7] I will discuss in detail the meaning of imagining in the other person's position later.

in the situation of the actual recipient. When considering serving a meal to a diabetic, I therefore should imagine myself in the position of a diabetic.

One may object that no passage about *shu* contains any explicit reference to the idea of imagining oneself in the other person's position. Furthermore, Confucius believes in universal human nature: "By nature, men are alike. Through practice, they have become far apart" (*Analects* 17:2). If people share the same nature, then perhaps they would have the same preferences and there would be no need to imagine oneself in another's position.

Yet universal nature, at best, only implies consensus on basic preferences (for example, health). Given people's different situations (for example, the difference between a diabetic and a non-diabetic), there is no reason to expect that consensus will be carried over to specific or secondary preferences (for example, diet) as well.

And Confucius does recognize the divergence between people's situations. The *Analects* points to the necessity of fine-tuning one's actions to fit one's social roles. The different social roles of fathers and sons, for example, determine different ways for dissenting opinion to be expressed. And Confucius himself interacts with his students according to their distinct temperaments (*The Analects* 1:15, 5:7; Lau 1979, Appendix: 2). Hence, reversibility in *shu* should include imagining oneself in another's position.[8]

4. Three Interpretations of "Putting Oneself in Another's Shoes"

So what does the *position* of the actual recipient include?

We can distinguish three interpretations. The first is that one should take into account *only the objective circumstantial features* of another's situation such as whether it is an emergency. In the context of Confucius' philosophy, one needs especially to consider things

---

[8] Most interpreters agree that *shu* involves imagining oneself in others' positions. See e.g. Nivison 1996, Ivanhoe 1990, and Lau 1979. However, Nivison and Ivanhoe believe that *shu* is the prerogative of social superiors in dealing with their subordinates, a view which I disagree.

such as social roles and the relevance of *li* (rules of propriety). In this interpretation, one *ignores the subjective features* such as values, beliefs, desires, dispositions, temperaments, commitments, tastes, etc. Consequently, one simply analyzes the situation according to one's own beliefs/desires/values. For example, imagining myself in the position of my friend who is in a financial crisis due to misfortune, I find that I would want my friends to give me generous material and moral support. In doing so, I do not consult my knowledge of my friend's character or her present psychological inclinations.

But this interpretation seems inadequate. The full effects of an action on a person are mediated through the subjective features about the person as well. Sometimes, whether an action (e.g. a kiss) benefits or harms a person depends on whether she loves or loathes it. And, once again, Confucius acknowledges subjective differences between people. For example, considering two students' differences in temperament, he advises one to immediately put into practice what he has heard, but warns another against doing the same thing (*Analects* 11:22). And he often asks students to express their own aspirations (*Analects* 5:26, 11:24).

Both the second and third suggestions count subjective as well as objective factors. And both recommend that one do so by *identifying* with the other person in the situation: imagining oneself as the other person, or taking the other person as one's hypothetical self. If I am deciding how I should treat Ann, I should first imagine that I am Ann. Such identification involves vicariously imagining her feelings and judgments.[9]

Now according to the second suggestion, putting oneself in another's shoes requires one to identify with the other person and react to the situation confronting her from *her* perspective.[10] What one would want to be done to oneself then is *what one's hypothetical self, i.e. the other person, wants to be done to herself in that situation.* For example,

---

[9] D. C. Lau (1979, 16) and Robert Eno (1990, 68) seem to hold this view.

[10] By perspective, I include the conglomeration of a variety of psychological states such as perceptions, beliefs, judgments, desires, values, and attitudes.

your daughter is a freshman in college. After failing several of her classes, she thinks that she lacks the intellectual caliber to pursue her dream career as a lawyer. Her reaction is withdrawal, depression and confusion. Under the second suggestion, you would therefore feel depressed and want to be left alone as she does.

According to the third suggestion, which follows Fingarette's interpretation of *shu* (Fingarette 1980, 384),[11] one also identifies with the other person. But instead of just reacting from the perspective of the other person, one criticizes it based on one's own perspective. In this way, *one takes one's own perspective as authoritative.* By one's own perspective, I mean one's present perspective, although it may have been altered by the experience of the imaginative exercise. For example, a man imagining himself as his wife may change his sexist belief that a woman's place is in the home. In brief, under the third suggestion, what one wants to be done to oneself *is what one would want to be done to one's hypothetical self after assuming and then criticizing the perspective of the hypothetical self from one's own perspective.*[12]

Let us return to the example of the daughter in college. Imagine that, contrary to your daughter, you value flexibility about aspirations and believe that performance in the first semester is not a reliable indicator of a person's intellectual ability, as the person may still be making adjustments to college life. Under the third suggestion, instead of feeling depressed, you would want for your hypothetical self sympathy, affirmation of her intellectual ability, and a challenge that she reconsider having rigid aspirations.

The third interpretation is the best interpretation. One appeal of the first interpretation is that by blocking out all subjective factors, it precludes the influence of problematic subjective features like false beliefs and perverse desires. However, it also throws the baby out with the bath water by excluding even relevant subjective features.

---

[11] Fingarette describes *shu* as involving two steps: (i) "I must imagine being you" and (ii) "To ask what I, Fingarette, would want, being that person in that situation." The second step therefore involves oneself being the critic of the other self.

[12] This is analogous to Peter Railton's suggestion that a person's good is what a fully-informed counterpart of that person would want *for her less-informed self.* See Railton 1986, 163-207.

The second interpretation reverses the advantages and disadvantages of the first interpretation by indiscriminately including all subjective features. In contrast, the third interpretation acknowledges the importance of subjective features. But through its recommendation of criticizing another's perspective, it also encourages one to weed out those subjective features that one finds problematic.

Moreover, the third suggestion seems more true to the spirit of analogical thinking in the sense of taking oneself as the measure for others. For it allows one's perspective to be authoritative in the imaginative exercise. In contrast, the second interpretation is merely about vicarious understanding, and its dictum, "Do unto others as *they* want to be done to them," is a far cry from, "Do to others as *you* would want to be done to you." Finally, the third interpretation, which emphasizes independent evaluation, coheres with Confucius' idea that an agent must critically evaluate others' perspectives. Confucius recommends making remonstrance against superiors (*Analects* 4:18, 18:1, 19:10), as well as giving advice to peers (*Analects* 14:7; 1:4).

5. *Shu* and *Ren* (benevolence), *Li* (propriety) and *Yi* (rightness)

To fully establish the third interpretation, we should see how it coheres with the other major Confucian philosophical concepts.

Shu and *Ren*

Ren (benevolence) in the *Analects* refers to an ethical ideal that encompasses many virtues such as courage, wisdom, integrity, respect ... etc. Among the various virtues, love or benevolence can be seen as quintessential. When asked about *ren*, Confucius says, "Love your fellow men" (*Analects* 12:22). In the same vein, affection for kin is emphasized. Filial piety and respect for one's elderly brother are taken as the root of practicing *ren* (*Analects* 1:2).

Confucius describes *shu* as the method of *ren* (*Analects* 6:30). Under our interpretation, it is obvious that *shu* is a method that yields a specific guide to actions. The question is whether it is a method of practicing *ren*. I think it is. For the method of *shu* involves one's identification with others: treating others as one's hypothetical self. Since one loves oneself, the identification implies that one should also love others. Furthermore as *shu* involves vivid visceral understanding, it enables an intimate emotional concern and sympathy for others. Consequently, the love involved is not some kind of unemotional will to benefit, as found in Mozi 's universal love (Graham 1989, 4). In this way, *shu* can be seen as capturing *ren*'s quintessential ingredient of love/benevolence.[13]

Shu and *Li*

It is unclear in the *Analects* whether *li* (propriety) refers only to rituals/ceremonial rules, or more generally to rules governing proper behavior in all contexts.[14] Whichever the interpretation, *li* provides concrete guidance to actions for a Confucian agent. *Li* therefore can also be described as a method of *ren*. However, this need not raise any problem about our interpretation of *shu*.

For Confucius can prescribe both *li* and *shu* as plural methods for practicing *ren*. *Shu* can supplement *li* in the following way. Since *li* embodies specific values, following it strictly implies inflexibility and inability to deal with all kinds of situations. Therefore, sometimes we need to use our discretion, or *quan* (weighing), to temper the rules. *Shu* under our interpretation can be seen as one specific way to *quan*.[15] Moreover, when we want an additional independent standard to check whether our behavior is appropriate, or when we want to arbitrate among rules of *li* when they come into conflict, we can also appeal to something like our notion of *shu*.

---

[13] Both Nivison and Fingarette give similar reasons for their claims that *shu* captures the spirit of *ren*. To Nivison, *shu* leads to the affirmation of common humanity and treating others like persons and not mere tools (see Nivison 1996, 76). Fingarette thinks that *shu* helps one to see others as "mon frere, mon semblable," highlighting the value of shared existence (see Fingarette 1980, 391).

[14] For the first view, see Graham 1989, 11. For the second view, see Benjamin Schwartz 1985, 67-68.

[15] Both Fingarette and Ivanhoe take tempering *li* as the main function of *shu*.

Perhaps there is another worry. Would Confucius prescribe something like our notion of *shu* given his prescription of *li?* We may have this question because the two prescriptions seem to be of diametrically different nature. *Li* emphasizes guidance that is external to the agent. In following *li*, the agent's input is minimal and confined merely to interpreting the rules and judging about their applicability to the situation. In most cases the agent plays no role in deciding about the content of the rules. On the other hand, *shu* in our interpretation assigns much more discretion to the agent. It allows the agent to follow her own desires and judgments in deciding what to do. Put differently, following *li* at best only amounts to an autonomous *ratification* of *li*. Following *shu*, on the other hand, may constitute an autonomous *initiation* of a principle for oneself. *Shu* embodies a greater extent of autonomy than *li*. Given their diverse orientations, one may wonder whether Confucius' explicit and unambivalent commitment to *li* is coherent with a recommendation to follow something like our notion of *shu*.

However, this worry can be put aside. There is incoherence only if prescribing *li* were meant to curb an agent's autonomy and prescribing our notion of *shu* were to facilitate a full expression of autonomy. But I believe that is not the case. Whether Confucius appreciates the intrinsic value of autonomy or not, he does not seem to show a distrust of autonomy in the sense of making independent judgment about what should be done. The rationale of prescribing *li* is not about checking one's autonomy. It is about internalizing *li*, which helps to nurture an attitude of respect (*jing*) and cultivate refinement (*wen*). Similarly, prescription of *shu* is about cultivating some other values, namely empathy and co-humanity. Since the virtues induced respectively by *li* and *shu* are consistent with each other, there is no incoherence in the prescription to follow both *li* and *shu*.

Shu and *Yi*

In the *Analects*, though *ren* (benevolence) is sometimes used to describe actions, it is mainly used to describe persons. *Yi* (rightness) is the word used to describe proper actions, especially actions which befit one's social roles, or are required by duty in a situation (Graham 1989, 11; Munro 1969,51). However, to find out what befits one's social roles or is required by duty we need to consider the variegated elements pertaining to a situation. *Shu* provides the means to make a proper consideration of these various factors. In other words, *shu* is a means to find out the content of an *yi* action.

6. *Shu*: Taking One's Own Perspective as Authoritative When Imagining Oneself in Another's Position: A Proposal

To recapitulate, *shu* involves imagining oneself in another's position, or taking another person as one's hypothetical self, and then takes one's own perspective as authoritative in criticizing the perspective of the other person. The question now is how such a critique should proceed. Since the text is mute on this issue, I would therefore propose a way to conduct the critique that I believe reflects the following relevant important values in Confucius' philosophy: benevolence (the promotion of others' interest), autonomy, and integrity tempered by the flexibility to make necessary concessions. Since the promotion of others' interests is an obvious value, I need to explain only the other values.

Autonomy:[16] Confucius always encourages his students to make their own judgments and praises students who take the initiative to think for themselves (*Analects* 7:8). And when they judge or choose wrongly, he criticizes but seldom interferes with their carrying out their choices (*Analects* 17:19, 5:26, 11:24).

Integrity: Confucius constantly warns against serving rulers who do not follow the Dao. For this would violate one's commitment to pursue the Dao (*Analects* 8:13, 14:3). He praises Bo Yi and Shu Qi, who starved themselves to death rather than betray their loyalty, as "not lowering their purpose or allowing themselves to be humiliated" (*Analects* 18:8).

---

[16] It is unclear whether Confucius values autonomy intrinsically, but we need not settle the issue here.

Flexibility: Being sensitive to the intricacies of situations, Confucius believes that sometimes one is justified in making concessions (in the sense of compromising one's integrity) for good reasons.[17] In the same passage that he praises Bo Yi and Shu Qi, he endorses the action of Liu Xiahui and Shao Lian who have "lowered their purpose and allowed themselves to be humiliated;" for they took office under bad rulers for the purpose of doing good to the people. His willingness to concede is obvious in his advice that when a person's remonstrance against his parents fails, he should still "resume an attitude of reverence and not abandon his effort to serve them. He may feel worried but does not complain" (*Analects* 4:18).

And the concession is not made only to one's social superiors. In discussing cases of stealing sheep, Confucius comments, "Fathers cover up for their sons, and sons cover up for their fathers. Straightness is to be found in such behavior" (*Analects* 13:18). Certainly, Confucius is not talking about fathers and sons who are accomplices. Rather, we can imagine that the one who does the cover-up is indeed sacrificing his integrity. To justify such compromise requires a strong reason, such as the need not to betray an important relationship. Whatever the reason(s), the point remains that sometimes concessions can be justified.

Taking into account these Confucian values, my proposal runs as follows:

First of all, to bring in one's own perspective as the authoritative perspective, one should bring in only beliefs[18]/desires/values that one *identifies with* and not those that one *merely has*. Beliefs/desires/values that one identifies with both motivate and have

---

[17] I am following Bernard Williams's interpretation of integrity as acting in such a way as to adhere to one's commitments. According to Williams, one's integrity is violated if one acts against one's deeply cherished principles, though all things considered, one may endorse the violation. See Williams 1981, 1-19.

[18] By beliefs, I mean both factual and evaluative beliefs.

one's *approval.*[19] Beliefs/desires/values that one merely has motivate as well. But they lack one's approval. In some cases, one may even want to do away with them. For example, a drug addict may identify with her desire to be healthy but reject her desire to have drugs, though the latter may be considerably more motivating than the former. Since only the beliefs/desires/values one identifies with truly represent one's best judgment, only they should serve as one's evaluation basis.

Thus a Rawlsian liberal would base her critique on the values of autonomy and equal respect for people, and a devout Christian fundamentalist on her Christian values. Still, both share some values that are less substantive than these—values that are more appropriately treated as instrumental in optimizing the efficiency of the hypothetical selves in achieving their desires. For example, they may hold it important to scrutinize the accuracy of the factual beliefs and seek the consistency among the values of the hypothesis.

Next, if one finds that some of the beliefs/desires/values of the hypothetical self diverge from one's own, one needs to determine if the divergence is a *conflict* or a *difference*. If they conflict with one's own, they will be considered as wrong (not necessarily in the moral sense) in light of one's own. But they will not be so judged if they are merely different.

One way in which people's beliefs/desires/values conflict is when there is a logical inconsistency between them. For example, belief in moral equality among humans conflicts with certain racist beliefs. On the other hand, beliefs/desires/values can be logically compatible with each other though they are different. The desire to develop one's artistic ability is logically compatible with, but different from, the desire to develop one's philosophical ability. Such different desires may still be unattainable simultaneously because of limitations on one's time, energy, and resources.

Alternatively, people may have shared beliefs/desires/values, but their divergence in the ranking of those beliefs/desires/values

---

[19] The approval can be hypothetical, not necessarily actual. For some of our desires may not be the objects of our conscious reflection, but they nevertheless would have our approval if we were to reflect upon them.

may still constitute a conflict. My opinion may conflict with yours if what I consider as most important is judged as least important by you. But whether it is a case of conflict or not perhaps defies a clear-cut answer and depends on factors such as the extent of divergence and the subject matter, as well as the individuals concerned. For example, in our ranking of artistic merits, only substantial divergence constitutes a conflict. However, in the debates between the environmentalists and the people in the lumber industry, a slight difference in priority sparks off serious fighting. For our purpose, it suffices to note that divergence in the ranking of things sometimes can be a matter of conflict.[20]

If one has determined that there is a case of conflict, one can then and *only then* take one's own beliefs/desires/values as guidance in determining what should be done. In case of difference, however, one should go by the beliefs/desires/values of the hypothetical self.

The rationale is as follows: The beliefs/desires/values of the hypothetical self should have a prima facie claim on our consideration. For one thing, forgoing these mental states involves costs. Not being able to pursue her beliefs/desires/values causes pain or at least discomfort to the hypothetical self. And it takes time and energy to help the hypothetical self to cultivate new beliefs/desires/values even if doing so is feasible and desirable. Furthermore, since beliefs/desires/values are often justified relative to the particular circumstances and constitution of an individual, it is reasonable to assume them to be apt for the person concerned, unless proven otherwise. Finally, to respect the autonomy of the hypothetical self, one should respect her beliefs/desires/values.

This prima facie claim should be overridden, however, and one's own beliefs/desires/values should guide one's action on the other's behalf, when those of the hypothetical self are *judged to be wrong* in the

---

[20] Note that divergence in ranking of values apply only to shared values and not to relative values. If my value properly described is "skiing-for-me," rather than "skiing," then it is only a relative value. And I share a value with another person only when, for example, both of our values are "skiing," instead of "skiing-for-me" and "skiing-for-her."

light of one's own. To allow oneself to be guided by these wrong beliefs/values/desires will only, in one's own judgment, set the hypothetical self on the wrong path, hence doing her a disservice instead of helping her. Also pursuing what oneself finds wrong violates one's own integrity. If I disapprove of the judgment of my hypothetical self on the issue of her right to euthanasia, I should not be required to go by it and help her to have euthanasia. Otherwise, my integrity would be violated and I would be, in my judgment, doing her a disservice rather than benefitting her.

Indeed, concern for one's integrity complicates the issue of how to deal with the different (but not conflicting) beliefs/desires/values of one's hypothetical self as well. Even though these mental states are not judged to be wrong, going by them may still violate one's integrity if doing so involves running against one's deep commitment(s). For example, while I do not judge the infliction of mild physical punishment on children to be wrong, it is also my principle not to physically discipline a child myself. Thus if my hypothetical self believes in physical discipline, I should allow and not criticize her for following her belief *herself*, all other things equal. I may even act in ways that can be seen as legitimizing her practices: I console her child after the punishment and warn him not to commit the wrong again but do not criticize his mother's action. However, guarding my integrity, I cannot involve myself too much in helping her to implement her beliefs. For example, I cannot comply with her request to execute the punishment on her behalf, if left with the responsibility to care for the child.

To recapitulate, one criticizes the perspective of the hypothetical self based on the beliefs/desires/values one identifies with oneself. When they diverge from the beliefs/desires/values of one's hypothetical self, the former should guide in case of conflicts and the latter in case of difference, provided that doing so does not violate one's own integrity. In case where one's integrity is threatened, one should allow the hypothetical self to pursue her beliefs/desires/values herself, but draw a limit to the assistance one is willing to provide.

Now we come to the final step of the critique: we have to fine-tune the claim that one should not be guided by the beliefs/desires/values of one's hypothetical self that one judges to be wrong, or that threaten one's integrity. What I have said so far seems close to the truth. But we should note that in some cases, one does need to compromise and go by these problematic beliefs/desires/values. One should treat them in the same way as one treats the beliefs/desires/values that one merely has but disapproves of. For example, whether it is one's own addiction to smoking or the sexist beliefs of one's hypothetical self, the disapproved belief/value/desire might still exert strong motivational force and be so deeply rooted in the concerned person's psychological structure that it is, in a sense, part of her. Consequently, as one should tolerate one's own instances of weakness of will and irrationality in going by the beliefs/desires/values that one disapproves of, one needs to concede to the problematic beliefs/desires/values of one's hypothetical self sometimes. For example, as much as I tolerate my own caving in to smoking, I should also tolerate the sexism-based self-image of my hypothetical self as a sacrificing mother. Consequently I might need to help her find a part-time, instead of a full-time job as she cannot bear to leave her baby for a long period of time.

Concessions can be costly. Going too far, one may have to relinquish one's own ideal or suffer psychological damages such as alienation. Nevertheless, if appropriately made, concessions need not be inherently problematic. And more importantly, in deciding the extent of concession, one should apply the same standard to oneself and to one's hypothetical self.

II. *Shu* and Caring

The application of *shu* in the context of caring seems a natural step. Like the Judeo-Christian saying, "love thy neighbor as thyself" (Leviticus 19:18), *shu* pertains to attitudes. It is not merely about extending identical treatment to everyone as the Kantian principle of universalization is. For, as we have seen, since *shu* involves taking another as one's hypothetical self, it therefore implies *favorable attitudes* toward another, such as caring for and loving her as one generally loves and cares for oneself. Consequently, actions following the prescriptions of *shu* can be seen as caring actions aiming to benefit others.[21]

Moreover, care ethicists often emphasize the role of emotions and contextual thinking in deliberation about caring (Gilligan 1982, 100-105). *Shu* asks us to vicariously *feel* what others *feel*, and not merely take cognitive note of what they think. In this way, *shu* calls for the full utilization of our emotions and not merely our intellectual analytical skills. It also requires contextual thinking by asking us to seek an intimate grasp of another's particular situation.

Specifically, *shu* might shed light on an important question in the ethics of care: in caring for another, how should we decide what to do? Swayed by our modern society's focus on individual autonomy, we, as caring agents, may tend to refrain from pushing forward our own perspective or even from helping action altogether. Hence some care ethicists make the following kind of recommendations:

> Trying to end a friend's pain, or to remove its source, encourages violation: by acting for her because we believe we are in a better position than she to handle the problem, we undermine her process and set aside her integrity. In other words, we indulge in paternalistic thinking.... I want to suggest that attending our friend in her pain, lending support, but not intervening to control.... If I focus on her and attend her process, she realizes that someone else understands what she is going through and this in itself is empowering. This is not to say that friends make no judgments in the situation.... Nor is this to say that the friends should never do anything (for example, when a lesbian asks for help in a custody case/ or in a case of job discrimination).... Thus

---

[21] We should note that *shu* does not imply *actually* according equal weight to one's own interests and those of one's hypothetical self. For *shu* only implies impartiality. And neither actual equivalent treatment nor actual equivalent consideration of interests follows from impartiality. Only application of the same standard does. An impartial teacher need not give every student the same grade. Similarly, impartiality in *shu* only implies applying the same standard to oneself and one's hypothetical self: using one's best judgment to decide what is the good for the person concerned. In this way, *shu* can allow me, for example, to give more weight to my mother's interests than mine when I consider that mothers merit gratitude from their children, especially aging mothers whose days of happiness are numbered.

we might choose to intervene for a friend, but we would do so only in very dangerous situations. (Hoagland 1988, 126-129)

Caring involves, for the one-caring, a "feeling-with" the other... The notion of "feeling-with" that I have outlined does not involve projection but reception. I have called it "engrossment." I do not "put myself in the others' shoes" so to speak, by analyzing his reality as objective data and then asking "How would I feel in such situation?" .... I do not project; I receive the other into myself, and I see and feel with the other.... (In engrossment) we enter into a feeling mode.... we receive what-is-there as nearly as possible without evaluation or assessment.... I allow my motive energy to be shared; I put it at the service of the other.... When this displacement occurs in the extreme form, we sometimes hear parents speak of "living for their children." (Noddings 1984, 30-31,33-34)

Ironically, these suggestions run directly counter to some of the central values in Gilligan's vision of ethics of care. The first suggestion by Hoagland overlooks Gilligan's criticisms of the so-called ethics of rights for its overemphasis on autonomy and independence. To Gilligan, such emphasis leads to a morality of non-interference, indifference, and individualism (Gilligan 1982, 22). In contrast, an ideal ethics of care balances independence and autonomy with interconnectedness and responsibility for the well-being of others. Hence, one should be ready to act on their behalf. Recognizing the problem of overprotection and infantilization of the cared-for should make us be cautious of, but not abstain entirely from, *initiating* helping actions. Hoagland suggests falsely that to be a sympathetic adviser or to be a paternalistic intervener are the exhaustive alternatives. She overlooks another alternative: to be an active caring agent while respecting the autonomy of the cared-for. Imagine that my close friend has just undergone a divorce. If I propose to do some errands for her and spend time with her children, am I acting paternalistically? I do not think so. There is a big gap between taking the initiative and forcing someone to go along with it. Indeed, depending on situations, the caring agent can be a team member, an assistant, or even a mentor to the cared-for.

Similarly, Noddings overlooks Gilligan's stress on the independence of the caring agent. Gilligan points out that when women understand their own identities as caring persons, they often feel impotent, confused, and untrue to themselves. This is because they suppress their independent selves by giving up their own legitimate claims or interests and *relinquishing their evaluations* of situations (Gilligan 1982, 128-150). Moreover, Gilligan includes recognizing the need for *personal integrity* as part of the moral vision of a mature woman (Gilligan 1982, 149). But if our caring actions are guided entirely by the perspective of the cared-for as Noddings suggests, we would be relinquishing our independence in judgment and, in some cases, even our integrity. It would hardly be right, for example, to lend money to our friend to buy cocaine just because she likes it.

But we do not need to refrain generally from initiating helping actions if we follow *shu*. For we can make contextual judgments and vividly grasp factors such as the importance of another's interests, her usual level of autonomy, her views about self-reliance, and the standing relationship between us and her. Consequently, we can decide whether to take positive actions on behalf of another. In this way, *shu* allows active caring.

Furthermore, since *shu* prohibits the caring agent from blindly following the perspective of the cared-for, it has two positive implications. First, we can avoid the problem of loss of independence of the caring agent. For *shu* requires the agent to make her own judgment and take it as authoritative.

Second, *shu* helps to ensure the promotion of the interests of the other person. Following *shu*, we are encouraged to grasp the perspective of the other person. Having this information is important because, in general, she is best positioned to know and care about her own interests. But this is not always the case. For she may be irrational and/or not well informed enough to know what is in her best interests. For instance, she may prefer smoking only because she is ignorant of the addictive effects of cigarettes. It may be argued, therefore, that *shu* allows us to better ensure another's interests by recommending us both to recognize and evaluate the other person's perspective.

One might object by pointing to cases where one has beliefs/desires/values inferior to those of the other person. We can imagine a reversal of values between the freshman daughter and her parent in our previous example. Moreover, Mill's point that people are the best judge of their own interests is generally true. Hence, *shu* implies the risk of rendering a disservice rather than a help to the other person by allowing us to impose our inferior perspective on her.

However, one may not be a better judge of one's own interests than another person, if, for example, the other party is in a better epistemic position. And it could be argued that, in the case of *shu*, the caring person *is* in a more privileged epistemic position than the cared-for person. For she has access to more data than the latter. She grasps two perspectives, her own and that of the other person, while the latter only considers things from one perspective.

Moreover, we should also note that the moral of Mill's point should be a presumption of validity, not infallibility, with regard to the other person's perspective. That is, one should assume the other person's perspective to be valid unless there is *clear evidence* of its being otherwise. This, however, does not preclude the critical evaluation of the other person's perspective as implied by *shu*. What is required, though, is that the caring person follow a much more stringent standard in evaluating the evidence grounding her judgments when she decides about actions on the other person's behalf than when she decides about actions on other occasions. Doing so will help her to ensure that she has clear evidence for the wrongness of the other person's perspective if she decides to act contrary to it. Of course, the risk of allowing the caring person to impose her inferior perspective on the other person remains. But it would certainly be much reduced if the procedures described were followed carefully.

1. Problems with *Shu*

Before I conclude, I would like to briefly mention two problems of *shu*. First, since *shu* recommends that one take one's own perspective as the ultimate evaluative standard, this may result in the imposition of one's perspective on others, hence not respecting their autonomy. I might discourage my sister from engaging in sports just because I, myself, see no value in them.

Certainly one's perspective may be revised through the imaginative exercise, and *shu* prescribes one to follow the other person's perspective when it differs from but does not conflict with one's own. But whether it is a case of conflict or mere difference is still judged from one's own perspective. If I am a Rawlsian liberal, respecting people's varying conceptions of a good life, I take my personal ideal of personal development as a value relative to myself, which therefore does not conflict with someone else's ideal of a laid-back life. But if I embrace the ideal of "survival of the fittest" as an absolutist value which applies to everyone alike, my ideal then would conflict with that of a laid-back life. Thus there is no strong guarantee for the respect of others' autonomy.

Another problem is that *shu* does not always provide enough guidance for doing the morally *right* thing, as opposed to the merely caring action. Caring actions are not always the same as morally right actions.[22] Imagine that I am a German Nazi. My close friend seeks my help to shelter her Jewish lover. Following *shu*, I can imagine her desperation and her deep attachment to her lover. However, if my Nazi beliefs are not shaken by the imaginative exercise, I might criticize my hypothetical self's blindness to the harm she is bringing on to herself and the German race. Though I can imagine that she hates betrayal by a friend, I have to protect her long-term interests, as well as my own integrity. I therefore decide to blow the whistle.

Shu does not reliably lead to moral rightness because it has no built-in mechanism to track the moral features of a situation. It itself does not point to specific moral values like filial piety, loyalty, courage, etc., as the virtue of *ren* (benevolence) does. And unlike *li* (rules of propriety), it does not lay down specific rules the following of which generally constitutes morally right action. Furthermore, *shu*

---

[22] Fingarette also recognizes the inadequacy of *Shu* in guaranteeing moral rightness (1980, 388). On the other hand, he believes that when we supplement *shu* with *li*, then we can reliably track moral rightness. I am skeptical of this conclusion as I do not see how putting two problematic means together can give us a perfect solution.

provides no bulwark against moral wrongs. It does not admonish, as does Kant's categorical imperative, against treating others as mere means. The ability to detect and arbitrate among features of moral import presumably resides entirely with the agent and the recipient of the action, whose perspectives, after all, are the only things *shu* considers. But the agent and the recipient could be anybody, including people who are just beginners on the road of moral cultivation.[23]

Perhaps *shu*'s incompleteness as a guide to moral rightness should not tell against its value in regards to caring actions. Instead, this feature of *shu* rightly highlights the important moral distinction between a caring action and a morally right action. And perhaps it is better to allow for this possibility of tension between morality and caring, so that a person can be caring despite her moral immaturity.[24]

What about the problem of paternalism? Does it warrant the rejection of *shu* as the moral guide to caring actions? I do not think so. It is unrealistic to search for a perfect moral guide that is free from any negative implication. The most we can hope for is to be alert to the pitfalls described above and to do our best to avoid them. And *shu* does offer compensating advantages, as we have seen. We should not, for example, overlook the fact that because *shu* involves identification with others, practicing *shu* can lead to the cultivation of a caring attitude and a sense of co-humanity with our fellow humans.

---

[23] My claim does not imply that Confucius' theory is formalistic or that *shu* is the Confucian procedural criterion of moral rightness. There is no such criterion because Confucius recognizes that the methods of *ren*, e.g. *li*, are not infallible guides to actions. This is why he highlights the importance of discretion (*quan*). Moreover, we should not forget that *shu* is supposed to be practiced by a Confucian agent whose moral sensitivity and framework are shaped by the practicing of *li* and the learning of the Confucian classics. Thus there are still some background constraints on the formalistic nature of *shu*.

[24] In describing *shu* as the one word that can serve as the guiding moral principle, perhaps Confucius means that it is *the* (most important) principle rather than the *only* principle.

These two attitudes, one might argue, are the bedrock of our moral sense.

2. Conclusion

To conclude, I have argued that Fingarette's interpretation of *shu* is right. *Shu* involves identifying with another person while criticizing the latter's perspective based on one's own. I have proposed a mechanism for developing this sort of critique, based on some significant Confucian values. Applying *shu* to the context of caring actions, I have shown that it can help to solve the problems of refraining from active caring and the caring agent's loss of independence and integrity. While *shu* has other problems, such as paternalism and incomplete guidance to moral rightness, these problems do not undermine the validity of *shu* in the context of caring actions.

Certainly, this does not suggest that we should be content with merely caring actions and stop striving to do the morally right thing. In the *Analects*, the morally right things are generally tracked by following the precepts of *li* or undertaking the deliberative process of *quan*. In another ethical theory, they may be tracked by something else. However the morally right thing is discovered, let us not forget another important point made in the *Analects*—the imperative to engage in incessant moral cultivation, which perhaps can help to connect caring with moral rightness. For a caring agent does not function in a moral vacuum. She operates within a particular moral framework and is guided by her desires and judgments. Hence she needs to seek the perfection of these things through moral cultivation. And virtues, which result from this process, would reliably lead to moral rightness, if caring alone does not.[25]

---

[25] I am grateful to my colleagues David Christensen, Arthur Kuflik, and Don Loeb for their incredibly generous help and stimulating discussion on this paper. I also thank Robert Eno, Chad Hansen, Donald Munro, Bryan Van Nordan, and Kwong-loi Shun for their penetrating comments. Last but not least, I am thankful to the anonymous referee for pushing me to probe more deeply into question of the connection between caring and moral rightness.

REFERENCES

Allison, Robert. 1982. "On the Negative Version of the Golden Rule as Formulated by Confucius," *New Asia Academic Bulletin* VIII. 1982.

——. 1992. "The Golden Rule as the Core Value in Confucianism and Christianity," *Asian Philosophy* 2 (2).

Brooks, Bruce and Brooks, Taeko. 1988. *The Original Analects.* New York: University of Columbia Press.

Eno, Robert. 1990. *The Confucian Creation of Heaven.* Albany: State University of New York Press.

Feng, Youlan. 1953. *A Short History of Chinese Philosophy.* Trans. by Derk Bodde. New York: The Macmillan Co.

Fingeratte, Herbert. 1980. "Following the 'One Thread' of the *Analects,*" *Journal of American Academy of Religion* XLVII/3, Thematic Issue 3.

Gilligan, Carol. 1982. *In a Different Voice.* Cambridge: Harvard University Press.

Hoagland, Sarah Lucia. 1988. *Lesbian Ethics.* Palo Alto: Institute of Lesbian Studies.

Ivanhoe, Philip. 1990. "Reweaving the One Thread of the *Analects,*" *Philosophy East and West* 40 (1): 17.

Kittay, Eva F. and Meyers, Diana T. eds. 1987. *Women and Moral Theory.* Totoowa: Rowman & Littlefield.

Marsha, Helen and Nielsen, Kai (eds.). 1987. *Science, Morality and Feminist Theory* (Canadian Journal of Philosophy, supplementary vol. 13). Calgary: University of Calgary Press.

Lau, D. C. (trans). 1979. *The Analects.* New York: Penguin.

Munro, Donald. 1969. *The Concept of Man in Ancient China.* Stanford: Stanford University Press.

Nivison, David. 1996. "Golden Rule Arguments in Chinese Moral Philosophy." In *The Ways of Confucianism: Investigations in Chinese Philosophy,* edited by Bryan Van Nordan. Chicago: Open Court.

Noddings, Nel. 1984. *Caring: A Feminine Approach to Ethics and Moral Education*. Berkeley: University of California Press.

Railton, Peter. 1986. "Moral Realism," *Philosophical Review* 95 (1986).

Graham, A.C. 1989. *Disputers of the Tao*. La Salle: Open Court.

Schwartz, Benjamin. 1985. *The World of Thought in Ancient China*. Cambridge: Harvard University Press.

Sidgwick, Henry. 1962. *The Methods of Ethics*. Chicago: University of Chicago Press.

Singer, Marcus. 1963. "The Golden Rule," *Philosophy* vol. XXXVIII, no. 146.

Thomas, Laurence. 1996. "Becoming an Evil Society," *Political Theory* 24 (2).

Williams, Bernard. 1981. "Persons, Characters and Morality." In his *Moral Luck*. Cambridge: Cambridge University Press.

8

Zhu Xi On *Ren* (Humanity) and Love: A Neo-Confucian Way Out of the Liberal-Communitarian Impasse

Yong Huang

The liberal-communitarian debate has played a central role in Anglo-American public discourse for the last decade or two (see Okin 1989, 46). In this article, I shall bring this debate into dialogue, beyond the limitations of time and space, with the Confucian tradition in ancient China. It is my contention that the principal concepts in this debate, the good and the right, are compatible with the fundamental Confucian ideas of *ren* (humanity) and love. Moreover, I shall argue, this debate has entered an impasse between the liberal insistence on "the right-prior-to-the-good" (RpG) and the communitarian espousal of "the good-prior-to-the-right" (GpR), while the Confucian discussion of *ren* and love, as represented in the neo-Confucian Zhu Xi's philosophy, can provide a way out of it. This article, therefore, consists of three parts: (1) the impasse of the liberal-communitarian debate on the good and the right; (2) the compatibility of the modern Western conceptions of the good and the right with the ancient Chinese ideas of *ren* and love; and (3) Zhu Xi's view of *ren* and love as an alternative to liberalism and communitarianism.

GpR or RpG: the Liberal-Communitarian Impasse

The liberal-communitarian debate is joined not only by philosophers, but also by theologians, sociologists, political scientists, and legal scholars. It can be roughly traced back to the publication of John

Rawls's instant classic *A Theory of Justice* in 1971 and Michael Sandel's systematic critique of it in his also highly acclaimed book *Liberalism and the Limits of Justice* in 1982. Other main figures actively participating in this debate include Bruce Ackerman, Donald Dworkin, and Thomas Nagel (liberals) and Alasdair MacIntyre, Charles Taylor, and Michael Walzer (communitarians). However, this debate has often been understood as one between the liberal emphasis on individual self-determination and the communitarian urge to conform to communal values (see Kymlick 1990, 207 & Bell 1993, 31). According to such an understanding, liberalism is the view that individuals can choose their ends independently of or prior to society, while society is regarded as the outcome of the negotiations between these individuals whose ends are already given. In contrast, communitarianism is the view that the ultimate order of explanation is community, only in terms of which can individuals choose and understand their ends.

Such an understanding, however, is misleading. On the one hand, liberals do not ignore the importance of community in their emphasis on individuality. For example, John Rawls denies that his theory of justice is an argument for a private society, in which persons have their competing and independent private ends, while institutions have no values in themselves (see Rawls 1971, 521). Rather, he argues,

> in the well-ordered society of justice as fairness citizens do have final ends in common. . . . [T]hey do affirm the same political conception of justice. . . . Besides, the end of political justice may be among citizens' most basic aims by reference to which they express the kind of person they very much want to be. (Rawls 1993, 202)

With this, another prominent liberal, Bruce Ackerman, entirely agree. For him, the tired debate on individualism and communitarianism "is based upon a false dichotomy. Political liberals do *not* seek to ground rights directly upon any notion of abstract individualism, Kantian or other. Their fundamental appeal is to community," a community united by public reason in a common dialogue, despite their different religious ideas of the good (see Ackerman 1994, 385-6).

On the other hand, communitarians do not deny the importance of individuality in their emphasis on the community either. For example, Charles Taylor whole-heartedly embraces the ideal of individuality, which means for him that "everyone has a right to develop their own form of life, grounded on their own sense of what is really important or of value" (Taylor 1991, 14). Therefore, Taylor agrees with liberals, seeing this ideal as a modern gain over the various premodern injunctions which commanded us to make sacrifices to the demands of supposedly sacred orders that transcend us. What Taylor wants to underscore is that individuality can be identified and nourished not by separating individuals from but by relating them to each other. In order to define one's individuality, one needs to presuppose two things. The one is the common meaning in terms of which one can define one's individuality: "I can define my identity only against the background of things that matter" (ibid., 40). The other is one's recognition of others: "my discovering my identity doesn't mean that I work it out in isolation but that I negotiate it through dialogue . . . with others" (ibid., 47). Michael Sandel, another communitarian, also makes it unmistakably clear that, in his debate with liberals, he has no problem at all with their claim that individual rights cannot be sacrificed for the sake of common good (see Sandel 1994, 1767). In this sense, he thinks that the term "communitarian" is misleading in characterizing his critique of liberalism, even though he himself still uses it for the lack of a more appropriate term. For "communitarian" implies that principles of the right should rest on the values or preferences that prevail in any given community at any given time, while he and his allies don't hold that view.

This is not to say that liberals and communitarians have exactly the same view of individuality and community. Obviously, they do not. However, their disagreement here can be understood properly only in terms of their more fundamental disagreement about our conceptions of the good and the right. In developing his anti-utilitarian theory of justice, for example, Rawls makes it clear that the "priority of the right over the good in justice as fairness turns out to be a central feature of the conception" (Rawls 1971, 31-32). In his argument against Rawls's liberalism, Michael Sandel also points out that, among the three debates that Rawls's *A Theory of Justice* initiates, the only one that engages communitarians is precisely the one about our ideas of the right and the good.[1] The problem he has with the liberal position is "not the relative weight of individual and communal claims, but the terms of relation between the right and the good" (Sandel 1994, 1767). According to Sandel, this issue is not only central to the communitarian critique of liberalism but has become the central concern of the liberal position itself as well, since Rawls now, in his *Political Liberalism*, has set aside the other two debates and concentrates solely on the one with communitarianism (see ibid., 1770).

The question is then what is meant by the good and the right. While in our everyday unreflective uses these two terms may seem interchangeable, they are profoundly different in moral discourse. Put in the most simplistic way, the right expresses an interpersonal or sociological concern, while the good has an idealistic or ontological connotation. In other words, we make a moral judgment in terms of right or wrong when our primary concern is other persons' interest. A conduct is right in this sense when it is beneficial or at least not harmful to others. Yet we make a moral judgment in terms of the good or bad when our main consideration is human nature and the fundamental reality of the world or universe. A conduct is good in this sense when it corresponds to this reality (see Hare 1963, 152). John Rawls thus regards our capacity for the good and that for the right as our two chief moral capacities. The former is the capacity

> to understand, to apply, and to act from the public conception of justice which characterizes the fair terms of social cooperation. . .
>
> [The latter] is the capacity to form, to revise, and rationally to pursue a conception of one's rational advantage or good. (Rawls 1993, 19)

---

[1] The other two are (1) the debate with utilitarians on utility or individual rights as the basis of justice and (2) the debate with libertarians on equality or market as the basis of distribution.

These two types of moral judgments are not always consistent. A good conduct is not necessarily right at the same time. For example, it may be good for Christians to live their life according to their unique understanding of God, the world, and human nature, while it is not right for them to impose this understanding upon others who have different understandings of those things. Similarly, a right conduct is not necessarily good at the same time. For example, seeing someone who is wasting his whole life on things like drinking, smoking, and gambling without providing any help may be right in terms of respecting another person's way of life but is apparently not good in terms of what should be considered as an authentic way of life.

Liberalism and communitarianism are best seen as two attempts to reconcile these two moral points of view. For liberals, since there are very different and incommensurable conceptions of what is the fundamental reality of the world, the task of moral philosophy is to develop a universally applicable conception of the right, which is not only derived independently of but has also to be used as a criterion to regulate different ideas of the good. This is precisely what the liberal RpG means. As Rawls maintains, people have to

> conform their conceptions of their good to what the principles of justice require, or at least not to press claims which directly violate them... The principles of right, and so of justice, put limits on which satisfactions have value; they impose restrictions on what are reasonable conceptions of one's good. (Rawls 1971, 31)

Rawls is willing to grant great importance to people's conceptions of the good, only if they support, or at least not contradict the pre-established principles of the right. It is in this sense that Rawls wants to distinguish between reasonable, rational, and sane conceptions of the good and unreasonable, irrational, and mad ones according to their consistence with the principles of the right or their lack thereof.

In contrast, for communitarians, since there are rival and competing conceptions of what is right, we need first to have a more fundamental understanding of the reality of the world and the nature of human life and only then can we use this understanding to judge which conception of the right is appropriate. This is exactly what the communitarian RpG means. As MacIntyre insists,

> a necessary precondition for a political community's possession of adequately determinate shared rationally founded moral rules is the shared possession of a rationally justifiable conception of human good. . . .[R]espect for and allegiance to that shared conception of the human good will have had to be institutionalized in the life of that community. (MacIntyre 1990, 351)

Thus, for MacIntyre, our view of whether something is right presupposes our view of the nature of the right; our view of the nature of the right in turn presupposes our view of the nature of the good; and our view of the nature of the good finally presupposes our religious and metaphysical understanding of the fundamental reality.

With this central disagreement between the liberal RpG and the communitarian GpR understood, perhaps we can now try to understand better their disagreement about individuality and community. As we have seen, liberals emphasize the importance of community as muchas communitarians. However, for communitarians, a community must be united with a shared idea of the good based on a religious or quasi-religious view of human nature and its place in the world. Yet for liberals, a community can only be based on a shared view of the right or justice which is fair to individuals with different religious or quasi-religious ideas of the good.[2] Similarly, communitarians emphasize individuality as much as liberals. However, for liberals, individuality means (among other things) that everyone has the freedom to choose one idea of the good over another. For communitarians, however, individuality is embodied, at least partially, in one's unique relationship to the common good of a society due to his or

---

[2] Rawls makes this distinction clear by maintaining that "justice as fairness does indeed abandon the ideal of political community if by that ideal is meant a political society united on one (partially or fully) comprehensive religious, philosophical, or moral doctrine" (Rawls 1993, 201).

her unique position in the society. In the final analysis, the disagreement between liberals and communitarians about individuality and community is not on the priority of the individual or the communal values but on the priority of the right or the good.

From the above, we can see that both the liberal and the communitarian positions have their strength, especially in each's criticism of the other. Liberals are right that, since there are many different and sometimes even conflicting ideas of the good, a political conception of the right, to be fair, cannot be based on any single idea to the exclusion of all others. Yet communitarians are also right that our conception of the right can have its meaning and play its role only when it is seen as a component part of our more comprehensive system of beliefs, which also includes our religious or quasi-religious ideas of the good. Thus, what is needed is to combine the insights of both liberals and communitarians into a coherent view to overcome their respective weakness. The problem shared by both liberals and communitarians is their common desire to ground our public discourse on a single foundation, either a religious or quasi-religious idea of the good or a social and political conception of the right. It is this common foundationalist assumption that prevents their debate from any significant achievement and leads them into the impasse between the RpG and GpR. It is here that I believe that Zhu Xi's neo-Confucian understanding of *ren* and love becomes significant in helping us move beyond this impasse. However, before I can proceed to argue for that, there is a prior question of the compatibility of the Western ideas of the good and the right with the Confucian ideas of *ren* and love.

The Good and the Right Verses *Ren* and Love: Their Compatibility

Just as the conceptions of the good and the right are central to the contemporary American public discourses, the ideas of *ren* and love are central to the ancient Confucian tradition. However, in what sense are these two pairs of concepts compatible? There seems to be no big problem with the compatibility of the Western idea of the good with the Confucian idea of *ren*. As we have seen, the good in the Western moral discourse is related to the question of what is good human life according to our understanding of human nature, which is usually accompanied by our religious or metaphysical conception of the fundamental reality of the world. Therefore, goodness is not a particular virtue of human being but is an ontologically oriented moral ideal of human life per se.

Now, the concept of *ren*, which is pronounced and was originally written the same as *ren* (meaning human), while having undergone great transformations in the Confucian tradition, has largely conveyed the similar meaning. Even in the view of the classical Confucians who don't make clear distinction between the metaphysical and experiential, *ren* is not a particular human virtue but is related to human nature, as is clear in the Confucius' saying that "*ren* is to be human" (Confucius 1971a, 20:5). What is expressed here is not that every human being is already a person of *ren*, but that, in order to become human, one needs to live his or her life according to the ideal of *ren*, which precludes all evils such as flattering, boasting, resentment, and covetousness, on the one hand, and embraces all virtues such as filial piety, wisdom, propriety, courage, and loyalty on the other.

Later in Song neo-Confucianism, the ideal of *ren* is understood in more clearly metaphysical terms. According to one version of such an understanding, *ren*, as the most fundamental character of human mind, has its root in the mind of Heaven and Earth, which is to give birth to things.[3] As pointed out by Wing-tsit Chan, although relating the idea of "giving birth" to *ren* can be traced much earlier, their identification is a new contribution made by Song neo-Confucianism, which culminates in Zhu Xi's philosophical system (see Chan 1955, 314). According to Zhu Xi, the reason that the human mind has the same character as the mind of heaven and earth is that, in their production by Heaven and Earth, humans and things

---

[3] This is related to the meaning of *ren* as seed of grain and kernels of peaches and apricots: when sown, they grow. Because of this double meaning of kernel and humanity, as Zhu Xi points out, "*ren* implies the spirit of life" (see Chan 1963, 632-633).

receive the mind of Heaven and Earth as their mind. Therefore, with reference to the character of the mind, although it embraces and penetrates all and leaves nothing to be desired, nevertheless, one word will cover all of it, namely, *ren* (humanity). (see Chan 1963, 593-94)

Just as production is the fundamental character of the mind of Heaven and Earth and includes all other characters such as flourish, advantages, and firmness, so *ren* is the fundamental character of human mind and includes all other characters such as righteousness, propriety, and wisdom.

Thus, not only as the ideal of perfect human being but also in its relation to our metaphysical understanding of the world, the Confucian idea of *ren* is indeed very close to the Western conception of the good. In contrast, the compatibility of the Confucian idea of love with the Western idea of the right or justice is not immediately clear. Thus, when searching for a Confucian conception of justice, people tend to focus on the concept of *yi* (righteousness) rather than love (see Roetz 1993, 111-118). The problem with such an approach, however, is that while the primary concern of the Western conception of the right is interpersonal rather than metaphysical, the Confucian idea of *yi* is fundamentally metaphysical rather than interpersonal, although in Confucian tradition, these two aspects are never entirely separated. For *yi*, together with *ren*, *li* (propriety), and *zhi* (wisdom), as pointed out by Zhu Xi, form human nature and are therefore a priori principles. Just as *ren*, *li*, and *zhi* have their external, experiential, and therefore more interpersonal feelings (love, respect and reverence, and right and wrong respectively), *yi* has its corresponding feeling of shame which is of a similar nature to love, respect, and reverence. Here, *yi*, as a metaphysical idea, underlines more what one feels no shame to do than what one thinks it appropriate to do in terms of other people's perspective, although, again, the Confucian tradition has never held that there is any gulf between the two.[4] As David Hall and Roger Ames point out, instead of referring to appropriateness to one's context, "*yi* denotes appropriateness to one's own person" (Ames & Hall 1987, 96). [5]

Of course, one may disagree that, if there is some problem comparing the Confucian idea of *yi* with the Western conception of the right or justice, the Confucian idea of love and the Western conception of justice seem to be inherently incompatible. While the latter is usually regarded as a rationally determined concept, the former is often seen as a sentimentally acquired feeling. In classical Confucianism, *ren* as human nature is often explained in terms of love as one's feeling of commiseration. In Song neo-Confucianism, this distinction is canonized in Cheng Yi's statement that "love is feeling while *ren* is nature" (see Chan 1963, 559). The main problem seems to be that only reason can pose universal moral obligations, while sentiment can be no more than local.[6] To use Richard Rorty's example of a parent in a famine, with food stored in the basement, we tend to regard him as having a rational conception of the right or justice if he shares the food with his neighbors, but as having only a sentimental feeling of love for his family if he fends his neighbors off with a gun (see Rorty 1995). Now it is one of the Confucian cornerstones, especially in its debate with Moists, that love is a feeling that is not impartial, universal, or indiscriminate but passional, personal, and distinct. According to Mozi, in order to avoid calamities, usurpation, hatred, and animosity, there is a need for universal love, which "is to regard other people's countries as one's own. Regard other people's families as one's own. Regard other

---

[4] Although in antiquity, as Mozi tells us, *yi* was purely individual: "in fact there were as many *yi* as there were people, and each approved of his own *yi* and disagreed with everyone else's" (Mozi, 14:11:1).

[5] This view was earlier expressed by Chung-ying Cheng, who emphasizes that *yi* "will enable one to respond naturally to a situation and to choose an action to one's own satisfaction.... [*Yi*] gives autonomy and independence as well as self-sufficiency to an individual and makes an individual a creative agent in which everything in the universe becomes meaningful to him" (Cheng 1991, 242; emphasis added).

[6] Perhaps in order to save the Confucian love from this narrow emotionalism, David Wong has made an attempt to rationalize the Confucian emotion, having in mind that the notion of reason implies generality (see Wong 1991, 31-44).

people's person as one's own" (see Chan 1963, 214).[7] Thus, Moists are espousing a conception of love similar to the Christian one which emphasizes universality and demands an equal love for all, including enemies. With personality, partiality, and discrimination taken away, love here is indeed almost indistinguishable from the rationalistic idea of justice, which is claimed precisely to be impartial, impersonal, and universal. Confucians cannot accept such an ideal of universal love. If enmity has also to be repaid by virtue, Confucius asks, "with what, then, shall virtue be repaid?" For him, we should "repay enmity with straightness, [and] repay virtue with virtue" (Confucius 1971, 14:36). The Confucian view is that love has distinctions and the most intimate one is family love. Perhaps because of this, there is a common criticism of Confucian love as inferior to the Moist or the Christian one (see Lin 1972, 170). Even those who want to defend Confucianism tend to choose to argue, unconvincingly, that the Confucian love, properly understood, stands for universal rather than differential love (see Allison 1990, 158-76).

Therefore, if the distinction between the universal reason and the parochial feeling is valid, it is certainly inadequate to bring the Confucian idea of love and the Western idea of justice together. Yet it is this distinction that is now under increasing criticism, especially in relation to the issue of justice and love that concerns us here. Feminists, for example, have pointed out that the sources of our conception of justice are not only reason but also feeling. A sense of justice at least partly depends on love, trust, and affection which originates from family (see Okin 1989, 229-249). Yet the more powerful deconstruction of this distinction is made by the pragmatist Richard Rorty. Following the line of William James's argument against the passion/reason distinction (see James 1956, 63-110), Rorty's main criticism is directed to the claim that a rational conception of justice is universal, while a sentimental feeling of love

---

[7] On this basis, Halk Jin Rah infers that, for Mozi, "love exists only when it reaches everybody; love disappears the moment it fails to include all people" (Rah 1978, 50).

or loyalty is parochial. According to Rorty, what we call justice or rightness is just a name for love of or loyalty to a certain large group. We therefore can always replace the term "justice" with that of loyalty to or love of the relevant group: one's fellow-citizens, or the human species, or all living things (see Rorty 1995, 4). The point he tries to make is that the sentimental feeling of love or loyalty is not necessarily local but can also be universal. Similarly, the rational conception of justice is not necessarily universal but may also be local. To return to his example mentioned earlier, the conflict a parent of a large family in a famine faces between sharing the food with his neighbors and keeping them for his own children only, is not a conflict between sentimental love of or loyalty to family and the rational justice or rightness to all. Rather it is a conflict between love for or loyalty to a small group and love for or loyalty to a large one.

This, of course, does not mean that we can simply reduce justice to love or loyalty in particular and rationality to sentimentality in general. Rather, it is to deny the distinction between the two. As William James pointed out, while reason is also passional, passion is not without reason. Thus, just as we can say that justice is nothing but a larger love, so we can also say that love is a small justice. Just as we can say that the parent in the above example faces the conflict between small love for his family and larger love for his neighbors, so we can say that he faces a conflict between small justice within his family and a larger one within his neighborhood. To be moral, even on the social level, is thus not to overcome one's sentimental love in order to realize impersonal justice. As Rorty points out,

> morality starts out not as an obligation, but as a relation of recip-
> rocal trust among a closely knit group, such as a family or clan.
> To behave morally is to do what comes naturally in one's dealing
> with your parents and children, or your fellow clan-members.
> (ibid., 5-6)

In this sense, moral progress is not a replacement of local love with universal justice nor universal justice with local love but the expansion of small love or justice to a larger one, "the expansion of the circle of beings who count as 'us'," the expansion that occurs "when families confederate into tribes, or tribes into nations" (ibid., 6).

Now, with the distinction between the universal reason and the particular sentiment abandoned, the compatibility of love in the ancient Chinese Confucian tradition with justice in the contemporary Western moral discourse becomes clearer. Confucians, as we have pointed out, stand against the Moist idea of universal love, but they don't thereby end up with a theory of self love, something held by Yang Zhu, whose famous motto is "each for oneself." Confucius makes it unmistakably clear that love is not to love oneself but is exactly "to subdue oneself and return to propriety" (Confucius 1971, 250). It is in this sense that Mencius sees both Yang Zhu and Mozi, whose teachings were popular throughout empire in his time, as the enemies of Confucianism. According to him, if these two teachings "do not subside and the way of Confucius is not proclaimed, the people will be deceived by heresies and the path of morality will be blocked" (Mencius, 3B:9).

Yet what is "the way of Confucius"? On the one hand, Confucians emphasize that family love, filial piety and brotherly respect, is the root of all love (Confucius 1971, 139). Family in Confucian tradition, as David Wong points out, "provides the first context in which love of others is learnt, and habits of thought, feeling and acting that compose this love form much of the foundation of the individual's character" (Wong 1989, 255). In this sense Confucians would whole-heartedly embrace the feminist idea of family as a school of justice (see Okin 1989, 17-24). On the other hand, however, Confucians maintain that love cannot be limited within the family but has to be gradually extended to all. Thus, immediately after advising a youth to be filial when he is at home, Confucius adds that, when he is "abroad, he should respect his elders.... He should overflow in love to all" (Confucius 1971, 140). In the same spirit, Mencius advises King Xuan of Qi to

> treat the aged of your own family in a manner befitting their venerable age and extend this treatment to the aged of other families; treat your own young in a manner befitting their tender

age and extend this to the young of other families. (Mencius, 1A:27)

Of course, if the Confucian love means nothing but to start from family love, which is then gradually extended to others, and finally realized in universal love, Moists may have no problem about it.[8] What Moists insist is that there must be a universal, impersonal, and indiscriminate principle of love, which could be applied to family first and to others only later. The main objection that Confucians have to this view is perhaps not its possible consequence of self-negation, as some scholars have pointed out (see Hitoshi 1986, 220-221). For Confucians, while there may be a common rule to measure one's own land and that of others, there is no common principle of love equally applicable to one's own parents and others. For love is a passion, a feeling, and an emotion which one first learns in family. When such a love is extended to all and becomes a universal love, it does not therefore become impersonal, impassional, or impartial as Moists insist. Here, as Zhu Xi points out, "if impartiality is to extend to the whole world and to eliminate the selfishness that divides the self and others, I am afraid that that impartiality is totally devoid of feeling, like the emptiness of wood and stone" (Zhu 1996, 32:19). In the Confucian view, one loves all not because one has grasped with a cold mind a universal imperative to love all and from this to infer that, since both one's parents and others are part of this "all," they are to be loved. Rather, since one first learns to love within a family, one can love others only in the sense and to the extent that one can make an analogy between these "others" and one's own family members. As a result, one's love of others, just as family love, is also a passional, partial, and personal one. It is here that we can understand the central Confucian claim that love has distinctions or discriminations. While Confucians do want to extend love to all, one loves different persons differently according to the different degrees to which one can make the analogy between them and one's parents.

---

[8] For example, the Moist Yi Zi feels it acceptable that "the practice of love begins with one's parents" (see Mencius, 3A:5).

That is why for Confucius, as is already alluded, one cannot have the same love for an evil person as for a virtuous one. Similarly, this is also the reason that Mencius claims that,

> in regard to [inferior] creatures, the superior man loves them but is not humane to them (that is, showing them the feeling due human beings). In regard to people generally, he is humane to them but not affectionate. He is affectionate to his parents and humane to all people. He is humane to all people and feels love for all creatures. (Mencius, 7A:45)

Here we have at least three most general distinctions of love (each of which can be further distinguished): affection to parents, love for all creatures, and humaneness to all human beings in the middle.

Zhu Xi On *Ren* and Love: A Neo-Confucian Way Out of the Liberal-communitarian Impasse

Attempts have been made to bring Confucianism into dialogue with contemporary liberalism and communitarianism. Yet more often than not these attempts have tried to ally Confucianism with communitarianism to combat liberalism. Here liberalism is understood as individualism, while communitarianism is identified as a collectivism (see Lee 1992 & Wong 1989). However, as we have seen, the central issue of the liberal-communitarian debate is not about individuality and collectivity but about the good and the right. Moreover, Confucianism is neither individualistic nor collectivist. It rather presents itself as an alternative to both Yang Zhu's individualism and Moist collectivism. Having established *ren* and love as the Confucian counterparts of the Western conceptions of the good and the right respectively, in this section, I propose to take a close look at Zhu Xi's view of *ren* and love to see whether it can help us better understand the relationship between the good and the right in the liberal-communitarian debate.

In appearance, we might still want to see Zhu Xi as a Chinese communitarian, since he seems to insist on the priority of *ren* over love, just as Western communitarians maintain the priority of the good over the right. For Zhu Xi not only follows Cheng Yi's view that *ren* is nature, while love is feeling; he further adds that "*ren* is the principle of love. Principle is the root, while love is the sprout" (Zhu 1997, ch. 20) and "*ren* is substance, while love is function" (ibid.). Yet, we can understand what Zhu Xi really means by such pairs of terms as substance and function, nature and feeling, and root and sprout only in relation to the two misunderstandings of Confucian ideas of *ren* and love that Zhu Xi wants to correct. One was made by many scholars before Cheng Yi. They "showed no concern for *ren*. Where the ancient sages used the word *ren*, they read as love" (Zhu 1996. 31:5). For them, the feeling of love is loftier and nobler than *ren*. Just as Western liberals give priority to the political idea of the right over the metaphysical conception of the good, these Confucians allowed the interpersonal love to determine the ontological *ren*. The other was the misunderstanding by scholars after Cheng Yi corrected the first one. In Zhu Xi's view,

> preoccupied only with the exposition of *ren*, they were remiss in the effort to hold onto the essentials and to immerse themselves in comprehensiveness... [they] removed their pursuits entirely away from love. They engaged themselves only in empty principles and empty discourses, and failed to arrive at any true understanding. (ibid.)

Just as Western communitarians give priority to the good over the right, these Confucians gave priority to *ren* over love.

For Zhu Xi, these people either try to understand *ren* independently of love or to understand love independently of *ren*. As a result, none of them correctly comprehends the true meaning of either *ren* over love. Thus, Zhu Xi's use of substance and function, nature and feeling, and root and sprout is not to emphasize the priority of *ren* to love but their inseparability. On the one hand, there is no *ren* as principle or substance without the function or feeling of love. In his letter to Lü Zujian, he argues that

> *ren*, of course, cannot be interpreted purely from the point of

view of function, but one must understand the principle that *ren* has the ability to function. Only then will it do. Otherwise, the term will be meaningless and cannot be explained.... One should not regard the original substance of *ren* as one thing and its function as another. (ibid., 47:26)

On the other hand, there is no love as function or feeling that does not present *ren* as its substance or principle. The substance must be able to present in the function and the function must be able to exhibit the substance. For Zhu Xi, "one must clearly see the principle in places where one applies oneself to the concrete task. Then the particular meaning will emerge" (Zhu 1997, ch. 20). For example,

> when one wants to gain a clear understanding of the meaning and content of *ren*, one will do well if one uses the concept of love as aid. When one realizes that *ren* is the source of love, and that love can never exhaust *ren*, then one has gained a definite comprehension of *ren*. Thus it is absolutely not necessary to search for *ren* in obscure places. (Zhu 1996, 31:5)

Moreover, Zhu Xi emphasizes that different people should find different places where *ren* can be both found and practiced, so that they can "personally realize it in the way relevant to themselves and not seek it outside" (Zhu 1997, ch. 20).

One objection to this interpretation is perhaps that Zhu Xi himself implies the priority of *ren* to love when he says that *ren* as substance is something before the mind is activated (*weifa*) and love as function is something after the mind is activated (*yifa*) (see Zhu 1996, 50:34). Yet, obviously, Zhu Xi here does not mean that first there is a functionless substance or nature and later it produces substanceless function or feeling. He makes it clear that

> the nature that is tranquil cannot help but be active, and the feeling that is active necessarily has a degree and measure. Thus whether the mind remains absolutely quiet or penetrates everything, it operates everywhere and penetrates thoroughly, in which case substance and function are never separated. (ibid., 32:24b-

25a)

In other words, in the substance there is already function and in the function substance remains. While Zhu Xi does hold that substance comes before function, he also affirms at the same time that function comes before substance. His emphasis here is that there is no gap between the two. From one perspective, we may say that A is before B, while from another perspective, we may say that B is before A (see Zhu 1997, ch. 1).

Therefore, although Zhu Xi uses such terms as substance, nature, and root to characterize *ren* and function, feeling, and sprout to characterize love, he does not hold the quasi-communitarian view that we need first to know what is *ren* and then from *ren* to deduce what is love. Indeed, for Zhu Xi, *ren* as nature is difficult if not impossible to see, while love as feeling can be easily perceived. Moreover, once you see the feeling love, you can see in it the principle *ren* too. Thus he argues that "there is this nature, and it issues forth as feeling. Because there are feelings we can perceive this nature, and because there are feelings so we perceive that originally there existed this nature" (Zhang 1991, 66).

This, of course, does not mean that Zhu Xi is here sliding back into a quasi-liberal view of the priority of love to *ren*. For Zhu Xi, one can know what is *ren* from what is love precisely because *ren* is the reason for love. His argument is that, if the feeling of love is good, there must be something more fundamental that makes it good and this for him is *ren*. Moreover, one's feelings can be either good, which is what they should be, or bad, which is what they should not be. In the case of the former, "the substance of his nature is operating and is revealed in them," while in the case of the latter, they "violate principle and lose their due measure and degree. They will then be merely expressions of selfish ideas and human desires" (Chen 1986, sec. 30). Only from good feelings can we see *ren* as their nature, while we can know whether feelings are good or bad only according to the presence or absence of *ren*.

Here, we seem to have entered into a vicious circle: in order to know what is *ren*, we first need to know what is love where *ren* exists. Yet in order to know what is love where *ren* exists we first need to know what is *ren*. In this case, if Zhu Xi ccould provide any alternative to the liberal RpG and the communitarian GpR, it seems that it can be nothing but to put these two contradictory views together. To someone who has a foundationalist, reductionist, and apodictic mentality, Zhu Xi's thinking is confused, illogical, and self-contradictory. Indeed, a couple of suggestions have already been made to overcome Zhu Xi's seemingly vicious circle. One is the solution offered by Li Zehou. According to Li, in Zhu Xi's emphasis on the inseparability of *ren* as noumenal substance and love as perceptual function, "perception itself achieves a significant status. And recognition and affirmation of the perceptual existence of man and the world inevitably leads to recognition of man's sensual desires and needs" (Li 1986, 557). In Li's view, Zhu Xi's problem, resulting from such confusion, is that he takes some transient and specific phenomenon as universally necessary and omnipresent "Principle of Heaven" and "Mandate of Nature" to repress and smother other phenomena. Li Zehou thus proposes his alternative: to separate the noumenal from the phenomenal and to derive the latter from the former.

The other suggestion is made by Donald Munro, who sees Zhu Xi's metaphysical picture as nothing but an explanatory fiction. According to his interpretation, in Zhu Xi,

> structural images were often used in discussions of theories employing "explanatory fiction" such as heaven, tao, principle, and human nature. This positivistic term refers to unobservable entities that supposedly cause all kinds of observable regularities in nature. (Munro 1988, 193)

Munro maintains that such explanatory fictions can only have unscientific reasons for their continued existence. For example, psychologically, they may "contribute to peace of mind by providing all phenomena with a structure that seems to explain how they are related;" aesthetically, they may suggest height and require reverential treatment (see ibid., 198). Yet rationally we can and perhaps should largely do without them.

Thus, unsatisfied with Zhu Xi's strategy of going back and forth between the metaphysical *ren* and experiential love, Li's suggestion is that Zhu Xi should start from the metaphysical and use it to order the experiential; in contrast, Munro's suggestion is that Zhu Xi should start from the experiential and see the metaphysical as only a fiction usable to explain the experiential. Yet it is my contention that, while there is definitely a circle in Zhu Xi's argument, it is not a vicious one. For Zhu Xi, our metaphysical conception of *ren* is neither foundational to nor founded on our interpersonal feeling of love. As is well know, Zhu Xi has an explicit theory of equilibrium (*zhong*) and harmony (*he*): the former as the state of mind before different feelings are aroused (*ren*) and the latter as the state of mind after these feelings are aroused and all attain due measure (love). I am here trying to suggest that Zhu Xi also has an implicit doctrine of equilibrium or harmony between these two states of the mind, i.e., between *ren* as substance or nature and love as function or feeling. What I mean is that, for Zhu Xi, our conceptions of love and *ren* have to be situated in a genuine reflective equilibrium and harmony, in which our understanding of *ren* cannot be separated from our understanding of love and our understanding of love cannot be separated from our understanding of *ren*. Moreover, our better understanding of love will lead us to a better understanding of *ren*, which in turn will bring us to a better understanding of love. In this open-ended process, while we can never get a final, absolute, and apodictic understanding of either *ren* or love, we do get a better and better understanding of both.

Thus, what seems to others the most problematic in Zhu Xi is precisely Zhu Xi's strength. In the Confucian discourse of the metaphysical *ren* and interpersonal love, Zhu Xi is not a foundationalist. Unlike those who want to first fix one term in order to determine the other, Zhu Xi appeals to their mutual supports and challenges. Nor is Zhu Xi an absolutist. Unlike those who want to get our ideas of *ren* and love right once and for all, Zhu Xi hopes that, through their continuous mutual supports and challenges, we can get an increasingly better understanding of both *ren* and love. Now it is this aspect of Zhu Xi that, I believe, can provide a forceful alternative to both liberalism and communitarianism and an effective way out of the impasse of the liberal-communitarian debate on the issue of the good and the right. In the spirit of Zhu Xi, what is needed here is neither the liberal RpG nor the communitarian GpR but a reflective equilibrium between G and R: i.e., between our religious and quasi-religious idea of the good and our social and political conception of the right, obtained through their continuous mutual supports and challenges. In other words, our idea of the good cannot be independent from our conception of the right and our conception of the right cannot be separated from our idea of the good. Of course, such an approach cannot guarantee that we will have a perfect idea of the good and that of the right at the beginning, but it does give us the promise that we can get an increasingly better understanding of both what is right and what is good.

REFERENCES

Ackerman Bruce. 1994. "Political Liberalisms," *The Journal of Philosophy* 91 (7).
Allison, Robert E. 1990. "The Ethics of Confucianism and Christianity: The Delicate Balance," *Ching Feng* 33 (3).
Ames, Roger & Hall, David. 1987. *Thinking Through Confucius*. Albany: State University of New York Press.
Bell, Daniel. 1993. *Communitarianism and Its Critics*. Oxford: Oxford University Press.
Chan, Wing-tsit. 1955. "The Evolution of the Confucian Concept of *Ren*," *Philosophy East and West* 4: 295-315.
————. (ed.). 1963. *A Source Book in Chinese Philosophy*. Princeton: Princeton University Press.
————. (ed.) 1986. *Chu Hsi and Neo-Confucianism*. Honolulu, University of Hawaii Press.
Chen, Chun. 1986. *Neo-Confucian Terms Explained*. New York: Columbia University Press.
Cheng, Chung-ying. 1991. *Confucian and Neo-Confucian Philosophy*. Albany: State University of New York Press.
Confucius. 1971. *Analects*. In *Confucian Analects, The Great Learning and The Doctrine of the Mean*, trans by James Legge. New York:

Dover.

Hare, R.M. 1963. *Freedom and Reason*. Oxford: Oxford University Press.

Hitoshi, Sato. 1986. "Chu Hsi's (Zhu Xi) 'Treatise on *Ren*'." In Chan 1986.

James, William. 1956. "The Sentiment of Rationality." In his *The Will to Believe and Other Essays in Popular Philosophy*. New York: Dover Publications.

Kymlicka, Will. 1990. *Contemporary Political Philosophy: An Introduction*. Oxford: Oxford University Press.

Lee, Seung-Hwan. 1992. *Virtues and Rights: Reconstruction of Confucianism as a Rational Communitarianism*. Ann Arbor, MI: Microfilms International.

Li, Zehou. 1986. "Some Thoughts on Ming-Qing Neo-Confucianism." In Chan 1986.

Lin, Timothy T'ien-min. 1972. "The Confucian Concept of *Ren* and the Christian Concept of Love," *Ching Feng* 15 (3).

MacIntyre, Alasdair. 1990. "The Privatization of Good: An Inaugural Lecture," *Review of Politics* 52.

Mencius. 1970. *Mencius*. Trans by D. C. Lau. London: Penguin Books.

Munro, Donald. 1988. *Images of Human Nature: A Sung Portrait*. Princeton: Princeton University Press.

Okin, Susan Moller Okin. 1989. *Justice, Gender, and the Family*. New York: Basic Books.

———. 1989. "Humanist Liberalism," in Nancy Rosenblum, ed., *Liberalism and the Moral Life*. Cambridge: Harvard University Press.

———. 1989. "Reason and Feeling in Thinking about Justice," *Ethics* 99.

Rah, Halk Jin. 1978. *The Political Relevance of Ren in Early China and Agape in the Theology of Reinhold Niebuhr*. Seoul: Seoul National University.

Rawls, John. 1971. *A Theory of Justice*. Cambridge: Harvard University Press.

———. 1993. *Political Liberalism*. New York: Columbia University Press.

Roetz, Heiner. 1993. *Confucian Ethics of the Axial Age: A Reconstruction under the Aspect of the Breakthrough toward Postconventional Thinking*. Albany: State University of New York Press.

Rorty, Richard. 1995. "Justice as a Larger Loyalty" (a paper presented at the 7th East-West Philosophers' Conference at University of Hawaii, January).

Sandel Michael. 1994. "Political Liberalism" (Review of Rawls's *Political Liberalism*), *Harvard Law Review* 107.

Taylor, Charles. 1991. *The Ethics of Authenticity*. Cambridge: Harvard University Press.

Wong, David B. 1989. "Universalism and Love with Distinction." *Journal of Chinese Philosophy* 16.

————. 1991. "Is There a Distinction between Reason and Emotion in Mencius?" *Philosophy East and West* 41.

Zhang, Boxing, ed. 1991. *Further Reflections on Things at Hand*. Lanham, Maryland: University Press of America.

Zhu Xi. 1996. *Zhu Weng Gong Wenji*. In *Zhu Xi Ji*, 10 vol. Chengdu: Sichuan Jiaoyu Chubanshe.

————. 1997. *Zhuzi Yulei*, 4 vol. Changsha: Yueluo Shushe.

9

Health Care Allocation and the Confucian Tradition[1]

Ruiping Fan

Health Care Allocation: Economical or Ethical?

How should health care be allocated? What is an ethically-justified health care system? Should everyone obtain equal health care according to need? If society does not have sufficient resources to meet all health care needs, how should scarce health care resources be distributed? What are the individuals and their families' responsibilities for their health security? What role should the state play in the proper allocation of health care? These have become primary questions in contemporary bioethical discussions and for public policy formulation all over the world.

Most are likely to agree that these issues are difficult. However, many seem to believe that the difficulty of these issues lies in the prohibitive expenses that health care generates. Indeed, contemporary health care involves ever-increasing financial costs that no state is able to undertake with ease. As medical sciences and technologies

[1] The first version of this paper was presented at the Second International Conference of Bioethics, National Central University, Chungli, Taiwan, June 26, 2000. I appreciate the questions raised by the audience and benefited from the discussion. I also wish to thank Dr. Xinyan Jiang and an anonymous reviewer for their comments and suggestions concerning earlier drafts of the paper. In particular, I am very grateful to my former mentor Professor Tristram Engelhardt for his preeminently insightful and stimulating conversations from which I have learned a great deal for finalizing the paper.

dramatically innovate and people's life expectancy significantly increases, all societies are confronted with sophisticated health care requirements as well as boosted health care expectations (regarding critical care, organ transplantation, and gene therapy for example) that are much more financially demanding than traditional therapeutic practices. Accordingly, many people come to see the issue of health care allocation primarily as an economical issue, namely, an issue of financial efficiency in using scarce resources. They appear to conclude that every society, facing the scarcity of resources, must address the issue of health care allocation in order to find out the most efficient way of distributing limited health care resources.

This is, however, a misunderstanding. It is true that health care financing has become an important subject for careful exploration. Nonetheless, the issue of health care allocation is much more than a technical issue of finance. It is first and foremost a foundational issue of ethics. The reason is as follows.

First, it is not the case that the issue of health care allocation would not exist if health care were comparatively inexpensive. Compared to human needs and expectations, resources are always scarce. The relative scarcity of resources constitutes an inevitable condition of human society, past, present, and future. Even in a society in which high-technology and high-cost medicine is not available and health services are thereby relatively inexpensive, all health care needs cannot be met. More resources can always be invested in enlarging the quantity and improving the quality of health care, such as in producing more physicians, providing more professional training for general practitioners, creating new and better medications, and so on. More resources can also be invested to promote the quality of a series of other health-affecting factors such as food, lodging, and sanitation that are important to people's health. However, the more resources spent on health needs and desires, the less resources left for other needs and concerns. Consequently, every society has to make trade-offs between health care needs and other needs (because resources are scarce in general) as well as between different health care needs (because health care resources are scarce in particular). The issue is: what are the legitimate grounds for making such trade-offs?

Efficiency is certainly a very important factor in allocating resources. No society wants its limited resources wasted. However, justice consideration comes before efficiency calculation. People are naturally concerned with justice in resource distribution. They want their societal resources to be allocated in a fair manner. Unfortunately, the requirement of justice and the concern for efficiency do not automatically go hand in hand with each other. A just health care allocation may not be efficient, while an efficient health care allocation may not be just. It would be ideal if we could establish a pattern of health care distribution that was both just and efficient. But this could not always be the case.[2] If we have to make a choice between two patterns of health care allocation, one efficient but unjust, the other just but inefficient, we ought to choose the latter, namely, a pattern of health care allocation that is just, although inefficient. We should stand ready to sacrifice some amount of efficiency for the sake of justice, because justice is a more basic value than efficiency in human society.[3] This is to say, society must first seek a just system of health care allocation, and secondly, within the limits of justice, attempt to manage the system as efficiently as possible.

The Dominant Contemporary Western Ideology of Health Care Allocation: Why Is It Illusory?

What is a just health care allocation? Evidently, there are as many answers to this question as there are major contemporary Western bio-

---

[2] David Friedman, holding an anarchist utilitarian understanding of health care allocation, argues that the free market mechanism (without government intervention) would naturally lead to a health care system that is both efficient and just. However, the judgment that such a system is just (in addition to being efficient) relies on his particular understanding of justice. Others who do not accept his anarchist utilitarian presuppositions would not accept this judgment. See Friedman 1991.

[3] As John Rawls points out, "justice is the first virtue of social institutions, as truth is of systems of thought. A theory however elegant and economic must be rejected or revised if it is untrue; likewise laws and institutions no matter how efficient and well-arranged must be reformed or abolished if they are unjust" (Rawls 1971, 3).

ethical theories, such as egalitarianism (Veatch 1991), utilitarianism (Singer 1976), redistributivism (Beauchamp and Childress 1994), and Rawlsianism (Daniels 1985). Interestingly, if we put the details and nuances of these theories aside, we can clearly find that they have all convergently shaped a dominant view of health care allocation, which constitutes, as I term it, a statist egalitarian ideology of health care. It is egalitarian because its core idea is that everyone should receive equal health care according to need. It is statist because it emphasizes that the state must, through compulsory taxation, enforce a national health care system to meet everyone's *basic* health care needs in an egalitarian manner. Essentially, in this ideology, the individuals' capacity to pay for health care should not affect the quality of health care that they receive, and the state must intervene so much as to maintain equal health care treatment to everyone according to need. This is why the ideology is both egalitarian and statist.[4]

This ideology, however, is illusory for the following reasons.

First, equal health care is impossible. There can be two types of equal care: equal best care and equal minimum "adequate" or "basic" care. Equal best care is simply impossible because resources are limited. If society sets up a goal to provide the best care for everyone, it would end up without resources left for other important goals. Equal minimum "adequate" or "basic" care—however "adequate" or "basic" is defined[5]—is economically possible, but is still practically im-

---

[4] Claiming that there is such a dominant ideology of health care allocation in contemporary Western society does not imply that there are no opposing ideas in Western bioethical exploration. It is well-known that, for example, H. Tristram Engelhardt, Jr., a libertarian bioethicist, has offered powerful arguments to show that the state does not have the moral authority to enforce an all-encompassing egalitarian package of health care in a large-scale pluralist state (Engelhardt 1996). However, if one checks the contemporary Western bioethical literatures concerning health care allocation, one can easily notice that most leading liberal bioethicists as well as their followers roughly hold such a statist egalitarian view as I describe in the text. It is in this sense that I state this ideology is dominant in the contemporary West.

[5] In fact, it is very difficult to define "adequate care" or "basic needs." The content of these notions is value-laden, depending on people's particular value judgments and expectations. In addition, some author worries that the meeting of even "basic"

possible. The issue is: after a basic tier of health care is defined and established, should the state allow any *better* basic tier of health care (including, for instance, a shorter waiting time, better physician and nurse services, high-quality medication, etc.) to be available for the affluent to purchase through special insurance plans or out-of-pocket payment arrangements? If the state allows such better tiers to be available, equal care is broken. On the other hand, if the state prohibits any better basic care, then the affluent may travel to other countries for better care, and physicians may immigrate to other countries for better careers, let alone the likelihood of a black market for better health care services inside of the state. This would further cause the risk of a drain on the state's resources and talents. In any case, equal care is extremely hard to maintain in a society. The only practically plausible goal might be attempting to achieve as much equal (basic) health care as possible.

Second, the free choices of the individual and the autonomy of the family would have to be restricted. If government was to enforce as much equal health care as possible, people's liberty to establish and purchase better health care for themselves and their family members would have to be restricted. Even if government only wants to achieve as much equal *basic* health care as possible, such liberty still has to be limited in order to rule out the threat by market-based private health care services on the ability of the basic egalitarian health care system. Otherwise the affluent would invest significantly in the private sector, good physicians would move to the private sector, the quality of the public sector would be discounted, and so on. The more equality is pursued, the less liberty can be allowed. But then the cardinal question is: why should people not have the freedom to use their own resources to pursue better health care for themselves and

---

health care needs would inevitably create a bottomless pit or a commitment to ever increasing health care investments with ever fewer returns so that society would be forced to forgo realizing other important social goals (e.g., Fried 1979, ch. 5). This paper contends that even if these notions can be appropriately defined and generally accepted in a state (through democratic decisions, for example) without causing a bottomless pit, it is still practically impossible to realize equal health care in the state.

their family members? In particular, under what circumstances should considerations of freedom defeat claims for equality?

Third, the consequences of attempting to seek as much equal health care as possible would be undesirable. If people granted government the authority to secure equal health care for everyone, the government would hold a strong or even exclusive power in collecting and distributing health care resources, and people would face a series of difficulties in supervising and restricting this government power. Among other things, there would be the challenge of effectively combating government health care bureaucracies and preventing escalating public health care expenditures, low efficiency, red tape, resource waste, and official inattention in government-controlled health care delivery. In short, how does one avoid the risk of obtaining a high-cost, low-yielding, and poor-quality health care system in the pursuit of equality?

Finally, government power tends to produce corruption, following Lord Acton's warning: "power tends to corrupt; absolute power corrupts absolutely." The power of health care allocation is no exception. In pursuing an egalitarian national health care system, government's power would become much too strong. Even if we were willing to sacrifice our free choices (for better health care for ourselves and our family members) in order to realize equality for everybody, we may still end up with intolerable health care inequality caused by government corruption.[6]

In short, the dominant contemporary Western health care ideology pushes us to engage in an egalitarian endeavor that is both illusory and costly. It turns out that, as I have shown above, (1) real

---

[6] The public choice theory developed by James Buchanan, the 1986 Nobel Prize laureate in economic science, is particularly helpful for us to understand the nature of government. Government consists of a group of humans called politicians. Just as every human makes choices based on one's own motives, desires, and values, politicians are no exception. It is not from the benevolence of the politician that we expect our welfare check, but out of his regard to his own, not the public interests. If governments are called upon to do more and more important things, Buchanan teaches us, the degree of popular democratic control over governmental decisions has to be gradually reduced. See Buchanan 1987.

equal health care is practically impossible, and (2) enormous moral and economic costs are involved in attempting to achieve as much equal health care as possible. In this case, we need to reconsider the basic assumption of the dominant contemporary Western health care ideology: namely, health care resources must be distributed by the state in an egalitarian manner. Many take this assumption for granted simply because they believe health care to be a basic human need. But they have overlooked that there is a conceptual gap between a "basic need" and a justified claim to "equality." Clearly, the moral emphasis has been placed on the claim to "equality," not on "need" itself.

Equality is a dominant value in the contemporary Western liberal account of human needs and welfare. For instance, John Rawls (1971) and Norman Daniels (1985) insistently argue that justice requires maintaining fair equality of opportunity. The state, they contend, must take positive steps (e.g., through educational system and health care service) to enhance the opportunity of those disadvantaged by social factors (such as family background) or natural lotteries (such as disease or disability) so as to ensure opportunity to be equal in the society. In this regard, if a societal goal is set up for seeking fair equality of opportunity, the autonomy of the individual and the family in securing better education or health care for himself or his family has to be restricted in order to maintain the scope and ability of a national equalitarian welfare system. In other words, following Rawls's and Daniels' view, the individual and family autonomy must be sacrificed in order to seek the so-called "fair equality of opportunity." Many of their followers seem to believe that this liberal egalitarian view is self-evidently justified.

Equality is by no means a dominant moral value in other moral visions or traditions, such as Confucianism, which holds a dramatically different value system from that of liberalism. Since liberalism has achieved a powerful ascendancy, there has been the conclusion that liberalism, as a moral and political vision, is superior to other moral accounts. This paper contends that, given the intractable problems involved in the dominant contemporary ideology of health care suggested by liberalism, we have good reason to draw on other moral traditions in order to determine the proper way of health care allocation. In particular, Confucianism cherishes "love with distinction" rather than "universal equality" regarding human welfare. It promises significant insights regarding contemporary health care distribution. The Confucian tradition may imply a health care system that is more justifiable than the system suggested by the egalitarian liberal ideology.

The Confucian Tradition: The Small Family and the Big Family

The Confucian tradition is well-known for emphasizing the importance of the family as well as promoting the individual virtues related to family relations, such as *xiao* (filial piety) and *di* (brotherly love). In a comparative sense, Western culture can be characterized as individualistic, while Confucian culture as familialistic (Fan 2002). As is well-known, Confucianism establishes the cardinal principle of *ren* (humanity) so as to display human nature as love or care in a relation-based and family-centered manner. The principle has been adopted in the Confucian tradition to guide both the individual in pursuing a full-fledged good life and to regulate society in shaping an appropriate political structure as well as formulating proper public policies. The good Confucian life is the life of learning and exercising the virtues and seeking the highest excellence (*zhi-shan*) throughout an entire life, in which the individual is cultivated, the family well regulated, the state rightly governed, and the whole world made peaceful (*The Great Learning*). A good society is one that conforms to the principle of *ren* in shaping its institutions and making its public policies. Presumably, as the principle of *ren* is the cardinal moral principle of society, a minimal requirement of a legitimate public policy should be non-contradiction with the basic requirement of *ren*. Accordingly, a Confucian answer to the question of what pattern of health care allocation a society should adopt must depend on an answer to the question of what the best application of *ren* is in the field of health care (Fan 1999).

Ren in its basic meaning concerns human relations. The essence of such relations, from the perspective of *ren*, is "loving" or "caring." Indeed, the principle of *ren* requires loving humans (*Analects*, 12:22). This requirement, however, is not equivalent to an egalitarian position of universal love. Instead, it requires one to love others according to the nature of one's relationships with them. In practice, this requirement is embodied by the Confucian guidelines of "love with distinction" and "love by gradation" regulated by Confucian rituals (*li*). In order to love others appropriately, one must take into account the distinctions, orders, and relative importance of one's relations to them (Chan 1955). This is because, for Confucians, different human relations convey different moral significance and require different ways of loving and caring, such as loving and caring as intimacy (*qin*) between parent and child, as righteousness (*yi*) between prince and minister, as different function (*bie*) between husband and wife, as appropriate order (*xu*) between older and younger, and as fidelity (*xin*) between friend and friend. Simply put, from the Confucian perspective of *ren*, it is improper for one to love a stranger as one's relative, or a remote relative as one would a close family member.

Confucians hold strong moral reasons for giving the family the first priority in the application of love. In the first place, Confucians take the family to be the root of love. One must start with the application of love in one's family, and then is able to extend it to other social relations. If one's caring for others cannot begin in one's family, it will not begin at all. Moreover, since our parents have given us so much, we owe them the most. For Confucians, a living being without a notion of gratitude would be a wild beast rather than a civilized human. Furthermore, it is human nature to give greater weight to the welfare of one's family. "Even if we do perceive the equal moral worth of human beings, we must recognize the power of the motivation that moves us to give priority to those particular people who stand in special relation to us" (Wong 1989, 260). Eventually, Confucianism holds that the family constitutes the essential pattern of human existence that is preordained by Heaven (*tian*), the ultimate reality. The human nature of giving priority to the family manifests the norm of the ultimate reality that requires no further justification. Accordingly, Confucians are naturally familialists and anti-egalitarians in the exercise of love. Although they are required to love all humans, they are also required not to love all humans equally or similarly.

What does this principle of *ren* imply for specific public policies, such as health care policies? In particular, does the Confucian requirement of love with distinction have any standing in the area of public policy formulation? Some may argue that it does not. As they see it, the Confucian requirement of love with distinction concerns only the cultivation of individual character and cannot extend to the area of public policy-making where the very problem is to determine what justice requires. This view is mistaken. It is true that to explore the problem of health care allocation is to determine what justice requires, and it is also true that the Confucian requirement of love with distinction concerns the cultivation of individual character, but it is misleading to believe that the Confucian requirement of love with distinction concerns *only* the cultivation of individual character and thereby should not be included into the Confucian view of social justice. In the first place, if *ren* is the cardinal moral principle of Confucianism, as is generally agreed, it has to be implicit in the Confucian view of justice, just as the principle of utility has to be implicit in the utilitarian view of justice and the categorical imperative in the Kantian view of justice. Second, if the requirement of love with distinction is an *essential* [7] requirement of the principle of *ren* as I have shown in the above, then this requirement has to be implicit in the Confucian view of justice. If the requirement of love with distinction was left aside, the Confucian principle of *ren* would no longer be the same principle. Third, whatever a complete Confucian view of justice turns out to be, the requirement of love with distinction has been embodied in the Confucian tradition with its emphasis on the family values and responsibilities for family members' welfare, as I will illustrate in the next section. Finally, even if the requirement of love with distinction, being implicit in the Confucian view of justice, cannot directly lead to many concrete suggestions regarding public policy-making, it sets down a side constraint on public policy. If a public policy made it impossible (e.g., illegal) for us to practice love with distinction, it would be an immoral or unjust public policy and should not be accepted by Confucians. This view will be further illustrated in the next section.

---

[7] By "essential" I mean a necessary condition for its basic character.

Some may also argue that "love with distinction" does not govern all human concerns. The more important moral requirement, it may be argued, is to do "what is right" (*yi*). It is not unknown that the Confucian notion "yi" (righteousness), in one of its multidimensions, is similar to the concept "justice." Accordingly, it may seem more appropriate to emphasize the role of "yi" rather than the requirement of love with distinction in talking about the Confucian position in health care allocation. This argument, however, is incomplete. The issue is not that we should not do what is right (*yi*). The issue is what is right, that is the content of *yi*. It is true that one of the meanings of *yi* (righteousness) is justice, if, by "justice," we mean giving everyone his or her due. But is the Confucian view of righteousness similar to the liberal view of justice? My answer is in the negative (Fan 1997). There are good reasons to support that love with distinction constitutes part of the content of what is right for the Confucians.[8]

Sometimes scholars use the Confucian notion of the state as a big family to support their proposal for state-imposed egalitarian wel-

---

[8] It is not uncommon that in the Confucian classics humanity (*ren*) and righteousness (*yi*) are juxtaposed in parallel as if they were unrelated different notions, with one (ren) emphasizing loving or caring, with the other (*yi*) emphasizing righteousness or appropriateness. For instance, in *the Doctrine of the Mean*, "ren is the characteristic element of humanity, and the great exercise of it is in loving relatives. Yi is what is appropriate, and the great exercise of it is in honoring the worthy" (ch. 20). Again, in *Mencius*, "the heart of compassion is the germ of humanity (*ren*); the heart of shame and dislike, of righteousness (*yi*)..." (2A: 6). In fact, Mencius was the first in the Confucian tradition to give the ideal of righteousness (*yi*) unprecedented importance. The reason for Mencius to do so, according to Wing-tsit Chan, is because "he bitterly opposed the Moist doctrine of universal love without distinctions. For this reason he often advocated humanity and righteousness together, for to him humanity was necessary to bind people together and righteousness was necessary to make distinctions" (Chan 1963, 50). If the basic requirements of both *ren* and *yi* are squarely opposed to egalitarian love without distinctions, then *yi* is better taken to be a derivative notion from the cardinal Confucian principle of *ren*: in addition to giving preferential treatment to one's relatives (and this constitutes the core of Confucian familialism), the Confucian morality also requires giving preferential treatment to the worthy (and this constitutes the core of Confucian elitism).

fare programs. As they see it, since Confucians take the state as a big family and all people are family members in the state, all people should receive equal treatment under a state arrangement. After all, if all individuals are our brothers and sisters, why should we distinguish them with different packages in taking care of their welfare? Indeed, Confucianism does hold a notion of a big family. Confucians understand that all people under Heaven (namely, all humans in the world, not just the people within a state) belong to a big family. As Confucius states it clearly, "all within the Four Seas [the world] are brothers" (*Analects* 12:5). In this sense, it is true that all humans are relatives. However, this notion of a big family makes sense in Confucianism only when it is used in contrast with the notion of a small family, namely, the traditional Chinese family of grandparents, parents, and children. All humans belong to a big family because they all came into being from the same ultimate sources, Heaven and Earth. But they also belong to different small families because they were reproduced by different human ancestors, and their nurturing and growing had to take place in different small families. And this, for Confucians, constitutes the normal way of human existence. Accordingly, Confucians must distinguish a small family from a big family, close family members from remote relatives—all people in the world are remote relatives, and only some people are intimate relatives. It is the requirement of the Confucian principle of *ren* that one's intimate relatives should receive one's preferential treatment.

Nevertheless, giving a moral priority to the small family does not mean that no moral weight should be given to the big family. Offering preferential treatment to one's close family members does not suggest that one should not care at all about the welfare of one's remote relatives. Evidently, it is the requirement of *ren* that one should extend love to others outside of one's small family. This is to say, the Confucian view of love holds a middle way between two extreme positions. One is the egalitarian doctrine that one should treat strangers as one treats one's family. The other is a doctrine that one should only care about one's close family members. Confucianism wants us to care about both the family and strangers, with more weight given to the small family. Of course, it would be very helpful if Confucianism could offer us specific guidance as to how love should be extended to others beyond our small families. However, it is unfair to demand Confucianism to offer such guidance through a deductive moral system, because no moral tradition with a requirement of love with distinction is capable of doing so. It may also be misleading to require Confucianism to do so because Confucianism takes the practices of love as presumptions in favor of the immediate, highly relation-relevant, context-sensitive, and creative in nature, all of which tend to preclude any concept of generalized or universalized rules or individual rights (Ames 1988). Nonetheless, with the clear general requirement of *ren* at hand, we can always attempt to inquire into the rich intellectual and exemplary resources stored in the Confucian tradition for practical instructions.[9] In exploring the appropriate way of dealing with the issue of health care allocation we face today, the Confucian tradition proves to be particularly insightful because it

---

[9] In an excellent essay regarding universalism versus Confucian love with distinctions, David Wong states: "I fault [Confucianism] for neglecting the real problems that come with emphasizing the necessity of love with distinctions when there is no clear way to extend that love into love for all" (1989, 265). His practical solution to the conflict between taking care of the family and aiding strangers is to "attempt to change the policies of our largest institutions so that much of the burden of aiding the stranger is taken on not by the individual who must then choose between the stranger and those close to him, but by entities with the greatest fund of resources" (ibid., 267). However, such a solution, if fully realized, may have essentially changed a Confucian society to an egalitarian liberal society. Although Confucians can support some collective acts undertaken by big "entities" such as government to aid people (as we shall show in the next section), they cannot arrange such acts as general welfare projects equally available to everyone so that the individual is free from the burden of making difficult decisions in choosing "between the stranger and those close to him." The role of the individual and family, in making decisions regarding the welfare of themselves, their family members, and others in society in a constantly relation-relevant and context-sensitive way, is always fundamental for nurturing the Confucian virtues as well as maintaining the Confucian structure of society. A society in which individuals do not need to make and practice such decisions is no longer a Confucian society. If Confucian sages set good examples in pursuing appropriate well-being for themselves, their families, neighbors, and others, contemporary people should not simply relegate these important issues to big "entities" like government for egalitarian arrangements and thereby free their hands from them.

takes seriously the moral fabric in which humans are born, care, suffer and die.

The Confucian View of Health Care Allocation: Toward a Harmonious Multi-Tier Health Care System

Traditional Confucian China has never attempted to establish an egalitarian national health care system. This non-action is consistent with the Confucian view of human welfare in general and health care welfare in particular. A Confucian evaluation on the contemporary egalitarian model of health care allocation endorsed by the dominant Western liberal health care ideology is inevitably negative. Under the strong version of this model, government enforces an all-encompassing egalitarian distribution of health care resources without even allowing the existence of better basic tiers of health care for voluntary purchases. Individuals are thereby prohibited from using their own resources to pursue better health care for themselves and their families. This model is inconsistent with the basic Confucian moral orientation of "love with distinction" or "care by gradation" under the principle of *ren*. It is in the Confucian moral virtues and sentiments that we are obliged to work hard to achieve better lives for our parents, children and siblings, health care welfare included. When a state health care system makes it impossible for us to practice such Confucian values (that is, when we are prohibited from spending our own resources to locate better basic medical services or health care insurance for our families), the system cannot be justified by the Confucian moral perspective. Instead, it violates a fundamental Confucian moral conscience.

Moreover, the Confucian moral perspective may not even support a modest version of egalitarian health care allocation. Under this latter version, government is to maintain as much equality of *basic* health care needs as possible, leaving non-basic needs to the mechanism of the free market. The problems is, seeking the egalitarian satisfaction of health care needs, however basic these needs are, is extremely expensive because needs inevitably vary to a great extent from individual to individual. Pursuing equality would urge government to levy heavy taxes on the people in order to achieve such an end. This, however, cannot be approved by the Confucian view. Confucianism supports that people in the local district should voluntarily assist each other in difficulty or sickness (*Mencius*, 3A: 3), but it never suggests that government should coercively collect resources and redistribute them for an egalitarian welfare goal or health care plan. To the contrary, Confucians always insist that "a government of *ren*... must make the taxes and levies light" (*Mencius* 1A:5:3). Confucius himself compared the heavy taxes and levies as aggressive wild beasts that attacked human lives. He admired the legendary sage kings, Yao and Shun, as the ideal models of leaders who ruled the country without taking aggressive redistributive acts (*Analects* 15:3). Similarly, Mencius insistently required the ruler to run a government with light taxes and levies. In short, according to Confucianism, government cannot be justified in extorting people's resources for egalitarian redistribution.

Instead, Confucianism has always enthusiastically advised people to make efforts with their families to gain good livings for themselves. The Confucian tradition understands that it is much more natural and secure for people to rely on their families than on government to pursue their welfare. At the same time, it emphasizes that a virtuous person should stand ready to give a hand to others in difficulty. The basic Confucian teaching puts it very clear that one must take care of one's family, assist one's friends in need, sustain one's neighbors in misfortune, and offer assistance to those in calamity. Although there are no absolute rules regarding how to divide or distribute these different obligations, one can always look at the examples of Confucian sages for guidance. Following Confucianism, a society cannot be good without ultimately depending on the good heart of its virtuous persons: the heart of filial piety (*xiao*) to their parents, loyalty (*zhong*) to their connections, and compassion (*ce yin*) to the suffering. If the enforcement of the state's egalitarian welfare programs dispensed individuals with the opportunities of performing such virtues, they would lose enthusiasm and strength for cultivating appropriate human relationships and would be relegated to non-virtuous beings blindly operating with whatever mechanisms were set up by the state machine. The society would then not be Confucian.

Accordingly, Confucianism does not support any state-imposed egalitarian welfare project. It relies on people's voluntary actions for welfare pursuit. But this does not mean that Confucianism does not support any state act in assisting people in difficulty. Confucians may, again, stand in the middle way between egalitarian liberals (who want the state through welfare to achieve a fair equality of opportunity) and libertarian liberals (who want noninterference from the state) regarding the role of the state in people's welfare. It is evident that, throughout history, Confucian scholars have always encouraged and even required the state to take limited acts in supporting special groups of people, especially (1) those who do not have complete families, such as widows, widowers, orphans, and the childless, (2) the handicapped, and (3) those who encounter unusual natural disasters, such as flood and famine. From the Confucian view, it is easy to understand why those people, with legitimate reasons, require special aid from the state. Those who don't have complete families lose the ordinary family reliance that people usually possess. The handicapped are not able to make their livings as effectively as the normal and usually cause life-long, extraordinary burdens on their families. Finally, natural disasters often occur unexpected and the victims find it hard to recover without assistance from outsiders. Clearly, this Confucian message is two-fold: on the one hand, government should be sympathetic to the unfortunate in society and offer them support; on the other hand, state assistance should be offered only in limited ways to extraordinary people or in emergent circumstances. State aid can only serve as an unusual rescue method and can never become usual means for life. As a well-known Chinese saying goes: "help the urgent, not the poor; support the weak, not the lazy." For Confucians, poverty due to laziness does not deserve help.

In short, the Confucian teaching is that people should not rely on state welfare programs to lead their lives. Although it is necessary and benevolent for the state to care about people's well-being and offer assistance to the unfortunate, the aim of such assistance is not fair equality of opportunity or equality of welfare at a particular level regardless of the character and condition of the assisted. The state should never substitute the role of people's families in the pursuit of opportunity and welfare. It is through the autonomy and effort of the family that Confucians believe they are obliged to seek better health care and welfare for themselves and their family members. Neither opportunity nor health care nor the good life can be secured by the state. In general, Confucians trust family care rather than state care. They want family responsibility rather than government bureaucracy.

What would these traditional Confucian insights and instructions mean for our contemporary society in attempting to establish the proper system of health care allocation? Specifically, if Confucianism is opposed to any egalitarian package of health care allocation, what will it have to offer regarding the appropriate ways of delivering health care to people? I think at least the three following ideas can be teased out from the Confucian tradition for our consideration.

First, it would support family savings for ordinary health care. Given that health care is basically a family obligation in the Confucian understanding, given that every family member needs some ordinary medical services for small health problems or preventive purposes (which can usually be handled in a clinic by family physicians without the need of involving medical experts, sophisticated facilities, or expensive medications), every family should have some resources saved and prepared beforehand for such ordinary health services for their family members. Since this type of health care is often needed and is relatively cheap, a family savings account for this purpose would be a good way to manifest family responsibility. Establishing such an account can also serve as an incentive for family members to care about their life styles, preserve their health, and prevent diseases in order not to drain on their families' resources for medical care. The savings accounts in the current Singaporean health care system may have reflected this Confucian idea of family responsibility.

Second, it would support the purchase of insurance plans for hospital and critical care. Some serious diseases or health problems need the care of a hospital with medical experts as well as advanced diagnostic and therapeutic facilities. Given the costs, insurance is the best way for people to share benefits and risks through the market mechanism. Government can certainly help organize some insurance plans or set up a public insurance plan to compete with other private insurance plans for people to choose. Confucianism would suggest that resources be left to people and their families for them to purchase appropriate insurance plans as they see fit for their family members. In the Confucian tradition, parents have a moral obligation to provide health insurance for their children, and adult children have a moral obligation to pursue health insurance for their elderly parents, if the latter are incapable of doing so by themselves. It is appropriate and legitimate for some individuals to be able to offer better insurance plans for their family members.

Finally, it may support establishing rescue projects for special cases. As Confucianism requires sympathy for the unfortunate, society may consider providing rescue projects to help the uninsured in special situations. But the targets of such projects should be extraordinary cases, such as those who do not have complete families or those who are handicapped. Confucianism would object to an egalitarian project that seeks to cover all the uninsured under all circumstances. Applicants for such relief should be considered based on their desert. At the same time, people should always be encouraged to help each other through voluntary charity and private foundations rather than relying on government projects. Finally, the state should not prohibit the purchase of better basic care. Appeal to fair equality of opportunity may not impede the prevenience of health care for family members. The autonomy of the family—in the sense that consensual relations within a given family to secure better educational or health care services for its family members should not be coercively interfered with by the state—is the cardinal value in the Confucian tradition.

Needless to say, these are only very general ideas and crude suggestions. They have to be developed into detailed proposals in order to guide public policy. But the general moral thought is clear: the pattern of health care allocation implied by the Confucian tradition would be dramatically different from the pattern recommended by the contemporary statist egalitarian ideology. While the statist egalitarian ideology demands equality, the Confucian view requires harmony with love with distinction—a harmonious multi-tier health care system in which family responsibility is emphasized, voluntary charity and mutual assistance are encouraged, and government rescue projects are supplemented without any egalitarian commitment.

Conclusion: Return to the Philosophy of Harmony from the Philosophy of Equality

Liberalism has been more and more influential in the contemporary world. All major world traditions are in retreat before liberal individualism and statism. However, liberal individualism, when it emphasizes the importance of individual independence, autonomy, and rights, tends to downplay the fact of individual interdependence (especially within the family) as an inevitable feature of human existence. What is worse, liberal statism wants individuals to rely on the state to maintain their welfare as equal as others. Thus the state has become the ultimate reliance in more and more individuals' life concerns. This liberal statist egalitarianism inevitably discounts the role of the family in society and separates people from state to state in the world. Indeed, when individualism and statism go hand in hand, the traditional functions of the family become been replaced by the state one after another. Not only can a state control its borders and not allow people to travel and communicate freely, it can also deprive people of their own resources and enforce illusory political ideologies.

Confucianism is neither individualistic nor statist. It is first and foremost familialistic. In the first place, Confucians recognize that a human being is not only an independent being, but is also a historical, social, and familial being. Since we are naturally born as the children of our parents or brothers of our sisters, we do not choose our original existential situations or familial roles. Given these metaphysical and existential conditions, we possess moral obligations to our family members. For Confucians, it is morally perverse to argue that children do not have any more of a moral obligation to their elderly parents in health care than any other persons in the society because children do not ask to be brought to the world in the first place (English 1979; Daniel 1988). For Confucians, it is deeply wrong to understand human moral obligations primarily according to individual decisions and contracts (Wang 1999).

Confucians do not first turn to the state for assistance, and the state is not their final concern. Though their ideal involves a net of multiple concerns ranging from the individual through the whole world (namely, individual cultivation, family regulation, state governing, and the whole world being made peaceful), the family always stands in-between the individual and the state to take care of the individual and grasp his or her loyalty. A peaceful world and the well-being of all people under-the-Heaven is their final concern, though this final concern cannot be realized through state-imposed egalitarian welfare plans. For Confucians, though the state certainly should shoulder certain responsibilities (such as maintaining a social order, protecting people from murder, fraud, deception, offering special assistance in unusual situations, and the like), the family should shoulder others (such as pursuing welfare for every family member).

When equality becomes a dominant value in society, the traditional virtue of harmony is in jeopardy. Indeed, what Confucianism has provided is not a philosophy of equality, but is a philosophy of harmony (*zhong he*) (Fan 1997). It holds that individuals be harmoniously treated according to their desert in a societal structure in which the family is a foundational community. For Confucians, harmony is not only a crucial value in nurturing individual character (*Analects*, 18:23), but it can also guide us in arranging social institutions and distributions (*Xunzi*, 9:2). Confucians never assume equality as a basic human fact or value. Instead, they perfectly understand the inequalities of individuals not only in respect of talent, knowledge and virtue, but also in terms of their familial relationships and social status. In this light, Confucians recognize that it is inappropriate to treat unequals as equals. An appropriate societal goal for Confucians is not to secure equality, but to pursue harmonious human relations. Essentially, since the family is the foundation of human community, Confucians hold that the common cause of the family should become every family member's cause and reliance and thus possess his or her loyalty.[10]

---

[10] Loyalty can be defined as the willing devotion of a self to the common cause of a community (Royce 1969, 902). Loyalty, as a virtue, has its irreplaceable importance. Among others, it furnishes us a personal solution of the hardest question of human practical problems, such as "for what do I live? Why am I here? For what am I good? Why am I needed?" In the early last century, American philosopher Josiah

To sum up, this essay argues that the dominant contemporary Western ideology in health care allocation is misleading because it strives for the impossible at the cost of overextended government power. This essay attempts to employ the long-standing intellectual and ethical resources of Confucianism for practical instruction and guidance. The Confucian tradition recognizes the family having the central status in society. The family is considered responsible for the welfare (health care included) of every family member, while the state, as an enlarged family, should offer only limited help to special groups of individuals in unusual situations. The state should not try to redistribute resources to maintain an egalitarian result of welfare by compulsory taxation or restrict the purchase of better basic care by appeal to fair equality of opportunity. This essay shows that this Confucian view still carries significant moral implications for the contemporary health care policy.

REFERENCES

Ames, R. T. 1988. "Rites as Rights: The Confucian Alternative." In *Human Rights and the World Religions*, edited by L. S. Rouner. Notre Dame: The University of Notre Dame Press.

Beauchamp, T. and Childress, J. 1994. *The Principles of Biomedical Ethics*, 4th edition. New York: Oxford University Press.

Bole III, T. J. and Bonderson W. B. (eds.). 1991. *Rights to Health Care*. Dordretcht: Kluwer Academic Publishers.

Buchanan, J. M. 1987. *Economics: Between Predictive Science and Moral Philosophy*. College Station: Texas A&M University Press.

Chan, Wing-tsit. 1955. "The Evolution of Confucian Concept *Ren*," *Philosophy East & West* 4 : 295-315.

—————. 1963. *A Source Book in Chinese Philosophy*. Princeton: Princeton University Press.

Confucius. 1979. *Analects*. Trans. by D. C. Lau. New York: Penguin Books.

Royce commented, "we as a nation, I fear, have been forgetting loyalty" (ibid. 899). But the more dangerous thing, I am afraid, is that more and more people have chosen the state as the object of their loyalty. They have forgotten the true meaning of the family.

Daniels, N. 1988. *Am I my Parents' Keeper?* Oxford: Oxford University Press.

Daniels, N. 1985. *Just Health Care.* Cambridge: Cambridge University Press.

Engelhardt, Jr., H. T. 1996. *The Foundations of Bioethics,* 2nd edition. New York: Oxford University Press.

English, J. 1979. *Having Children: Philosophy and Legal Reflections on Parenthood.* New York: Oxford University Press.

Fan, R. 1997. "Confucian and Rawlsian Views of Justice: A Comparison," *Journal of Chinese Philosophy* 24 (1997): 427-456.

————. 1999. "Just Health Care, the Good Life, and Confucianism." In *Confucian Bioethics,* edited by R. Fan. Dordretcht: Kluwer Academic Publishers.

————. 2002. "Reconsidering Surrogate Decision-making: Aristotelianism and Confucianism on Ideal Human Relations," *Philosophy East & West* 52:3 (forthcoming).

Fried, C. 1979. *Right and Wrong.* Cambridge: Harvard University Press.

Friedman, D. 1991. "Should Medicine be Commodity? An Economist's Perspective." In Bole III and Bonderson.

Mencius. 1970. *Mencius.* Trans. D. C. Lau. New York: Penguin Books.

Rawls, J. 1971. *A Theory of Justice.* Cambridge: Harvard University Press.

Royce, J. 1969. "The Philosophy of Loyalty." In *The Basic Writings of Josiah Royce,* V.2, edited by J. J. McDermott. Chicago: The University of Chicago Press, 855-1013.

Singer, P. 1976. "Freedom and Utilities in the Distribution of Health Care." In *Ethics and Health Care Policy,* edited by R. M. Veatch and R. Branson. Cambridge: Ballinga Publishing Company, 175-193.

Veatch, R. 1991. "Justice and the Right to Health Care: An Egalitarian Account." In Bole III and Bonderson.

Wang, Q. 1999. "The Confucian Filial Obligation and Care for Aged Parents." In *Confucian Bioethics,* edited by R. Fan. Dordretcht: Kluwer Academic Publishers.

Wong, D. B. 1989. "Universalism versus Love with Distinctions: An Ancient Debate Revived," *Journal of Chinese Philosophy* (16): 251-272.

Xunzi. 1990. *Xunzi* vol. II. Trans. by John Knoblock. Stanford: Stanford University Press.

10

A Pragmatic Insight on Morality and Its Distinct Metaphysical Foundations [1]

Bo Mou

I. Introduction

Although, strictly interpreted, the term "pragmatism" refers to a specific philosophical school or movement that rises in the late nineteenth century and the early twentieth century and was highlighted and formulated by modern or contemporary American philosophers Peirce, James and Dewey, some important aspects of its spirit are shared and advocated in other philosophical traditions in distinct ways. In this paper, by focusing on the aspect of its metaphysical foundation, I examine one pragmatic strategic insight on human morality to the effect that no pre-set and fixed moral rules or principles should be taken as the final absolute moral authority. Instead, attention needs to be paid to the moral agent's own moral experience that responds to the felt demands in concrete situations. The pragmatic insight was explicitly presented by Dewey and also suggested by Laozi in the *Daode Jing* in their distinct ways. Through a comparative examination of how the pragmatic insight on morality is arrived at on the basis of some distinct metaphysical foundations in Dewey's and Laozi's accounts, I intend to show that the pragmatic insight in question captures something important about the nature of human moral-

---

[1] The original version of this article, under the title "A Pragmatic Insight Regarding Morality: From A Comparative Perspective," was published in P. Weingartner, G. Schurz and G. Dorn eds. 1997, 659-64. This revised version deletes one section on Confucius' approach in the original version and makes a significant revision of the section on Laozi's relevant Daoist view.

ity that a promising moral theory cannot afford to ignore. Also, from a metaphysical point of view, Dewey's and Laozi's distinct approaches to the pragmatic insight could jointly contribute to, and enhance our understanding of, the strategic insight and overcome each other's limitations.

My strategy in the following discussion is this. First, in the rest of this section, I highlight two basic orientations in ethical studies and its connection with the pragmatic insight under discussion. Second, I present Dewey's basic point of view in this regard. My discussion of Dewey's view in this aspect is relatively sketchy because Dewey has presented his own basic view on the issue in quite clear terms, and I do not intend to further elaborate Dewey's view on the issue. Instead, I focus more on considering some relevant possible challenges for the sake of the comparative examination of the pragmatic insight. Third, through an elaboration of the opening message of the *Daode Jing*, I discuss how Laozi looks at the issue from a distinct metaphysical vision. The emphasis of this writing is on how Laozi's approach could complement Dewey's point in regard to the pragmatic insight.

Indeed, in the field of ethical studies, theorists are contentious and divided by their deeply conflicting intuitions and goals. Nevertheless, there seems to be one common orientation shared by many accounts within the orthodox approach in ethics regarding the rightness of acts: they are rule-oriented. Their primary focus is on working out some fixed moral rules or principles that supposedly determine the rightness of acts. Some of those accounts consider those fixed moral rules or principles as being commanded from without. For example, in the case of divine command theory, such a moral rule is this: whatever God permits, prohibits, or commands is right, wrong, or obligatory respectively. In the case of ethical egoism, such a moral rule is this: one ought always to maximize one's own personal good as an end. In the case of Kantianism, such a moral principle is Kant's categorical imperative, which states that you act only according to that maxim which you can at the same time will that it should become a universal law. And, in the case of (act) utilitarianism, such a moral rule is this: an act is right if and only if it produces at least as great a balance of good over bad in its consequences for all people affected as any other act available to the agent. The aforementioned orientation might be called "moral legalism." In contrast, another way of thinking, though giving a role to moral rules and principles, maintains that the rightness of a moral agent's acts depends crucially on those relevant particular elements in concrete situations in which she performs her acts. The latter orientation might be called "moral particularism."[2] The kernel of the latter orientation is an insight on human morality that is considered to be pragmatic in character: no fixed rule reigns supreme as the final, absolute moral authority; moral judgments cannot ignore various felt demands of concrete situations. This strategic insight has been explicitly delivered by Dewey.

II. Dewey: Instrumental Character of Moral Rules and Unique Character of Concrete Moral Situations

The aforementioned pragmatic insight in Dewey's philosophy is influenced by Charles Darwin's work on evolution. Darwin's account criticizes the static world view and replaces what Dewey calls its "assumption of the superiority of the fixed and final" and its "treating change and origin as signs of defect and unreality" (Dewey 1978, 3) with a dynamic world view which is characterized in terms of change, growth, process, evolution, and emergence. Dewey emphasizes the impact of Darwin's work on philosophy. For it is to redirect our thinking to reflect this evolutionary reality: our bodies and our minds have evolved, and our institutions and our values have evolved as well. Its primary impact, as Dewey sees it, lies in this: philosophy needs to abandon searching for "absolute origins and absolute finalities" and instead to seek "specific values and the specific conditions that generate them" (Dewey 1978, 10). This general pragmatic perspective regarding the direction of philosophical inquiry bears especially upon Dewey's approach to morality, especially in regard to how to look at the relation between those formulated and fixed general moral rules and principles and particular and concrete situations.

---

[2] For a clear discussion of the distinction between moral legalism and moral particularism, see Holmes 1993.

Dewey's approach in this connection seems to have two basic points, a negative one and a positive one. The negative point is highlighted by his following remarks:

> A moral principle, such as that of chastity, of justice, of the Golden Rule, gives the agent a basis for looking at and examining a particular question that comes up. It holds before him against taking a short or partial view of the act. It economizes his thinking by supplying him with the main heads by reference to which to consider the bearings of his desires and purposes; it guides him in his thinking by suggesting to him the important considerations for which he should be on the lookout. A moral principle, then, is not a command to act or forbear acting in a given way: *it is a tool for analyzing a special situation....* [But] The moral quality of knowledge lies not in possession but in concern with increase. The essential evil of fixed standard and rules is that it tends to render men satisfied with the existing state of affairs and to take the ideas and judgments they already possess as adequate and final. (Dewey 1936, 309-12)

Dewey's point in this passage is that no fixed rule or principle reigns supreme as the final, absolute moral authority. For a rule, as a tool, emerges inductively or conventionally from the consideration of past situations to analyze present or future situations. This tool is subject to modification with respect to present and future situations not only because it is supposed to be an instrumental guidance generalized from concrete situations but also because there are unique situations in which an appeal to the moral rule does not apply. In this way, a general moral rule is neither logically nor empirically a priori to particular and concrete situations.

One might immediately challenge: if the right or wrong is not determined by the fixed moral rules, then by what? It seems to Dewey that the right or wrong is "determined by the situation in its entirety, not by the rule as such" (Dewey 1936, p. 309). Dewey's point is that one needs to appeal to concrete situations to whose felt demands a moral agent's own moral experience of approval or disapproval responds. In concrete situations, there are significant elements other than the given rule(s) or principle(s) alone to be considered. The particular features of the situations, consequences, the lessons of the past, the ends-in-view that guiding ideals suggest are worth pursuing, the goodness of certain acts (such as caring, considerateness, compassion, and interpersonal love) and their associated thoughts, motives, and intentions, etc. also need to be considered. Those elements in concrete situations appear as the felt demands of concrete situations to which a moral agent's own moral experience needs to respond in certain ways.[3] This does not mean that a moral agent necessarily assesses the aforementioned elements in a very conscious way; they might spontaneously respond to the felt demands of concrete situations. In this way, the ultimate justification of our moral judgments lies in moral experience that responds to the felt demands of concrete situations in their entirety.

In this way, Dewey explicitly and clearly presents the pragmatic insight under discussion in terms of his evolutionary view of world and his general pragmatic methodological guiding principle. Note that, as suggested in the preceding presentation, Dewey's view here involves various interesting and significant issues concerning the metaphysical foundation of moral rules and principles, the nature of situated moral experience, the moral foundation in human nature, etc. What I focus on in this writing, as indicated at the outset, is the issue of the metaphysical foundation addressed in the pragmatic insight on morality under discussion. In the following I thus concentrate upon some possible challenges to Dewey's version of the pragmatic insight in regard to its metaphysical foundation.

Indeed, there seem to be several questions that one might raise to challenge Dewey's view. First, though the world keeps changing and maneuvers in dynamic process, is there still some unifying force that runs through all those "specific values and the specific conditions" or "special situations"? If yes, then would there be something general or universal among those specific situations? For such a unifying force would reveal itself in concrete situations in certain uniform ways. Second, if the answers to the above two related questions are yes, could such a unifying force and its uniform ways be somehow captured or formulated in our thought and then in our language?

---

[3] Cf., Holmes's elaboration of Dewey's positive point in his 1993, last chapter.

Third, if some formulated moral rules or principles do capture such a unifying force and its uniform ways to some extent, can we still say that those formulated rules or principles merely have its instrumental value and can be employed only as a tool? To my knowledge, Dewey does not explicitly answer those questions or, at least, those questions as explicitly phrased in the preceding ways. Nevertheless, based upon his line of thought in this connection, especially his Darwinian world-view orientation, we can still figure out his possible responses and so find out what challenges his version of the pragmatic insight under discussion would be facing. On the one hand, Dewey's background of experimental science and his Darwinian evolutionary world view might let him stop short of metaphysical vision towards the afore-mentioned unifying force whose entirety seems beyond experimental verification, or at least he would suspend a metaphysical commitment to it. On the other hand, whether or not Dewey makes a metaphysical commitment to such a unifying force, he clearly renders any formulated rules or principles short of such metaphysically heavyweight import when he emphasizes their instrumental character. Now the challenges to Dewey's version of the pragmatic insight are these. First, if there does exist some fundamental unifying force running through the world or universe, then, though no fixed and formulated rules reigns supreme as final and absolute authority, one would have need to do justice to such a unifying force and its uniform ways in one's account of the metaphysical foundation of the pragmatic insight. Second, in such an account, one would also need to provide an explanation of, or at least some insight on, the relation between such a unifying force and its uniform ways if any, on the one hand, and any formulated rules or principles that are intended to capture them, on the other hand. Third, if some formulated moral rules or principles do somehow capture such a unifying force and its uniform ways to some extent, one's account of the pragmatic insight needs to do justice to some value of those formulated rules or principles that go beyond their mere instrumental value. Without meeting those challenges, an account of the pragmatic insight regarding morality cannot go far in the sense that it would be incomplete and, worse, go with some relativistic character. For those metaphysical concerns that are somehow related to the pragmatic point under discussion clearly go beyond what Darwin's theory of evolution or any experimental scientific account could deal with on its own. They thus demand some fundamental metaphysical insights beyond mere Darwinian evolutionary world view or any account exclusively based upon experimental science. In this aspect, I will show in the next section that some of Laozi's fundamental metaphysical insights in the *Daode Jing* provide us some guiding visions. These guiding visions are not merely externally complementary to Dewey's view in this regard in the sense that Laozi teaches and reminds us of something that Dewey's approach goes short of but that does not directly engage with those metaphysical imports of Dewey's approach. They actually more substantially and internally complement Dewey's view regarding the metaphysical foundation of the pragmatic insight under discussion. They provide something that would reflectively answer those challenges raised to Dewey's approach and constructively contribute to a due metaphysical foundation which would prevent the pragmatic insight either from running into a certain kind of moral relativism or from indiscriminately rendering those moral rules or principles expressed in our language merely instrumental in nature.

III. Laozi: Dao in Language-Engagement and Genuine Dao

Dewey, in the classical American pragmatic tradition, explicitly elucidates the pragmatic insight by giving a rational analysis of why fixed and formulated (moral) principles cannot be taken as final (moral) authority on the basis of the evolutionary world-view, and in more or less scientific terms. Laozi, in the classical Chinese philosophical tradition, captures the same pragmatic insight through his visions on the dialectical relation of the fundamental metaphysical *Dao* of the universe to its language expressions. Through, directly and explicitly or indirectly and tacitly, meeting the three challenges aforementioned, Laozi's approach reveals something important regarding the pragmatic insight. That is, the pragmatic insight is not incompatible with the human being's persistent pursue after some eternal and ultimate values or even with their finite formulated expressions. In the following, I will make points through briefly explaining one of Laozi's most fundamental insights in this aspect, which is succinctly suggested in the opening message of the *Daode Jing*.[4]

One of Laozi's most fascinating teachings in his *Daode Jing* is its first six-character aphorism in Chapter 1 which, according to one prevailing standard translation-interpretation, is paraphrased as follows:

> "The way that can be spoken of is not the constant way" (Lau 1963, 5) or "The *Dao* that can be told of [in language] is not the eternal *Dao*." (Chan 1963, 139)

One thing is clear. Laozi explicitly maintains that there *is* the eternal or constant *Dao* as the ultimate unifying force evolving and operating throughout the universe, which might as well be called 'the metaphysical *Dao*'. But, how to capture this constant and eternal *Dao*? Is any language engagement with the ultimate concern like the eternal *Dao* doomed to fail to capture the genuine *Dao*?[5] According to one standard paraphrase, the cited passage is considered to reveal one fundamental insight which appears to be strikingly similar to that of Wittgenstein's idea about the spoken and the unspoken that is sometimes delivered this way: Language expressions or formulations cannot really capture what those expressions or formulations aim to say. The genuine *Dao* has to be captured in a way that is beyond language. It is often said that, in Laozi's case, contemplation of the *Dao* in silence requires sharply distinguishing the eternal *Dao* from what can be formulated or captured in (or by) language. In other words, the genuine *Dao* is fundamentally and intrinsically different from "the *Dao* that can be formulated," for the two are simply opposed to each other. I think that this interpretation fails to comprehensively capture what is actually delivered by the opening message of the *Daode Jing*. Indeed, Laozi teaches that one needs to contemplate the eternal *Dao*

---

[4] The discussion in this section is partially based upon my discussion of the opening message of the *Dao Jing* in Author 2.

[5] By "language engagement with the ultimate concern" I mean any reflective endeavor to capture (reach or characterize) an ultimate concern through our language.

without the dominance of the fixed formulation of *Dao* so as to reach the vantage-point from which one can achieve one's comprehensive understanding of the eternal *Dao*. What is also interesting and significant is to elaborate Laozi's insight about why various formulated and fixed (moral) principles are rather limited and cannot exhaust the eternal *Dao*. Does he think that, as what the standard interpretation literally means, the *Dao* that can be spoken of *is not* genuine *Dao*? In what sense? Does he reject any language expression and characterization, or language engagement, of the eternal *Dao*? Indeed, the *Dao*, or the fundamental unifying force that runs through the universe and its Way in which all things pursue their courses, is subject to eternal change and dynamically evolves in the universe. Any attempt to identify the eternal *Dao* with some formulation in terms of finite and fixed words or speech thus cannot *exhaust* the eternal *Dao*. However, that does not amount to saying that the eternal *Dao* cannot be (partially or somehow) captured in terms of language or cannot be reached in language. Laozi himself endeavors to characterize or, more generally speaking, *reach* the eternal or genuine *Dao* in a variety of language engagement throughout eighty-one chapters of the *Daode Jing*.[6] It is evident from Laozi's own language engagement in the classic that Laozi does not consider a language engagement with the eternal *Dao* as a sin. Rather, because the eternal *Dao* manifests or reveals itself in all things in various concrete, or, one can say, finite, situations, the *Dao* can be partially captured in terms of (finite) language related to (finite) concrete situations. Indeed, to capture the *Dao*, a moral agent needs to focus on her felt demands of concrete situations where the genuine *Dao* manifests itself. She thus can contemplate her situations and felt demand in terms of language. Due to all this as well as due to the syntactic and semantic structure of the Chinese *original* of the opening sentence of the *Daode Jing* which clearly consists of two statements (one affirmative while the other

---

[6] There is some important difference between the phrases "being reached" and "being (descriptively) characterized": the former is to cover a variety of ways to talked about the *Dao* through language engagement, far more than what the latter denotes. For example, among others, rigid designation falls under the former but not under the latter.

negative),[7] a more suitable paraphrase of the first six-character aphorism in the opening message would be this:

> The *Dao* can be reached [in language], but the Dao that has been characterized is not identical with, or cannot exhaust, the eternal [constant] *Dao*.

Here Laozi suggests a two-sided guiding vision regarding the ultimate concern and its language engagement, which consists of a positive finite point of view and a negative transcendental point of view. On the one hand, in the first assertive claim of the opening sentence, Laozi positively affirms the possibility and adequacy of the language engagement with the *Dao*: Any part or dimension (even the eternal dimension) of the *Dao* can be somehow talked about or reached in language, though any of such talks is finite in character in the sense that what it reaches is one finite part or dimension *of* the *Dao*. That is, the *Dao* still can be told even if being told in a finite point of view: (i) the finite point of view might be reasonable to the extent that it is true when it does capture a certain aspect or dimension or layer of the genuine *Dao*; (ii) it would be true when it does not claim its finite characterization of one part or aspect of the *Dao* as exclusively or exhaustively true and render false others that capture the other parts of the same entire *Dao*; (iii) different or even opposite finite points of view can be held about one and the same thing, when they capture various aspects or development stages of the same thing. On the other hand, in the second (negative) claim, Laozi alerts us to the limitation of the finite point of view and emphasizes the transcendental character of the *Dao* as the ultimate concern; for any finite language-engagement of the *Dao* cannot *exhaust* the entirety of the eternal and constant *Dao*. This point of view is transcendental because it transcends the finite point of view so as to capture the *Dao* of things in a holistic way and to realize the limitations of the finite point of view.

---

[7] For my detailed discussion of the semantic and syntactic structure of the opening sentence, see Bo Mou, 2000.

In this way, in the opening passage, Laozi takes both positive and negative looks at the finite point of view.

In my preceding interpretative elaboration of the opening message of Laozi's *Daode Jing* in view of his whole ideas in the classic, one can see that the two points of the pragmatic insight on morality as Dewey explicitly delivered are also captured in Laozi's teachings: (1) Any formulated rules or principles in terms of finite language cannot exhaust the eternal and constant *Dao* that evolves itself in ever-changing process and thus cannot reigns supreme as the indiscriminate final authority in all relevant concrete situations. (2) Since the eternal *Dao* reveals itself in all things in various concrete situations, to capture the *Dao*, a moral agent needs to primarily focus on her felt demands of concrete situations where the genuine *Dao* manifests itself.

Now one interesting question is this: Could Laozi's insight in this connection meet the three challenges raised to Dewey's version so as to contribute to, and enhance our understanding of, the pragmatic insight on morality under discussion? In my opinion, the answer is yes, though some interpretative work is needed to elaborate Laozi's relevant points. Laozi makes three significant points through his dialectical transcendental approach. First, rejecting fixed and formulated (moral) rules as final (moral) authority amounts neither to denying the existence of the fundamental unifying force nor to discarding the pursuit of the eternal *Dao* that runs through all the things in the universe. It is still our mission to pursue the ultimate principle, the eternal *Dao*, which reveals itself in its dynamic and evolving process.

Second, as the first affirmative statement of the opening message of the *Daode Jing* teaches us, the eternal genuine *Dao* can be somehow reached or captured in finite language (in the sense and to the extent explained before). So those 'formulated' moral rules and principles—indeed, any language expression, you can say, is a kind of formulated thing—could partially or to some extent capture the genuine *Dao*. That does not amount to saying that all of them do capture the genuine *Dao*, and much less to saying that any of them could exhaust the eternal *Dao*. For the eternal *Dao* dynamically manifests itself in various individual things in various concrete situations. So, when one captures something uniform through a certain pattern of concrete situations and expresses it in language, what has been captured could be some part or aspect of the genuine *Dao* that reveals itself in those situations. If so, what has been captured would be the *Dao* in language-engagement. The point is that the genuine *Dao* and the *Dao* in language-engagement cannot be sharply and dualistically separated and distinguished.

Third, because the genuine and constant *Dao* can be reached in language, as Laozi positively affirms, those formulated (moral) rules in terms of language could, to some extent, somehow capture parts or dimensions or layers of the genuine *Dao*. Those formulated rules that do more or less capture the genuine *Dao* would have their intrinsic value that goes beyond their mere instrumental value.

The preceding discussion shows how, and in what sense, some of Laozi's fundamental metaphysical insights in the *Daode Jing* provide us some guiding visions. One can also see how those visions are not just externally complementary to Dewey's view in the sense that Laozi merely teaches us something that Dewey's approach goes short of, without directly engaging with those metaphysical imports of Dewey. As a matter of fact, they internally or more substantially complement Dewey's view regarding the metaphysical foundation of the pragmatic insight under discussion. They provide something that would reflectively answer those challenges to Dewey's approach, as mentioned at the end of the first part of this section, and they constructively contribute to a due metaphysical foundation which would prevent the pragmatic insight either from running into a certain kind of moral relativism or from indiscriminately rendering those moral rules or principles expressed in our language merely instrumental in nature.

It is noted that, like Dewey's case, for the sake of the focus of this writing, some other relevant ideas in Laozi's *Daode Jing* are not examined here. For example, Laozi's insight on the relation between superior virtue and inferior virtue in Chapter 38 of the *Daode Jing* is closely related to the pragmatic insight on morality discussed here and the nature of moral experience. A more comprehensive treatment, which also discusses the issues of the nature of moral experience that responds to the felt demands in concrete situations and the moral foundation in human nature, is given in another writing.

*   *   *

In brief, converging from their distinct metaphysical perspectives, Dewey and Laozi deliver the same kind of pragmatic message on morality to the effect that no pre-set and fixed moral rules or principles should be taken as the final absolute moral authority but, instead, attention needs to be paid to the moral agent's own moral experience that responds to the felt demands in concrete situations. However, this pragmatic insight is based upon Dewey's and Laozi's distinct metaphysical guiding visions or world views. An interesting question is whether two visions could complement and so enhance each other. On the one hand, Laozi's naturalistic cosmic-metaphysical world view is essentially consistent with the evolutionary world view to the extent that both consider nature or universe as changing, growing, processing, and evolving on its own course. At least as far as those parts of the universe that are reached by human experience are concerned, our understanding of Laozi's Daoist cosmic-metaphysical world view could be supplemented by Dewey's evolutionary world view in its more or less scientific terms. On the other hand, as far as fundamental metaphysical vision is concerned, Dewey's evolutionary world view could be enhanced and substantively complemented by Laozi's Daoist cosmic-metaphysical world view which transcends what our experience, understood in its narrow sense, has so far reached. Moreover, Dewey's clear and detailed analysis of *how* moral rules could play their *instrumental* role can handily come to one's aid in one's actual applications of moral rules in concrete situation, while Laozi's teachings on the dialectic relation between the *Dao* in language-engagement and the genuine *Dao* would let us keep an eye on, and bear in mind, something that moral rules and principles might deliver beyond their mere instrumental value.

REFERENCES

Chan, Wing-tsit (trans.). 1963. "The Lao Tzu (*Tao-Te Ching*)," in his *A source Book in Chinese Philosophy*. Princeton: Princeton University Press.

Dewey, John. 1936. *Ethics* (revised edition). New York: Henry Holt and Company.

——. 1978. *The Middle Works, 1899-1924, Vol. 4: 1907-1909*, edited by Jo Ann Boydston. Carbondale: Southern Illinois University Press.

Holmes, Robert. 1993. *Basic Moral Philosophy*. Belmont: Wadsworth Publishing Company.

Laozi. 1995. *Daode Jing*. In *A Source Book in Chinese Philosophy*, complied by Wing-Tsit Chan. Taipei: Chu Liu Book Company.

Lau, D. C. (trans.). 1963. *Lao Tzu: Tao Te Ching*. Penguin Books.

Mou, Bo. 2000. "Ultimate Concern and Language Engagement: A Re-examination of the Opening Message of the *Daode Jing*," *Journal of Chinese Philosophy*, 27 (4): 429-39.

Weingartner, P. Schurz, G. and Dorn, G. (eds). 1997. *The Role of Pragmatics in Contemporary Philosophy*. Kirchberg, Austria.

11

"Three Teachings are One": The Ethical Intertwinings of Buddhism, Confucianism and Daoism

Jay Goulding

Introduction

This paper argues that the idea of Buddhist ethics is one of in-betweenness. Historically, Buddhism stands in-between Confucianism and Daoism. Philosophically, it stands in-between Confucian virtuousness and Daoist cosmology. As such, Buddhist ethics navigates a realm of in-between that we call "the Void." Simply put, Nagarjuna's Middle Way (Madhyamika, *Zhongguan Pai* 中觀派) influences early *Sanlun* 三論 (Three Treatises) Buddhism to reach emptiness as the between of heavenly principles and earthly phenomena. This in-between is attractive to both Confucianism and Daoism because it activates the neutral "ways of nature" in terms of issues of rebirth and the soul's immortality. It also offers meditative strategies, which lead to ethical conduct. By curtailing daily desires, Buddhists attempt to embrace all things with compassion (*karuna*). Wisdom (*prajña*) becomes the realization that all *dharmas* are empty. The ethics of a good life is the teaching of this wisdom of emptiness to all persons. Ironically, the interweaving of Buddhism, Daoism, and Confucianism in the early creative days of the 3rd to 7th century found renewed life in the 18th century Qing Dynasty where outsider Manchu emperors, for the most part, allowed the above traditions to flourish simultaneously. The murky beginnings of Chinese Madhyamika Buddhism find beginnings again in an era which has no pretensions to past history.

Hence, the "matching meanings" (*geyi* 格義) of 4th century Buddhism and Daoism reappear in the literature of the 18th C. novel, *Dream of the Red Chamber (Hong Lou Meng* 紅樓夢). Because of the folding back of Chinese history, this paper will "match meanings" of Buddhism and Daoism throughout, moving liberally back and forth from early to late dynasties. Throughout this recursive process, we keep philosophical focus on the centre of the Void to which all phenomena fall.

Buddhist Ethics?

When we first hear the expression "Buddhist ethics," it sounds puzzling. For those with a passing acquaintance with Buddhism, it seems natural that Buddhism is itself ethical and need not be explained as such. For those with more intimate knowledge of Buddhism, the expression is rather parodoxic. Some of the confusion might stem from the two words—"Buddhism" and "ethics" - in either their English rendition or their Chinese (*fojiao* 佛教 and *daode* 道德). In English, "Buddhism" conjures up the idea of gentle, loving, passive monks leading meditatively blissful lives and contemplating the bubbles in a dish of soapsuds. "Ethics" might invoke an intricate combination of absolute moral values and the practical application of questions of right and wrong, good and bad. For the English reader, then, Buddhism and ethics might seem to be a comfortable "metaphysical" fit, given that both terms represent a universal appraisal of two unknowable dimensions, one from the East and the other from the far recesses of the Western *psyche* (ancient Greece). Hermeneutically, the very language that we use as a horizon of understanding becomes the topic. "Buddhist ethics" emerges as a topic itself, which relies on an East-West nexus.

The Chinese understanding of "Buddhism" and "ethics" is equally problematic. When Buddhism, as a multitudinous fragmentation of Indian traditions arrives in China, it is also seen as a gelatinous whole (see Hurvitz, Watson et al. 1999, 433). The Chinese are not acquainted with its many dimensional schisms nor are they interested. Instead, they functionally appropriate it for the already established traditions of Daoism and Confucianism. The meditative techniques of Buddhism could seemingly be grafted into the Daoist mission of longevity or equally so into the Confucian cosmological order. Since the Chinese had no word for Buddha, they invented one (*fo* 佛) which was composed of two radicals: a man and a form of negation or a man and rope binding two sticks (see Li 1993, 89). Buddha was "not a man" or "the negation of man." Kenneth Henshall, a Japanese etymological expert, sees the Chinese character representing the binding and "unwinding" of a person, he who appears to be but is not a person (see Henshall 1988, 245). Since they could not read Sanskrit, the Chinese of the 3rd and 4th C. looked back into their own Daoist classics to try to understand Buddhism (see Thompson 1973, 66). Some Chinese scholars even held the fanciful belief that Buddhism was a distorted form of Daoism coming back into China after Laozi's trek to India (see Smart 1998, 115; Dumoulin 1988, 79). From the first moment of its introduction to China, Buddhism was in-between: in-between East and West, in-between Heaven and Earth, in-between Daoism and Confucianism. As such, its ethics was also in-between.

From scholarly quarters, Buddhism was initially viewed in an ambivalent way by the Chinese. It seemed to be without a socially viable ethics. Unlike Confucianism, it did not have a system of language and practice which supported societal levels of moral behaviour but rather focussed on individual attainment of "enlightenment" (*sambodhi*) and "wisdom" (*prajña*). On the other hand, this very absence of social ethics allowed Buddhism to meld into the Confucian cosmology while opening up the Void between the Daoist extremities of Heaven and Earth (cf. Zürcher 1972).

Grappling with ways of integrating Buddhism into already established philosophical positions, the First Patriarch of the Pure Land School, Hui-yuan, consistently utilizes a variation on the technique of "matching meanings" (see Dumoulin 1988, 67) by explicating Buddhism in terms of Daoism (Laozi and Zhuangzi). In regard to Buddhist meditation, Heinrich Dumoulin relates: "In Taoism, the depth of reality is called primordial nothingness; this same reality is grasped by prajña when it sees through the emptiness of all things" (1988, 67). Hui-yuan's teacher, Dao-an (4th C.) provides a good example of

Daoist language in the teaching of Indian Buddhist "meditative breathing":

> The breathing technique known as Anapana refers to the inhaling and exhaling the breath. Tao and Te rest in all places, there is no place that they are not to be found. Anapana is the use of breathing to achieve inward integration. There are four meditation techniques which make use of the functions of the body. Through breathing exercises we pass through the six stages toward integration. Bodily exercises lead through four stages toward concentration. These steps consist of taking away until we have reached the point of complete non-activity. The stages consist of forgetting and forgetting until we have done away with all desire. By non-activity we come into accord with things. By non-desire comes harmony in our affairs. By being in accord with things we can see into their nature. Through harmony in our affairs we can accomplish our missions. Accomplishing our mission, we make all that is consider itself as the other. Seeing into the nature of things, we cause the whole world to forget the self. Thus we eliminate the other and we eliminate the self. This is to achieve integration into the one. (Tripitaka, Lv, 43. quoted in Thompson 1973, 67)

As Thompson observes, this passage from the Buddhist canon Tripitaka (*San Zang Jing* 三藏經—doctrinal records, writings on discipline, philosophical writings) is replete with Daoist imagery. Laozi's strive toward nothingness is augmented by Zhuangzi's *wu wei* 無爲 as nondoing (see Thompson 1973, 67). In the above quote, the *dao* as the cosmological way of the universe and the *de* as virtue, lead us to the Chinese notion of "ethics" as *daode*. Looking closer at the etymology of the *hanzi* 漢字 we see *dao* 道 as composed of "movement" and "chief/main," the "chief means of direct movement" (see Henshall 1988, 53); *de* 德 is a composition of radicals, one part from oracle bones indicating "path and direction" together with "an eye staring straight ahead" representing "integrity" and finally a "heart" added in bronze inscriptions (see Li 1993, 58). To speak, to conduct oneself, to exert oneself in harmony with upright principles is the essence of "virtue."

Together, the Confucian cosmological "way of being" alongside the Daoist "way of the water" compose the virtues of everyday "ethics." It is not a far cry to see that the Confucian virtues of *ren* (仁 benevolence), *li* (禮 propriety, decorum), *yi* (義 righteousness, duty), *zhi* (智 wisdom, knowledge) and *xin* (信 faithfulness, fidelity) might anticipate the Noble Eightfold Path of Buddhism. Ninian Smart divides this Path into the following parts:

> ... right views, right aspiration, right speech, right conduct, right livelihood, right effort, right mindfulness, and right contemplation. The first two concern the preliminary frame of mind of the aspirant; the next three are the ethical requirements; and the final three concern the meditative training needed for contemplative or mystical knowledge of the ultimate truth and for the serenity that goes with it. This attainment of peace and insight is called *nirvana*. (1967, 417)

Right speaking, right conduct, right livelihood as the "ethical" components of the Eightfold Path fit neatly into the already established idea of *de*. On this account, what is of interest in the unique development of Chinese Buddhist ethics is the notion of "emptiness." The eminent Zen philosopher, Daisetz Suzuki observes that 2nd C. importation of Mahayana Buddhist texts into China found scholars unsure about *sunyata* (emptiness, *kong* 空) but more comfortable with alikening "emptiness" to the Daoist *wu* (無 nothingness) (1970, 48-49). These were the Prajñaparamita (perfection of wisdom) Sutras, "The Sutras of the Wisdom that Reaches the Other Shore" which included the Diamond and Heart Sutras (see Schuhmacher and Woerner 1989, 274; Conze 1973; 1975).

Sanlun's Middle Path

The translations of Nagarjuna by the Indian scholar Kumarajiva (344-413) and subsequent commentaries by Jizang (吉藏 549-623), which form the central texts of the *Sanlun* School, bear the uncertainty between Sanskrit and Daoist concepts of which Suzuki speaks. This flux, however, is not without merit. It helps illuminate the tri-partite blending of Buddhist, Confucian and Daoist views of morality as they relate to and through emptiness. Blessed with a Chinese mother and a Parthian father (see Hurvitz, Watson et al. 1999, 438) Jizang possessed intimate knowledge of both Sanskrit and Chinese. In developing the *Sanlun* School, he is aware that the Sanskrit word *sunyata* as "emptiness" is equally related to an idea of "fullness" as illustrated in the *Prajñaparamita* literature. Emptiness connects to *prajña* (wisdom) in so far as we view the universe through the Buddha's eye. After all, *nirvana* is itself "like a magical illusion... a dream" as the *sutra* states (quoted in Williams with Tribe 2000, 135). Thus, the Chinese translations of *sunyata* oscillate necessarily between *kong* as emptiness, *wu* as nothingness and a variety of negatives such as *fei* 非 and *bu* 不. For example, Kumarajiva translates various expressions of Nagarjuna's in *Zhonglun* (中論 Middle Treatise) as follows: "emptiness" or "not existence" (*fei you* 非有), "not nothingness" (*fei wu* 非無), not existence and non-existence (*fei you wu* 非有無), "not empty" (*bu kong* 不空), "emptiness that is not emptiness" (*kong bu kong* 空不空), "not empty not not emptiness" (*fei kong fei bu kong* 非空非不空), "emptiness of emptiness" (*kong kong* 空空), "non-existent emptiness" (*wu kong* 無空), "empty nothingness" (*kong wu* 空無) and existent emptiness (*you kong* 有空) (see Jizang 1994, 6, 56, 61). All of these point to the "suchness" of the empty nothingness (*kong wu ru* 空無如) (Jizang 1994, 61; cf. Digital Dictionary of Buddhism, www.acmuller.net) which is at the heart of Middle Way ethics. An emptiness which is not empty, has at its centre a polarity of *yin-yang* (陰陽). Movement from the centre of stillness negates both the ideas of universal and particular. All phenomena fall to "the middle path." This preserves the Indian idea of eighteen emptinesses as names of the Perfection of Wisdom:

> emptiness of the subject, emptiness of the object, emptiness of subject and object, emptiness of emptiness, great emptiness, ultimate emptiness, conditioned emptiness, unconditioned emptiness, infinite emptiness, emptiness without beginning or end, emptiness of non-repudiation, emptiness of the essential original nature, emptiness of all dharmas, emptiness of own-marks, emptiness of non-apprehension, emptiness of non-existence, emptiness of own-being, emptiness of the non-existence of own-being.... (Conze trans. 1973, 197)

Not only did Buddhist emptiness provide Daoists with new meditative practices but also affirmed reliance on nature. In this respect, early Chinese Buddhism of the 4th and 5th C. ironically introduces an ethics to the "Dark Learning" amalgamation of Confucianism and gnostic traditions. As E. Zürcher aptly puts it: "...the universal law or rather process of karmic retribution—was given a different meaning: that of a *moral* principle working through the universe..." (1972, 73). Realizing that there are no beginnings and no sources, the Buddhist does away with desire by emptying his self of any need for seeking origins. Since all things are empty, the compassionate person directs every being toward *nirvana* (see Cheng 1982, 14). This moral principle stood in-between existence and non-existence amidst dependent co-arising (*yuan qi* 緣起) where all things are devoid of inherent nature. As Nagarjuna relates:

> I salute the Buddha,
> The foremost of all teachers.
> He has taught
> The doctrine of dependent co-arising,
> [The reality of things is marked by]
> No origination, no extinction;
> No permanence, no impermanence;
> No identity, no difference;
> No arrival, no departure. (quoted in Cheng 1982, 16)

From this early age period, the relationships among Buddhism, Confucianism and Daoism reveal a cosmologically motivated ethical engine that drives the three philosophies. For example, the upright person typically holds righteousness (*yi*) as paramount, enacting it through propriety (*li*) benevolence (*ren*) and fidelity (*xin*). As Richard Smith puts it: "...*yi* served as a spring controlling the tension between *ren* and *li*" (1994, 145). But as Mencius relates, a man would naturally abandon the propriety (*li*) of not touching a woman's hands in public in order to reach out to his drowning sister-in-law. In this case, *yi* mollifies *li* while displaying *ren* or as Smith explains "...*yi* mitigates *li*, but makes manifest *ren*" (1994, 145). We see here a tripolar rotation of these virtues which are simultaneously universal and particular. As Cheng Chung-ying argues, "the polarities" of *dao* (the way) and *de* (virtue) unite in "moral self-cultivation": "The *dao* as a philosophical term in Confucius, refers also to the way that things are generated and moves on in a state of moral order and in a state of onto-cosmological harmony" (2000, 222). Confucian morality gives rise to a "religious consciousness" (see Cheng 1991a, 284-292) which is a "dynamic unity" somewhere between *ming* 命 as "objective nature," fate, limitations of life and irrationality on one hand (see 1991a, 285) and *xing* 性 as "subjective nature" of lived experience as it connects to both "the universal" and "the particulars" of human interaction (see 1991a, 280). The onto-cosmological harmony of which Cheng speaks is one field through which Confucian, Daoist and Buddhist ethics appear. One mitigates the other, while manifesting a third. The three are phenomenologically interwoven and layered through thousands of years of practice despite having very distinct histories.

While Buddhism originally arrived in time to interpolate ongoing political debates between Confucians and Daoists, it also disappeared at various points of Chinese history. At some points, Confucianism was strong and Daoism waned. At others, such as the Six Dynasties (386-587), Confucian texts were interpreted through Daoism. This was precisely the time when Kumarajiva arrived to translate several Mahayana texts (see Suzuki 1970, 49). While Daoism was well received during the late Ming, it was frowned upon in the Qing in favour of both Confucianism and Buddhism (see Smith 1994, 165-66). Nevertheless, the already established dipolarity of *yin-yang* relationships through Daoism became mutually conditioning for both Confucianism and Buddhism. It allowed all to appear and re-appear at various moments. Ethically, these intricate relations allowed a person to be both "a good Chinese" and "a good Buddhist" (see Hurvitz and Tsai 1999, 422). We can see this trend of ethical in-betweenness from early Chinese Buddhist history, possibly the time just after Kumarajiva (see Ch'en 1964, 36-37) when Mouzi writes:

> The questioner said, "If the way of the Buddha is the greatest and most venerable of ways, why did Yao, Shun, the Duke of Zhou and Confucius not practice it? In the Seven Classics one sees no mention of it...Why do you love the way of the Buddha and rejoice in outlandish arts?...Permit me the liberty, sir, of advising you to reject them." Mouzi said, "All written works need

not necessarily be the words of Confucius, and all medicine not necessarily consist of the formulae of Bian Que. What accords with rightness is to be followed, what heals the sick is good. The gentleman-scholar draws widely on all forms of good and thereby benefits his character. (Hurvitz and Tsai 1999, 422)

Mouzi's ethics involves pragmatism where the proof of the pudding is in the eating: "...what heals the sick is good."

Whereas both Confucianism and Daoism had established a bridge between Heaven and Earth in terms of nothingness and being, Buddhism helped open a third space, that of the Void. Buddha's Four Noble Truths paved the way: life is an unending cycle of birth and death in a suffering universe; the origin of suffering is selfish desire; the removal of suffering means the removal of desire; the removal of desire points to the Eightfold Path. Ethical behaviour appears at the practical juncture of the action in its tensions with these pathways of decision. Jan Yun-hua (1991) argues that the prominence of Confucian filial piety in the Han Dynasty forever changed Buddhism. The willingness of Buddhism to negotiate with Confucian law quickly dispelled the cries of "unethical." The Buddhists shaved their heads, took no wives and often had no stable homes. All three of these behaviours violated laws of filial piety. Yet Buddhism was willing to elevate the notion of ancestral reverence to equal that of Daoism and Confucianism. Hence, "Chinese Buddhism" was a new formation which included elements from both Chinese and Indian civilizations (see Jan 1991, 36). Not merely "an ethical principle" but rather "a cosmological virtue," filial piety became much more important for Buddhists in the Han Dynasty. The Buddhist Zong-mi (780-841) insists: "Starting with the primal beginning a great virtue that fills the space between Heaven and Earth, common both to humans and gods, nobles and humbles, what is respected as the [fundamental] principle both by Confucianists and Buddhists, is the Way of Filial Piety alone" (quoted in Jan 1991, 31).

China particularly liked the idea of a *bodhisattva* who stayed behind in order to help others rather than move on to Buddhahood. This is a basic morality of Mahayana Buddhism. But if the *bodhisattva* were the "most passionately altruistic" of persons (see Hurvitz and Tsai 1999, 419), why did Buddha go on to *nirvana*? This cosmological conundrum plays out in the doctrine of Three Bodies (*Trikaya* 三佛, 三身). The Buddha possessed three bodies: the Body of Transformation which lived on Earth, the Body of Bliss which lived in Heaven, and the Body of Essence as *nirvana*, "the ultimate Buddha, who pervaded and underlay the whole universe" (Hurvitz and Tsai 1999, 420). If we align these in a chart, some interesting ideas spring forth.

As a "middle kingdom" (*zhongguo* 中國), China floats between Heaven and Earth, and Heaven and the barbarians. The Buddhist additions help navigate the Void between Heaven (Nothingness) and Earth (Being), the invisible and visible, the unreal and the real:

Heaven 天	Body of Bliss	Nothingness 無
Void 空	Body of Essence	Void 空
Earth 地	Body of Transformation	Being 有

By sinking into the middle, the Buddhist would always be in the right position for moral rectitude. The above chart is encapsulated in the Madhyamika expression, *kong jia zhong* (空假中)—unreality, reality, the mean doctrine (see Soothill and Hodous 1937, 276). Emptiness as the middle doctrine eliminates both extremes of unreality (*noumenon*) and reality (*phenomenon*). The myopic monk thinks he sees flies in his begging bowl. His illusion is real although the flies are not. All phenomena are the same. There are no ultimate principles. Why try to champion the real over the false when in fact all existence is merely empty (see Hurvitz, Watson et al. 1999, 436-37)? While phenomenal events are fleeting and ephemeral, emptiness alone remains. The person of emptiness is the person of moral rectitude who helps all others reach *nirvana*.

Similar to this Buddhist middle path, Zhuangzi tells us to embrace the Dao Pivot: "Then the Pivot begins to obtain its middle point of the circle, and -with it, it responds till there-is-no end" (Wu 1990, 141). The Dao Pivot allows us to make the right decision through a myriad of possibilities: "There is none like judging things with the standard of the illumination of clarity" (Wu 1990, 141).

Hence, Buddhist ethics or Daoist ethics are always in-between each other. To make a moral decision is to walk the "double walk" (*liang xing* 兩行) between them. Our "goodness" lies in-between the Monkey Keeper's "morning three, evening four" and "morning four, evening three": "…the holy man harmonizes them with (this-) yes and no of things, and rests in the heavenly balance" (Wu 1990, 142). Buddhist teaching also echoes the Daoist Liezi. Liezi's neighbour has a wooden face and a nothing mind. He "hears nothing" and is "not distracted;" he "sees nothing" and is "not attracted;" he "says nothing" and does "not argue." His virtue is as perfect as a blank wall. If there is no difference between hearing and not hearing, seeing and not seeing, speaking and not speaking, then he will be empty, that is all (see Wong 1995, 113-114).

The idea of *ren jian* (人間) as a person in-between Heaven and Hell is omnipresent throughout Chinese history. In terms of ethics, it allows people to be secure that they are doing the right thing at the right time by being in the right place. The right place is not only an ontic experience but also a cosmological one. Life itself is the right place; being between Heaven and Earth is the right place. The Daoist Yuan Ji (210-263) of the Wei-Jin Period said: "If the sage has no house, Heaven and Earth will contain him; if the sage has no master, Heaven and Earth will own him; if the sage has nothing to do, he is free to walk under Heaven and on the Earth" (quoted in Zhang 1993, 308). This idea might well flow into the more modern Chinese expression for ethics (*lunli* 倫理) as the "order" of "human relations."

In respect to the form of ethics, Buddhism and Daoism are mutually interlocked and self-correcting. Buddhism provided a plethora of mythological themes for sculptors, painters, poets and writers. Consistent with the Confucian onto-cosmology, the practice of artwork physically manifests moral images. For example, the Stele with Deified Laozi and Shakyamuni Buddha from the Northern Wei Dynasty, Xiping reign is dated in the 6th century. On one side of the statue is the mustached Laozi, wearing a Daoist hat and holding a fan. On the other side is Shakyamuni with his *urna* (bump at the top of his head), an *usnisa* (hair on his forehead) and raised right hand with the sign of fearlessness (see Little 2000, 169). Such artwork gives rise to folktales of Buddhism and Daoism. For example, one stormy day, a Buddhist monk entered a temple to find a statue of Shakyamuni on the right side of the mantle while Laozi rested on the "lucky" left. Quickly, the monk, his hands and clothes dripping wet, changed the statues. Shortly afterward, a Daoist priest came into the temple, his hands and robes soaked with rain. When he saw the statues, he felt it his moral obligation to change them in order to favour the revered Laozi. For a month it rained and the monk and the priest did their duty, switching the statues with their wet hands until the statues dissolved. Shakyamuni addressed Laozi: "For so long we sat together; now these two shatter our tranquillity" (see Zhai 1998, 16-17). There is a Confucian moral to this story. Respect cannot be gained by moving to a supposedly better position. Buddhism and Daoism are eternal partners, each respecting their moral stances. Buddhism looks toward the next world through the annihilation of this illusionary one while Daoism looks to longevity in this very life by whisking away illusion by means of Laozi's "way of the water."

"When the Unreal is Taken for the Real..."

Buddhist ethical life is not merely attainable through rigorous monastic training and contemplation. A scholar of 18th century literature, Dore J. Levy writes: "Monks, nuns and lay practicioners have traditionally availed themselves of a variety of intellectual, artistic and even physical disciplines, all of which, undertaken in the right spirit, were accepted as valid paths to the insight that would supercede them" (1999, 140). This also included poetry. The scholar Yan Yu of the Song Dynasty (13th C.) suggests: "One should speak of poetry as one speaks of Chan...Just as the essence of Chan is arational illumination, the essence of poetry is likewise arational illumination" (quoted in Levy 1999, 140). In "Chan Historiography and Chan Philosophy," Cheng Chung-ying speaks of the "visual" phenomenology of language in Chinese Chan:

> ...Chinese language like Chinese painting reconstructs reality from a holistic point of view: the whole is constitutive of the world and the mind. What is presented in the language is not simply what is represented in the language, for there is the invisible or the yin part of reality existing side by side with the yang

part of the reality. Hence language also speaks of that which is
beyond the language... Speaking is not a matter of language alone
but of non-language (including silence) as well. (1996, 500-501)

Given a three millennia flux of Chinese philosophical life, the
Qing Dynasty (1644-1912) stakes claim to a unique period for its
various forms of Buddhism and consequent ethical expressions. Although Manchu rulers adopted Confucianism as their main align-
ment, four forms of Mahayana Buddhism flourished: *Chan* 禪, *Tiantai*
天台 (Celestial Platform), *Jingtu* 淨土 (Pure Land) and *Huayan* 華嚴
(Flower Garland). In this regard, Harold Roth, Sarah Queen and Nathan Sivin argue for a "syncretism" throughout Chinese philosophy.
What happened in the Qin State through Huang-Lao (Huangdi and
Laozi) as an amalgamation of Confucian, Mohist and Legalist philosophies "synthesized... within a Daoist framework" (Roth et al.
1999, 235), had its Buddhist counterpart in the Qing. As a conventional saying goes: "The Tiantai and Huayan Schools for doctrine; the
Meditation and Pure Land schools for practice" (Hurvitz, Watson et
al. 1999, 436). The notion of a Buddhist ethics arises amongst and
between these intermingled forms. While *Tiantai* held to the centre of
the Mahayana school as the "Truth of Emptiness," *Huayan* focussed
on the *yin-yang* polarity of "coexistent" pairings of universal-
ity/speciality, similarity/difference and integration/disintegration (see
Smith 1994, 169). *Chan* promoted rigorous training which included:
"...physical shock—such as shouting and beatings—and the use of
puzzling sayings, stories and conversations known as gongan" (公案)
(Smith 1994, 170) to free the mind/self from the search for "absolute
truth." Pure Land was attainable by the chanting of Amitabha's name
and absence of the five violations (killing father, mother, arhat; hurt-
ing the Buddha's body; disrupting the monastic community) (see
Hurvitz, Stevenson et al. 1999, 483).

Reminiscent of the early *Sanlun* flux, Cao Xueqin's (曹雪芹)
Qing novel *Dream of the Red Chamber* (written 1754-1760) represents
the poetically ethical folding of Buddhism and its Daoist partner. An
amorous story of Bao Yu and his competing lovers Bao Chai and Lin
Dai Yu, it challenges Confucian virtuousness in an era of flux. Two
questions are important: (1) Can Bao Yu navigate the meditative

worlds of Buddhism and Daoism on one hand, while fulfilling his Confucian duties on the other? (2) As the immortal Stone comes to Earth and Bao Yu reaches for Heaven, will they meet in the Void (see Miller 1975; 1981)?

These questions are entertained throughout the adventure by means of *gongan* (公案) styled poetry prose. The characters whirl and swirl around one repeated couplet in particular, at times embracing it, at times rejecting it, at times gasping at its cosmic implications and at times grasping for its insubstantial substance. It is a wheel of fortune that spins out the fates of hundreds of characters. This couplet appears on the stone arch in the Land of Illusion. A Buddhist monk and a Daoist priest move at will through the arch but no mortal can follow them. The beginning of the story sees them contemplating both immortality and daily desire; the conclusion sees them escorting Bao Yu away from the mortal world, his "obligations fulfilled" (his "karma complete") (see Tsao 1958, 327; cf. Cao 1986, 359). The daily world of the Red Dust's carnal desires is as much an illusion of material pleasures as is any pretension to knowledge of the really real. The novel tests our worth: can we wipe the dust from the mirror and see our "true" selves? Throughout *Red Chamber*, both Earth and Heaven gravitate into the Void, falling to the centre of stillness. We dwell in this Void with all its paradox and contradiction, dancing around this couplet (Cao 1990, 5, 36):

假	作	眞	時	眞	亦	假
jia	zuo	zhen	shi	zhen	yi	jia
無	爲	有	處	有	還	無
wu	wei	you	chu	you	huan	wu

Wang Chi-Chen, a professional translator writes:

> When the unreal is taken for the real, then the
> real becomes unreal;
> When non-existence is taken for existence, then
> existence becomes non-existence (Tsao 1958, 7, 42)

Another scholarly translator, David Hawkes writes:

> Truth becomes fiction when the fiction's true;
> Real becomes not-real when the unreal's real. (Cao 1973, 55,
> 130)

Although these translations are adequate for study, a more phenomenological (and fanciful) translation might read:

> The false is taken for true,
> when the time is right for true to become false;
> When "non-doing" (doing as an undoing) exists everywhere,
> being returns to nothing. (my translation)

In the first line, "false" and "true" are pastimes of Buddhist monks, ceaselessly contemplating their earthly and heavenly implications until they "awaken" (*wu* 悟) and disappear into the nothingness (*wu* 無) of the Void. Once again, the Madhyamika Doctrine of the Middle is the key to Chinese Buddhist morality, which exposes the illusions of both falsehood and truth in favour of the emptiness (*kong* 空) of the mean. The first expression of the second line is *wuwei* 無為 the Daoist action of non-action from Laozi and Zhuangzi (see Wu 1990, 488). For the Daoist, not striving, not searching, not struggling is the way to the Void. The best teacher is the one who falls behind. Each day "forget" one thing until there is nothing to remember and be "free." As *Red Chamber*'s Daoist priest explains: "For if you are free, you'll forget, and if you forget, you'll be free" (Tsao 1958, 13).

In regard to the ethical resolution of his dilemma, Bao Yu chooses to walk Zhuangzi's "double walk." After much to do, he writes the prefectural exams to satisfy Confucian obligations to his family and then pursues his religious dream of becoming a monk. He disappears into a snow squall with the Buddhist monk and the Daoist priest each holding one of his hands. Part of Jia Bao Yu's decision is arrived at by conversation with his double Zhen Bao Yu, his "reflection in a mirror" (see Tsao 1958, 322). "Jia" is a pun on "false" and "Zhen" on "true" as in the above couplet. Bao Yu's upright resolve is spontaneous and perhaps in heed of Cao Xueqin's opening chapter warning:

> Pages full of idle words
> Penned with hot and bitter tears:
> All men call the author fool;
> None his secret message hears. (Cao 1973, 51)

Here we see the 18th century doubled back into the ancient past. For Buddhists such as Cao, the words are not important but the meaning is.

On this account, Cao's novel recalls Dao Sheng (360-434), Madhyamika disciple of Kumarajiva, who follows Zhuangzi in forgetting the trap (words) and catching the fish (reality) (see Dumoulin 1988, 74). Obviously, Cao is a proponent of Zhuangzi's *yan wu yan* 言無言 (words without words):

> The fish trap exists because of the fish; once you've gotten the fish, you can forget the trap. The rabbit snare exists because of the rabbit; once you've gotten the rabbit, you can forget the snare. Words exist because of meaning; once you've gotten the meaning, you can forget the words. Where can I find a man who has forgotten words so I can have a word with him? (Watson, ed. 1968, 302)

Following up on Cao's "matching meanings," the above Daoist wisdom is itself mirrored in various Chan *gongan*. From the *Wumenguan* 無門關 (*The Gateless Gate*), we see "Trapped in Words":

> A monk asked Yumen about the line, "Radiant light silently
>   illumines the universe."
> Before the monk had even finished, Yunmen abruptly said,
>   "Aren't these the words of the scholar Zhang Zhao?"
> The monk replied, "Yes."
> Yunmen said, "You're trapped in words."
> Later, Zen master Sixin brought this up and said, "Now, tell me
>   where did the monk get trapped in words?" (Cleary 1993,
>   174)

Forget the words if you have grasped the meaning; idle talk strays from *dharma* (法). The above verse implies Zhuangzi's fishing metaphor:

A line is cast in the waters;
The greedy will be caught;
if your mouth opens just a bit,
your life is completely lost. (Aitken 1990, 235)

In forgetting the words but realizing the meaning, Bao Yu follows Zhuangzi. His poetic musings in the inner chambers show him the way. It is this resolve that allows him to balance the tragedy and ecstasy of his life.

Forever leading us back to *Red Chamber*, Daoist and Buddhist metaphors become conduits of right conduct; they are fluid passages between Heaven and Earth; they are traces of Chinese ethical thinking as related through archaic fables and stories. These literary instruments are the slashes between the worlds of reality and fantasy which the Chinese use to enact moral decisions. They are indeed the onto-cosmological tools of which Cheng speaks. Rather than privilege one world (the real) over another (fantasy) or one medium (us) over another (our mirror images), Buddhism and Daoism serve to disintegrate the barriers between the two. These endemically phenomenal crossings make Chinese philosophy simultaneously one of visibility and invisibility, of corporeality and ideationality, of reality and fantasy.

In this respect, John Ferguson writes about the ethics of Mysterious Tally, supposedly compiled by the mythical Huangdi:

> This book is largely devoted to ethical discussions in which an attempt is made to fit the one side of the tally which covers the visible phenomena around us with the other half which relates to the unseen world. It discusses the hidden harmony which exists in all animate things where only discord appears on the surface and reconciles the apparent disagreements between the seen and the unseen. (Ferguson and Masaharu 1964, 17)

This flow of experiential existence/non-existence renders the world a flux of infinite possibilities. The world is a seamless flow of the visible and invisible. As Tai Xu, the great synthesizer of the eight Buddhist Schools insists: "There are many tributaries of the *Dharma*, yet the source is only one" (quoted in Sheng-Yen 1991, 59). That source is the "True Suchness" of the immediate awakening of the *Chan* and *Tiantai* Schools which Bao Yu exhibited in his awareness of Zhuangzi's "double walk." Bao Yu is an example for all of us. As the Venerable Chan master Sheng-Yen writes: "An emancipated saint is influenced by purity, while an ordinary person is influenced by delusion; whether one is influenced by purity or delusion, is a saint or an ordinary person, the nature of True Suchness is unchanged" (1991, 56). Therefore, Buddhist "awakening" is intimately tied to the dual worlds of reality and non-reality, existence and non-existence. Suzuki further clarifies "suchness" as "Reality in its 'isness'": "Some may say, 'There cannot be any meaning in mere isness.' But this is not the view held by Zen, for according to it, isness is the meaning. When I see it I see it as clearly as I see myself reflected in a mirror" (1970, 16).

The Empty Mirror

Buddhist "awakening" does not dispel myth or demystify allegory but thrives in it. In contrast, Western enlightenment often separates the living from the dead, privileging the existing visible over the non-existing invisible. Historically, the Chinese do not so discriminate. David Hall and Roger Ames quote G. K. Chesterton as a dedication for their book on China, *The Democracy of the Dead*:

> Tradition means giving votes to the most obscure of all classes, our ancestors. It is the democracy of the dead. Tradition refuses to submit to the small and arrogant oligarchy of those that merely happen to be walking about. All democrats object to men being disqualified by accident of birth; tradition objects to their being disqualified by accident of death. (front page to Hall and Ames 1999)

China's ethics relies on the boundarylessness of both the living and the dead, of the present and of the past and of the yet to come. Thus, we see the reverence for the Bodhisattva who remains behind on the slash between past and future. No metaphorical image better exemplifies this phenomenal crossing than that of Chinese mirrors. Huangdi's polished stones, the mirrors of Heaven and Earth, reflected the energy of both through their reliance on the middle. His magical mirror reflected the interior of whosoever looked into it (see Williams 1976, 277). In Chapter 12 of *Red Chamber*, Cao tells the story of the lovesick Jia Rui who is approached with a magical mirror by a Daoist priest. Of this Mirror for the Romantic, Cao's priest speaks:

> This object comes from the Hall of Emptiness in the Land of Il-
> lusion. It was fashioned by the fairy Disenchantment as an anti-
> dote to the ill effects of impure mental activity. It has life-giving
> and restorative properties and has been brought into the world
> for the contemplation of those intelligent and handsome young
> gentlemen whose hearts are too susceptible to the charms of
> beauty. I lend it to you on one important condition: you must
> only look into the back of the mirror. Never, never under any
> circumstances look into the front. (Cao 1981, 251)

Unfortunately, Jia Rui looks in the front of the mirror and is mesmer-
ized by his lover Xi-Feng who "beckons" him into the mirror world
where "his ravished soul floats" into lustful incarceration. Eventually,
he cannot escape his own desire, his lifeless eyes stare into the empty
mirror which falls from his grasp. Jia Rui's friends and relatives
"curse" the priest and attempt to burn his mirror which floats away
from them. The Daoist relates the moral of the story: "It is you who
are to blame, for confusing the unreal with the real! Why then should
you burn my mirror?" (1981, 253).

There is nothing in the Chinese mirror but flowers. *Jinghua shui-
yue* 鏡花水月, "flowers in the mirror, moon in the water," is not only a
key expression of Li Ruzhen's Qing Dynasty novel about the incarna-
tion of flowers (see Li Ju-Chen 1965) but refers to the frivolity of
nonconsequence. The more you search for the truth, the less likely
you are to find it. The Daoist mirror of retribution coupled with the
Buddhist empty mirror of no-self reflect the Chinese versions of
"awakening." However, Zhuangzi cautions:

> Do not be an embodier of fame; do not be a storehouse of
> schemes; do not be an undertaker of projects; do not be a pro-
> prietor of wisdom. Embody to the fullest what has no end and
> wander where there is no trail. Hold on to all that you have re-

ceived from heaven but do not think you have gotten anything.
Be empty, that is all. (Watson, trans. 1968, 97)

For Zhuangzi, the "perfect" person has a mind-mirror "... going after
nothing, welcoming nothing, responding but not storing" (Watson,
trans. 1968, 97). The mirror can become the moral "enlightenment,"
simultaneously resource and topic, coupling cosmological order with
personal uprightness. For *Red Chamber*'s Jia Rui, however, the mirror
"as both his temptations and the means to transcend them" remained
as "a symbol of his unenlightened mind" (Levy 1999, 77-78).

Alongside the Daoist mirror of retribution, the Buddhists display the "empty" mirror of no-self. The mind is a mirror, the body is
a *Bohdi* tree. Clear the Red Dust of desire from the mirror and gaze
upon your true self. Hui Neng, the Sixth Patriarch further disrupts
this image of the mirror: "There is no mind, there is no mirror"
(Yampolsky 1967, 130-32). In the 8th century, Fa Zang 法藏, pro-
genitor of *Dharma* Buddhism (*Huayan*), creates a hall of mirrors in
order to answer Empress Wu of the Tang Dynasty's challenge: show
me the Totality of *Dharma* (see Chang 1994, 22-24). These mirrors
reflected and refracted thousands of light-fragmented images of the
Buddha, "one in all, all in one—the mystery of realm embracing
realm ad infinitum" (Chang 1994, 24). Thus, Fa Zang shows Empress
Wu that Chinese ethics arise through infinite interdependence as a
"Suchness" (*ru* 如). "Suchness" (*ru*) stands at the empty centre of
principle (*li* 理) and phenomenon (*shi* 事). "Principle" as heavenly and
"phenomenon" as worldly meet together in the infinite co-existence
of the Void. The decisiveness of ethical life crosses through the middle of this emptiness. To achieve emptiness is to become a moral
person. In the Buddhist vocabulary, the two terms (*li shi*) taken together are like salt and pepper: "Noumena and phenomena, principle
and practice, absolute and relative, real and empirical, cause and effect, fundamental essence and external activity, potential and actual;
e.g. store and distribution, ocean and wave, static and kinetic" (Soothill and Hodous 1937, 360). Our chart now looks like this:

Heaven 天	Body of Bliss	Nothingness 無	Principle 理
Void 空	Body of Essence	Void 空	Suchness 如
Earth 地	Body of Transformation	Being 有	Phenomenon 事

Fa Zang's golden lion is a good example of the above. The gold represents the static world and the lion the dynamic world. The gold is a formless form which manifests in every part of the phenomenal lion: one in all, all in one. The same occurs in Chinese Buddhist ethics—one in all, all in one—the cosmological in the everyday and the everyday in the cosmological, the noumenal in the phenomenal and the phenomenal in the noumenal (see Chang 1994, 156). Mutual interpenetration (*xiang ru* 相入) and identity (*xiang ji* 相即) are mainstays of Fa Zang's worldview. All phenomena intertwine with each other; all phenomena are manifestations of principle; all phenomena are empty. Each different phenomenon is identical. Hence we see the "noumenal" (*li*) within the phenomenal (*shi*) (see Ch'en 1964, 316-320).

During the Qing, the Manchu took their name from the Manjusri Buddha (*Wen-shu* 文殊), with a sword in his right hand and a lotus and a book in his left; he is depicted throughout Chinese art and literature as riding on a lion (see Williams 1976, 126, 264). In the 18th C., the multiple forms of Buddhism and their respective moralities were like the correlational organs of the *dharma* lion which Fa Zang describes. Each particular contained a universal; each universal contained a particular. As well, the ethical message of the golden lion is similar to Zhuangzi's interpretation of the white horse: "To use a horse to show that a horse is not a horse is not as good as using a non-horse to show that a horse is not a horse" (Watson trans. 1968, 40). Zhuangzi is responding to the sophist Gongsun Lung's white horse is not a horse (*bai ma fei ma* 白馬非馬) that claims that "horse" is naming a shape; "white" is naming a colour. Therefore, a "white horse is not a horse" (see Graham 1989, 85). Yet, Zhuangzi like Fa Zang goes a step further than logic. He is providing a moral template for action as "the ontological consistency of self-so-ness" (Wu 1990,

197). As Kuang-ming Wu argues: "...we can afford to affirm things in their differences (using a no-horse to show that a horse is no-horse), accepting everything as 'such'" (Wu 1990, 196). This "such" is parallel to the Buddhist *tathata*, the "Suchness" beyond all phenomena. As Wu writes: "We must illuminate all in the life of Heaven, that is in naturalness, as-they-are-ness. We must explain (fingers as) non-fingers with non-fingers. This is a judgmental consistency of rightness" (1990, 197). Fa Zang's golden lion in its correlational interdependence also parallels Zhuangzi's judgement: "Heaven and earth are one pointer; myriads of things are one horse" (Wu 1990, 141). Buddhism and Daoism stand arm in arm in metaphor and parable as they "match meaning."

Chinese morality combines both mind and body. When the mind alone thinks, then the body disappears into oblivion (withers away). When the body thinks, then the mind disappears (transdescends) into it. Thriving on the intertwining of mind and body, Chinese body thinking moralizes its practice in and through these parables of lived experience (see Wu 1997). The stories and allegories are part of a communicative body and through them we live. To recognize this is part of our "awakening." Understand by not understanding, do by not doing, see by not seeing are keynotes to virtuous body thinking which allows the Buddhist and Daoist to proceed beyond the paradox of existence/non-existence into the lived experience of myth, thereby permeating the mirror-world of visible and invisible. But you need a "place" from which to unravel the knots of conventional knowledge. For Buddhism, it is the Void (*kong* 空); for Daoism, it is the hollows (*qiao* 竅). Zhuangzi writes of the Daoist hollows:

> "... For-the-moment now I have lost me-myself,
>   do you understand it?"
> "Do you hear men's piping, and are yet to hear heaven's
>   piping?"
>
> Tzu Yu said, "I venture-to ask-about their secret ways."
> Tzu Ch'i said, "Well, the Huge Clod belches out breath;
>   its name is called wind.
> This is well if only there-is-no starting-up; once it starts-up,
>   then myriads of hollows rage-up howling.

Do you alone not hear them roaring, roaring?"
"...Fierce wind relieved, then multitudes of hollows are made
    empty..."

Tzu Yu said,
"Earth pipings—these, then, are multitudes of hollows only.
Men's pipings—these, then, are rows of bamboo tubes only.
I venture-to ask-about heavenly pipings."
"... Huge understanding widens, widens;
    small understanding is picky, picky.
Huge words, burn, burn; small words chat, chat." (Wu 1990, 135-
36)

These stanzas are replete with the phenomenological crossings of
experience, of visibility and invisibility, of the real and the unreal, of
big talk and of small talk, of the ruminations of philosophers and of
common folk. They make and unmake the moral person in a chaotic
vortex that is both empty and full of primordial vapour. Like the rip-
pling of the butterfly's wings, the hollows are the craters of creation,
Laozi's hubs of the wheels, the Buddhist emptiness. The expression
"the hollows are made empty," *qiao wei xu* (竅爲虛) (see Wu 1990,
133) is not to be taken lightly. "Empty" is not "nothing." Like Fa
Zang's hall of mirrors, it is full of the invisibility of what is, what is
not and what might be. As a fulcrum of creativity and uncreativity, it
is a primal 'awakening.' The Chinese characters themselves tell a tale.
Qiao is a hole or an aperture, as in the seven apertures of your face;
wei as a verb from the famous Daoist rendition *wuwei* 無爲 means do,
make, mean, call (see Wu 1990, 487); *xu* is an empty void—hollow,
unreal, and groundless. This is an ancient Chinese moral proclama-
tion of body thinking without grounds or what we might call "making something out of nothing."

   In Chinese history, Buddhist ethics is correlational and mutually
conditioned by both Daoism and Confucianism. As eternally linked
partners, the three create a template of virtuousness that interweaves
with *yin-yang* cosmological principles while manifesting through daily
practice. Thus, we have the old Chinese saying: "The three teachings
are one" (*san jiao he yi* 三教合一) (Eberhard 1986, 289). Confucianism
acts to contextualize Buddhist right conduct by linking up to virtues
such as filial piety. Confucianism's onto-cosmology harmonizes both

Buddhist and Daoist ethics between objective and subjective life that might otherwise be disconnected from society (see Cheng 1991b, 127). Buddhism helps clarify the rectitude of the Confucian upright person by promoting extreme humility while walking the "double walk" with Daoism. Daoism tells Buddhism to live each day for living's sake, not to simply live each day for dying. As Wu relates: "Zhuangzi's 'living' in death makes life enjoyable; we live as if we were already dead" (1990, 15): "The Buddhist awakening to knowledge dissolves our ignorance. Zhuangzi's awakening to uncertainty (are we dreaming or awakened?) amounts to our knowledge of ignorance, affirmation of uncertainty. Buddhists awaken out of dreaming; Zhuangzi wakes up to dreaming" (1990, 227). Bao Yu's decision is an ethical example of the melding of the three philosophies. Buddhism takes him to emptiness through poetry and singing; Confucianism sobers him to the world of everyday moral obligations; Daoism helps him dream his own nothingness. His moral decisions revolve around balancing the three. The scroll of Liu Xiang, the divinely illuminated Han scholar, which Bao Yu initially discarded, became a *gong- an* for his double walk:

> To know through and through the ways of the world is Real
> Knowledge;
> To conform in every detail the customs of society is True
> Accomplishment. (Tsao 1958, 39)

Having satisfied his worldly Confucian obligations of filial piety, Bao Yu was free to take the tonsure. He was "free" to "forget" as the Daoist priest advised:

> We all envy the immortals because they are free,
> ...But fame and fortune we cannot forget....
> ...But gold and silver we cannot forget...
> ...But our precious wives we cannot forget...
> ...But our sons and grandsons we cannot forget...
> ...But how few of the sons are filial and obedient! (Tsao 1958, 13)

All those who do "forget" are protected under the virtues of the Buddhist umbrella. As the punning old saying goes: "Buddhist umbrella, no law (no hair), no heaven" (*heshang dasan wufa wutian* 和尚打傘無法[髮]無天).

Conclusion

In conclusion, Buddhist ethics of the Middle Way is often invisible. It has neither a specific language nor specific pragmatics as Confucianism does. Rather, it resides in-between. It emerges through daily experience, thus attesting to its onto-cosmology. By leveling both "principles" and "phenomena" into a vortex of emptiness, it equates dependent co-arising with *nirvana*. Life is neither simply the way of virtue (Confucianism) nor the way of the water (Daoism) but something in-between. By extinguishing desire, we can arrive at life. Life is "suchness." All *dharmas* are empty, yet all interpenetrate as Fa Zang's golden lion teaches. Each is identical in its difference. In some respects, Buddhist ethics is the undoing of ethics as worldly obligations (Confucianism) or celestial obligations (Daoism). Yet it draws strength from both these traditions. Its "realization" can arise in both this world and the next. Emptiness is not a retreat from the world of morality but an entrance back into it. As Nagarjuna's followers, Kumarajiva and Jizang of the *Sanlun* maintain, emptiness is not nothingness. *Sunyata* is both full and empty. It both is and is not. The dynamics of the two—being and non-being—lead to and from the Void, that is to and from the middle, the in-between of Heaven and Earth. Mouzi and Zhuangzi remind us that we need not harp on the words in order to get to the meaning, that is to get it "right," so to speak. In *Red Chamber*, Bao Yu oscillates between fulfilling his Confucian familial duties and taking the tonsure. He is in-between. It is "good" if he supports the household; it is "good" if he leaves to become a Buddhist monk. His solution is that of the Daoist "double walk." All of the above exemplify the ethical crossings of Buddhism, Confucianism and Daoism as the way of China, "the Middle Kingdom" which echoes the slogan "three teaching are one."

REFERENCES

Aitken, Robert. 1990. *The Gateless Barrier: The Wu-Men Kuan* (Mumon-kan). San Francisco: North Point Press.

Cao, Xueqin. 1973. *The Story of the Stone.* Volume 1: The Golden Days. Trans. by David Hawkes. London: Penguin.

————. 1990. *Dream of the Red Chamber (Hong Lou Meng* 紅樓夢). Rao Bin (ed.). Taibei: Three People's Book Office.

Cao, Xueqin and Gao, E. 1986. *The Story of the Stone.* Volume 5: The Dreamer Wakes. Trans. by John Milford. London: Penguin.

Chang, Garma C. C. 1994. *The Buddhist Teaching of Totality: The Philosophy of Hua Yen Buddhism.* University Park: Pennsylvania State University Press.

Ch'en, Kenneth. 1964. *Buddhism in China. A Historical Survey.* New Jersey: Princeton University Press.

Cheng, Chung-ying. 1991a. "Dialectic of Confucian Morality and Metaphysics of Man: A Philosophical Analysis." In his *New Dimensions of Confucian and Neo-Confucian Philosophy.* Albany: State University of New York Press.

————. 1991b. "The Nature and Function of Skepticism in Chinese Philosophy." In his *New Dimensions of Confucian and Neo-Confucian Philosophy.* Albany: State University of New York Press.

————. 1996. "Chan Historiography and Chan Philosophy: A Review Essay on Bernard Faure's Chan Insights and Oversight," *Journal of Chinese Philosophy* 23: 489-507.

————. 2000. "Confucian Reflections on Habermasian Approaches: Moral Rationality and Inter-Humanity." In *Perspectives on Habermas, edited by* Lewis Edwin Hahn. Chicago: Open Court.

Cheng, Hsueh-li. 1982. *Nagarjuna's Twelve Gate Treatise.* Dordrecht: D. Reidel Publishing Company.

Cleary, Thomas (trans.). 1990. *Book of Serenity: One Hundred Zen Dialogues.* Hudson: Lindisfarne Press.

————. 1992. *The Blue Cliff Record.* Boston: Shambhala.

————. 1993 *No Barrier: Unlocking the Zen Koan.* New York: Bantam.

Conze, Edward (trans.). 1973. *The Short Prajñaparamita Texts.* London: Luzac & Company.

————. 1975. *The Large Sutra on Perfect Wisdom.* Berkeley: University of California Press.

de Bary, W. Theodore and Bloom, Irene (eds.). 1999. *Sources of Chinese Tradition. Volume I.* 2nd ed. New York: Columbia University Press.

Dumoulin, Heinrich. 1988. *Zen Buddhism: A History Vol. 1 India and China.* New York: Macmillan.

————. 1990. *Zen Buddhism: A History Vol. 2 Japan.* New York: Macmillan.

Eberhard, Wolfram. 1986. *A Dictionary of Chinese Symbols: Hidden Symbols in Chinese Life and Thought.* London: Routledge.

Ferguson, John C. and Masaharu Anesaki. 1964. *The Mythology of All Races.* vol. VIII. New York: Cooper Square Publishers.

Graham, A. C. 1989. *Disputers of the Tao: Philosophical Argument in Ancient China.* La Salle: Open Court.

Hall, David L. and Ames, Roger T. 1999. *The Democracy of the Dead: Dewey, Confucius, and the Hope for Democracy in China.* Chicago: Open Court.

Henshall, Kenneth G. 1988. *A Guide to Remembering Japanese Characters.* Tokyo: Charles E. Tuttle.

Hurvitz, Leon, Daniel Stevenson, Daniel, Yampolsky, Philip B., and Chun Fang-Yu. 1999. "Schools of Buddhist Practice." In de Bary and Bloom.

Hurvitz, Leon and Tsai Heng-Ting. 1999. "The Introduction of Buddhism." In de Bary and Bloom.

Hurvitz, Leon, Burton Watson, Daniel Stevenson, Geprge Tanabe, and Wing-tsit Chan. 1999. "Schools of Buddhist Doctrine." In de Bary and Bloom.

Jan, Yun-hua. 1991. "The Role of Filial Piety in Chinese Buddhism: A Reassessment." In *Buddhist Ethics and Modern Society* , edited by Charles Wei-hsun Fu and Sandra A. Wawrytko. New York: Greenwood Press, 27-39.

Jizang. 1994. *The Middle Treatise, The Hundred Treatise, The Twelve Gate*

Treatise (Zhonglun, Bailun, Shi'er Menlun 中論, 百論, 十二門論).
    Shanghai: Ancient Publication Society.
Levy, Dore J. 1999. *Ideal and Actual in The Story of Stone.* New
    York: Columbia University Press.
Li Ju-Chen. 1965. *Flowers in the Mirror.* trans. Lin Tai-yi. Berkeley:
    University of California.
Li Leyi. 1993. *Tracing the Roots of Chinese Characters: 500 Cases.* Beijing:
    Beijing Language and Culture University Press.
Little, Stephen. 2000. "The Beginnings of Religious Taoism" in
    Stephen Little with Shawn Eichman. *Taoism and the Arts of
    China.* Chicago: The Art Institute of Chicago and University
    of California Press, 163-188.
Miller, Lucien. 1975. "Masks of Fiction in *The Dream of the Red Cham-
    ber.*" Arizona: University of Arizona Press.
————. 1981 "Naming the Whirlwind: Cao Xueqin and Heideg-
    ger." *Tamkang Review* vol. XII no. 2 (Winter): 143-164.
Roth, Harold, Queen, Sarah and Sivin, Nathan. 1999. "Syncretic Vi-
    sions of State, Society and Cosmos." In de Bary and Bloom.
Schuhmacher, Stephen and Woerner, Gert (eds.). 1989. *The Encyclope-
    dia of Eastern Philosophy and Religion: Buddhism, Taoism, Zen, Hin-
    duism.* Boston: Shambhala Press.
Sheng-Yen Venerable. 1991. "Four Great Thinkers in Modern Chi-
    nese Buddhism." In *Buddhist Ethics and Modern Society,* edited
    by Charles Wei-hsun Fu and Sandra A. Wawrytko. New
    York: Greenwood Press.
Smart, Ninian. 1967. "Buddhism." In *The Encyclopedia of Philosophy.*
    Vol. 1 and 2, edited by Paul Edwards. New York: Macmillan
    Publishing and The Free Press.
————. 1998. *The World's Religions.* 2nd ed. Cambridge: Cambridge
    University Press.
Smith, Richard J. 1994. *China's Cultural Heritage: The Qing Dynasty,
    1644-1912.* Boulder: West View.
Soothill, William Edward and Hodous, Lewis. 1937. *A Dictionary of
    Chinese Buddhist Terms.* Delhi: Motilal Banarsidass.
Suzuki, Daisetz T. 1970. *Zen and Japanese Culture.* Princeton: Princeton
    University Press.

Thompson, Laurence G. 1973. *The Chinese Way in Religion.* Encino: Dickerson Publishing.

Tsao Hsueh-Chin. 1958. *Dream of the Red Chamber.* New York: Anchor.

Watson, Burton (trans.). 1968. *The Complete Works of Zhuangzi.* New York: Columbia University Press.

Williams, C.A.S. 1976. *Outlines of Chinese Symbolism and Art Motives.* New York: Dover Publications Inc.

Williams, Paul. 1989. *Mahayana Buddhism: The Doctrinal Foundations.* London: Routledge.

Williams, Paul with Tribe, Anthony. 2000. *Buddhist Thought: A Complete Introduction to the Indian Tradition.* London: Routledge.

Wong, Eva. 1995. *Lieh-Tzu: A Taoist Guide to Practical Living.* Boston: Shambhala.

Wu Jingrong, editor-in-chief. 1979. *The Pinyin Chinese-Engli Dictionary.* New York: John Wiley and Sons.

Wu, Kuang-ming. 1990. *The Butterfly as Companion: Meditations on the First Three Chapters of the Zhuangzi.* Albany: State University of New York Press.

——————. 1997. *On Chinese Body Thinking: A Cultural Hermeneutic.* Leiden: The Brill Publishing Company.

Yampolsky, Philip B. 1967. *The Platform Sutra of the Sixth Patriarch.* New York: Columbia University Press.

Zhai, Howard. 1998. *101 Classic Chinese Fables.* Richmond: Dragon Fly.

Zhang, Shi-Ying. 1993. "Heidegger and Taoism" in John Sallis (ed.) *Reading Heidegger.* Bloomington: Indiana.

Zürcher, E. 1972. *The Buddhist Conquest of China: The Spread and Adaptation of Buddhism in Early Medieval China.* Leiden: E. J. Brill.

Index